from Lemons *to* Lemonade

in the New Legal Job Market

Winning Job Search Strategies
for Entry-Level Attorneys

from Lemons *to* Lemonade

in the New Legal Job Market

**Winning Job Search Strategies
for Entry-Level Attorneys**

RICHARD L. HERMANN

DecisionBooks

SEATTLE, WASHINGTON

Published by LawyerAvenue Press and its imprint, DecisionBooks

Interior design by Rose Michelle Taverniti
Cover design by Elizabeth Watson
Cover concept by Sandra Imre

Volume discounts available from LawyerAvenue Press. Email to
editor@LawyerAvenue.com, or write to Avenue Productions,
4701 SW Admiral Way #278, Seattle WA 98116

Library of Congress Cataloging-in-Publication Data

Hermann, R. L. (Richard Lee)
  From lemons to lemonade in the new legal job market : winning job search
strategies for entry-level attorneys / Richard L. Hermann.
     p. cm. -- (The new lawyer survival guide ; v. 1)
  ISBN 978-0-940675-68-1 (alk. paper)
  1. Law--Vocational guidance--United States. I. Title.
  KF297.H437 2012
  340.023'73--dc23
                            2011042536

For my dear friends, the Shomakers:
Ed, Michele, David, Thomas and Devin,
all exceptional exemplars of
high-order lemonade production.

CONTENTS

ACKNOWLEDGEMENTS

My thanks go out to my entry-level attorney counseling clients who taught me so much about nuances of legal job hunting, and whose questions, triumphs, and disappointments provided the insight that gave rise to *From Lemons to Lemonade in the New Legal Job Market*. I owe special thanks to my wife, Anne M. Hermann, whose constant encouragement, wise counsel and cogent critiques contribute so much to making my books so much better than they would be if left to my own devices.

ABOUT THE AUTHOR

Richard L. Hermann (Cornell Law, 1974) is a professor at Concord Law School, teaching the nation's only full-semester course in Legal Career Management, and his blog appears weekly at www.legalcareerweb.com. Hermann is a frequent speaker and presents numerous webinars on legal career topics. He co-founded Federal Reports Inc., the leading U.S. provider of legal career information, AttorneyJobs.com, and Law Student Jobs Online (both now the property of Thomson Reuters). He was a principal in Nationwide Career Counseling for Attorneys and Sutherland Hermann Associates, a legal outplacement and disability insurance consulting firm.

Hermann is the author of many books on legal careers, including:

- *Landing a Federal Legal Job: Finding Success in the U.S. Government Job Market*
- *Managing Your Legal Career: Best Practices for Creating the Career You Want*
- *The Lawyer's Guide to Job Security*
- *The Lawyer's Guide to Finding Success in Any Job Market*
- *JD Preferred: 600+ Things You Can Do with a Law Degree (Other Than Practice Law)*
- *The ALJ Handbook: An Insider's Guide to Becoming a Federal Administrative Law Judge*

INTRODUCTION

THE BACKGROUND

As a result of the Great Recession, nearly eight percent of attorneys at the 250 largest U.S. law firms were laid off in 2009–10, in addition to those attorneys terminated by state and local governments, and from corporate and small law firm positions. Meanwhile, the number of law school grads able to enter the legal work force has declined sharply, and entry-level lawyers are competing not only against each other—and jobless attorneys with experience—but also against law grads from the classes of 2009 and 2010.

Like the overall U.S. economy, the traditional legal job market may be three years into what could very well become a "lost decade." The pain, anguish and frustration felt by law students and recent grads is palpable and perfectly understandable. This book will demonstrate why it does not have to be.

This past year, the University of Maryland Law School hosted a panel discussion on "*Is Law School a Losing Game?*"

This was just the latest and boldest expression of increasing concern within the legal community about the value of a legal education in the face of crushing debt upon graduation and a very tight traditional legal job market. It followed a cascade of articles, webcasts, and other published ruminations within the profession on whether the current law school model has become obsolete. To my knowledge, the Maryland panel is the first time that a law school has admitted that law school might be a lemon.

Law school, however, is no lemon. In fact, law school and legal education are not only relevant, but can be the basis for a career that is both remunerative and satisfying in other ways.

However, this book is intended to compensate for the largest omission in the law school curriculum: *how to position yourself to find a good job, build a satisfying legal career, and how to cope with—and make lemonade from—all the other lemons in your search for work.*

I maintain that entry-level attorneys *can* compete effectively for jobs—even against attorneys with several years of experience—if they follow some or all of the 21 strategies described in this book to enhance their competitive status. Each of these strategies has a track record of success, which I attribute to (1) their positive impact on the job hunter's self- esteem, self-confidence and overall ego, and psychological affect, and (2) because they will impress and imprint your foresight and sophistication on employers, and make you memorable when it comes to decision time.

Whenever I speak to graduating law students or recent graduates, someone in the audience invariably raises the following issue: *"Almost every legal job I see advertised asks for at least 2–3 years of experience. How can I compete for these jobs if I lack that experience?"*

The more of the book's strategies you adopt (and adapt to your particular situation and preferences), the more effective your legal job search is likely to be, and the more upside there is likely to be to your legal career down the road.

After all, what good is professional training if a rewarding job is not possible?

—Richard L. Hermann, January, 2012

SECTION ONE
THE UNTAPPED LEGAL JOB MARKET

CHAPTER 1

12 Legal Lemons: An Introduction

You can't make lemonade without lemons. And in the current legal job market there is no shortage of lemons to be squeezed. A dozen such lemons, described and dissected in this first chapter, are having a huge impact on legal employment. As you read about them, keep in mind that, while they appear at first glance to present serious obstacles to legal job seekers and career builders, they also represent opportunities for those attorneys clever enough to circumvent them using the strategies put forth in this book.

Lemon #1: Too many lawyers

Inflation is defined by economists as a rise in the general level of prices of goods and services over a period of time. When price levels rise, each unit of currency buys fewer goods and services. Consequently, inflation also reflects erosion in the purchasing power of money. Inflation is usually caused by an excessive growth of the money supply. What we are witnessing in the legal job opportunity market is something very similar.

An "inflated" number of attorneys seeking a relatively static—and in some sectors a declining number of mainstream attorney jobs.

When I graduated from law school in the mid-1970s, the attorney population in the U.S. numbered 250,000. The American Bar Association says that there are currently approximately 1.2 million attorneys (JD degree holders) in the United States. The Bureau of Labor Statistics calculates that there are approximately 900,000 "mainstream" legal jobs (i.e., jobs with law firms, corporate in-house counsel offices, and government law offices). Do the math: *there are too many lawyers pursuing too few mainstream legal jobs.* It is not a pretty picture. And approximately 44,000 new law school graduates are added to the attorney population each year!

Furthermore, The Great Recession has impacted attorney job opportunities in several ways in addition to the ones discussed above that increased lawyer inflation:

First, law school enrollment spiked due to college graduates who could not find work and decided to go to law school in hopes that the economy would right itself while they were learning the law. While this appears to be a temporary phenomenon, it nevertheless complicates the current legal job scene.

Second, legal employers drastically cut back on hiring.

Third, older attorneys are deferring retirement because their pension plans took a tremendous hit.

Lemon #2: The experience gap

Surveys reveal that only two percent of all attorney jobs advertised at any given time are open to entry-level lawyers. That means that 98 percent of advertised attorney positions require some experience. This presents a real dilemma for 3Ls and recent law grads who enter the job market without any experience, or should I say any "countable" experience. Legal employers tend, at first glance, not to consider summer jobs or positions held during law school to be countable experience for the purpose of their hiring needs.

Lemon #3: The timing issue

Most hiring of graduating law students occurs early in the fall semester of their 3L academic year. Law firms, the occasional corporation, and a handful of government agencies appear on campus to interview candidates, and then customarily hold follow-up interviews in their offices. Offers are then made and hiring of the next spring's graduates is locked down for the year. The conventional wisdom is that the fall hiring season is the end of the exercise for entry-level attorneys. However, the conventional wisdom is not always all that wise. *Needs arise in all seasons of the year.* This has always been the case, but is even more so today than ever before. The accelerating pace of change that marks 21st century society is largely responsible for this development. Change comes so rapidly, and unanticipated consequences are so frequent, that legal employers like everyone else, must constantly adjust their business models on the fly. Technological advances and their cascade effects barrage us from all sides all the time, and the law must constantly play "catch-up" in order to accommodate the new technologies. What this means to entry-level lawyers is that job opportunities do not always lend themselves to predictable timing considerations.

Lemon #4: Top-ranked candidates only need apply

Approximately 500,000 attorneys, or more than 40 percent of all lawyers, work for law firms. The majority work for large and medium-size law firms.

These firms employ fairly consistent recruitment and hiring procedures, and follow a predictable (fall) hiring schedule.

But the criteria that large law firms apply in their recruiting of new law grads eliminates the overwhelming majority of candidates *before* the hiring process even begins. There are few exceptions to the following criteria that typically apply to competitors for these prized jobs: Law review (preferably on the basis of grades, not a writing competition), and high class rank (top 10–15 percent; top 25–30 percent if attending a top-rated law school). This does not leave a great deal of room for candidates without these qualifications. Exceptions are so infrequent that they soon become legendary and the stuff of anecdotes. One of my best friends graduated with poor grades from a top-50 law school, yet managed to obtain an associate position with a premier law firm in Pennsylvania. He persuaded the law firm hiring officials to set aside his law school performance in favor of his strong personality, interpersonal and intangible skills, and entrepreneurial bent.

> **Entry-level attorneys aren't just hired in the Fall. Hiring needs occur throughout the year.**

Lemon #5: Law grads are a luxury

For most of their history, law firms have been collegial collections of convivial colleagues who maintained a certain level of civility in dealings with each other and with opposing counsel. That idyllic world is now rapidly disappearing, replaced by one of Darwinian competition that is more akin to Thomas Hobbes than Rousseau. To wit:

- Client loyalties are not what they once were, and the pressures on corporate clients to cut costs and be more efficient impact negatively on their outside law firms.
- Competition for clients is now so intense it consumes many more hours of law firm time than ever before.
- Corporate client defections are way up as clients seek to pare their outside counsel costs and cost-cutting becomes a primary criterion for selecting an outside law firm.
- Competitive bidding for corporate clients has proliferated as evidenced by corporations publishing Requests for Proposals and instituting formal contracting processes. Losing a major client no longer means merely the loss of business. It may also mean the loss of key partners, associates and even whole practice groups who, spooked by the loss of one or more clients, seek greener pastures elsewhere. In some cases, it can even mean the sudden demise of the law firm.

What all this means for entry-level attorneys is that law firms no longer have the luxury of hiring large numbers of new associates fresh out of law school, investing hundreds of thousands of dollars in mentoring and training them, and letting attrition determine which ones ultimately survive. The number of law firms that have scaled back their entry-level hiring is legion. More ominous, those firms that have drastically cut back or eliminated their summer associate hiring programs indicate that near-term entry-level opportunities will be limited.

Lemon #6: The domino effect of the billable hour

Law is the last of the so-called "learned professions" that continues to bill for its work by the hour. While this has been a bonanza for law firms, it is increasingly perceived as a negative by clients, many of whom suspect that hourly billing is principally a means of "padding" bills.

The first warning shot across the bow was fired by clients who engaged legal fee auditing firms to go into law firms and subject their billing records to close examination. Regardless of what this invasive scrutiny discovered, it made law firms very uncomfortable. Increasingly, clients armed with much more insight into their outside counsel billing practices balked at paying by the hour, forcing firms to change their practices if they wished to retain their clients. Many law firms still object to project billing because, they argue, it is impossible for them to accurately predict the amount of time and effort that a legal project might take. This is despite the fact that virtually every company, law firm corporate clients included, must operate under such seemingly unpredictable conditions all the time.

While the billable hour is the bane of almost all law firm associates (and lately partners), movement away from this traditional billing practice is bad news for entry-level attorneys. It inevitably means fewer job opportunities in firms that luxuriated in billing out novice associates with no experience at princely rates to their corporate clients. The impulse to hire large numbers of associates to over-staff legal projects and bill accordingly has been severely weakened.

Lemon #7: Corporate streamlining of outside counsel

In a single year in the mid-1990s, a Fortune 10 energy company downsized its outside counsel force from 1,100 law firms to 30! This radical surgery was shocking to the legal community, but very intriguing to corporate America. Since then, more and more companies have followed suit and have pared down their own outside representation. As much as anything, this has compelled law firms to focus on how to compete with each other for business.

They have had to concentrate increasing attention on selling what they have to offer, which means having a clear understanding of their "value proposition," i.e., what is it that differentiates them from, and elevates them above, their competitors, making them worthy of assignment in the eyes of their client corporations. This has been a gut-wrenching exercise for law firms, one that is ongoing and likely will never end. As this book goes to press, most U.S. law firms have not yet devised an acceptable answer to this question. Fewer corporate clients, of course, mean fewer employment opportunities across the board, whether for experienced or entry-level lawyers.

Lemon #8: Client aversion to junior associates

A recent development, one very detrimental to routine law firm hiring of new associates, complicates the new paradigm confronting law firms: an increasing number of client companies tell their outside counsel that they do not want to see first- or second-year associates working (translation: billing) on their projects. Paying out $300/hour for a green attorney with little or no experience has become increasingly unacceptable to corporate general counsels who must write the checks. Corporate clients are demanding more for their money. This development is both a major threat to the comfort zone of the billable hour and a mandate to law firms to re-think their recruiting methodologies. The recruiting conundrum requires a balance between bringing in young lawyers and processing and mentoring them through the experience pipeline, and redirecting recruiting efforts away from new law grads and toward experienced attorneys. What makes this even more vexing is the bad habits that experienced lawyers may bring with them, as opposed to the clean slate presented by entry-level attorneys who can be much more easily molded into what the firm wants.

Lemon #9: Diversity for some not all

Law firms throughout their history have, for the most part, paid politically correct lip service to the concept of a diverse professional work force. While many firms "talked the talk," few actually "walked the walk." That began to change around the turn of the century (20th to 21st) when a handful of corporate clients announced that their outside counsel hiring decisions would be based, in part, on law firm diversity. In the past decade, this movement has spread and now, diversity has become a part of almost every company's outside law firm evaluation criteria. This is a very positive development for minority, women, and LGBT attorneys. Unfortunately, this paradigm shift has not yet had much positive impact with respect to disabled attorneys and zero impact with respect to retaining or hiring of aging attorneys.

Lemon #10: The career associate blues

As this book goes to press, a handful of large law firms have carved out a special class of associates called "Career Associates." These are attorneys who enter the firm with the clear understanding that they are not on the partnership track. In addition, they are not paid anything close to the salaries that partnership track associates command, which in 2011 means up to $160,000 for first-year associates. In return, Career Associates have to work fewer hours and thus are able to balance work with their outside lives. While the law firms that are going this route tout this as something new and innovative, it really is not. Many firms have had something similar to this category for years, usually called Staff Associates or Senior Associates. If there is a difference, it is probably that the vast majority of Staff or Senior Associates transferred to that status from the partnership track within the same law firm. Career Associates, on the other hand, so far appear to be new hires.

Lemon #11: Government opportunities in a downturn

A large number of my law student and recent law graduate clients over the years operated under the misconception that, if the barriers to entry-level legal employment by law firms and corporations were too difficult to overcome, they could always fall back on the government.

While federal, state and local governments hire an impressive number of entry-level attorneys each year, they hire many more experienced lawyers. U.S. government agencies do currently offer 19 different honors programs for entry-level attorneys (see Appendix A), and the Department of Justice maintains by far the largest such program, employing approximately 120 attorneys. Nineteen may sound like a great many programs, but in reality it is not when you realize that more than 130 federal government agencies *do not* have such a program. And if and when these agencies do hire entry-level attorneys, they do so intermittently as the need arises.

A handful of state government agencies nationwide also offer honors employment programs to entry-level lawyers, but, like so much state legal hiring, they have suffered due to The Great Recession and its budget-constraining aftermath. Many programs have been cancelled completely, with no indication when they might be revived. Similarly, state civil service hiring examinations for attorneys have also been severely cut back or frozen due to the fiscal crisis affecting virtually every state.

Local government entry-level legal hiring has also suffered due to the economic downturn, but to a lesser extent than state attorney hiring. Overall, state and local government legal hiring is way down, whether for entry-level or experienced attorneys. This is not likely to change in the near term, given that 49 states are constitutionally required to balance their annual budgets. Combine that with the end of the $400 billion+ of stimulus money states received from the federal government from 2009—2011, funds that enabled states to defer some of the harsh realities they would have otherwise had to face much earlier, and the near future does not look very promising.

Lemon #12: The in-house obsession with experience

How entry-level attorneys are perceived by, and fare with respect to, corporate in-house counsel offices, the scenario is much less complicated than in law firms. For companies, legal experience is king, period. If you do not have at least a few years of it, you probably will not find a job in a corporate in-house counsel office. While not an absolute assertion, this is probably the closest thing to one. The only exceptions are the following:

- A handful of very large corporate in-house counsel offices have a history of some entry-level hiring. IBM and AT&T fall into this category, although their commitment to hiring a few entry-level attorneys every year is waning. The insurance industry has always hired some entry-level lawyers. This may be in the process of receiving a boost from the Patient Protection and Affordable Care Act of 2010 (healthcare reform), Pub. L. 111–148.
- An "in-bred" company employee who acquires a law degree occasionally has a shot at moving directly from law school into an in-house position with his or her company.
- A small or start-up company may feel that it needs an in-house attorney and, for economic reasons, cannot afford one with experience (this is, however, extremely rare).

For the most part, however, corporate general counsel offices have a traditional bias against entry-level lawyers. Given the increasing complexity of both the legal and business environments in which they operate, this is not likely to change.

While most of the paradigm shifts affecting private practice, and the in-house bias in favor of experience, and the misconceptions about the economics of nonprofits, and the erroneous view of government-as-employer-of-last-resort, appear to have an adverse effect on entry-level attorney hiring, *there are ways to launch a successful legal career in each of these dominant employment sectors*. The "recipes" for legal lemonade that comprise the heart of this book are only tangentially related to the paradigm shifts and resulting obstacles. Most of them derive from creative, common-sense initiatives that have a lengthy track record of success, and that you can invoke to position yourself to make yourself an attractive legal employment candidate with a competitive advantage over your entry-level competitors. They may even level the playing field when you are pitted against attorneys with experience.

These strategies have been tested in the real world by many of my legal career transition counseling clients and been found to work. What follows is a detailed description of the most effective means of coping with the "downsides" of being an entry-level attorney in a highly competitive legal world.

CHAPTER 2

JD-Preferred: Looking Outside
the Mainstream

For the purposes of this book, *mainstream* legal practice is defined in terms of where attorneys work...as attorneys.

That means law firms (large, medium, boutique, small and solo practices), for-profit corporations (both publicly-traded and closely-held), government law offices (federal, state, local, regional and special district), nonprofit legal offices (such as the general counsel offices of trade and professional associations, colleges and universities, hospitals, museums, foundations, and public interest and advocacy organizations), and the law offices of international organizations and multilateral development agencies (such as the United Nations Secretariat, World Bank, International Monetary Fund, World Trade Organization, and World Health Organization).

Unfortunately, the "macro" problem that graduating attorneys face is one of simple demographics: there are just not enough mainstream legal job opportunities to absorb the entire attorney population. Extrapolating from statistics gathered by the American Bar Association and the federal Bureau of Labor Statistics, the current "shortfall" of attorney jobs is around 250–300,000. That means that only 900–950,000 of the 1.2+ million attorneys in the United States work in mainstream legal jobs. The U.S. economy simply does not produce enough new mainstream attorney jobs to absorb the annual influx of newly-minted lawyers.

As dismal as these statistics are, they should not be a cause for depression and despair.

Looking *Outside* the Mainstream

Despite all of the handwringing and public anguish by bar leaders, some legal educators, and much of the legal and general media, they are completely tunnel-visioned.

For them, there is only the mainstream and, for many of them, that does not even include jobs outside of major law firms! Don't listen to them. They are looking at only one port in a sea of possible jobs. Moreover, you can discount much of the drumbeat in the mainstream media about there being no jobs for lawyers. Doom-and-gloom stories sell newspapers and magazines and, once these publications adopt that point-of-view, they do not want to hear an opposing view.

One of the great advantages of a legal education is its fungibility. Attorneys can do a great many things and can fit into numerous employment sectors and niches that fall outside the definition of mainstream legal practice.

As I hope you'll see, this chapter will reveal the importance of expanding your job-search horizons to include the immense—and growing—array of *law-related* job opportunities outside of mainstream law. If you reject or discount these possibilities, you do yourself a great disservice.

Let's begin.

Back in the 1990s, I wrote *JD Preferred! 600+ Things You Can Do with a Law Degree (Other Than Practice Law)*. The premise was that a legal education lends itself to a vast array of possibilities—at the time, at least 30 categories, ranging from Academic Administration to Transportation—and that there was no better background than law for someone who wants to maximize his or her employability. Virtually all of the job titles in the book came from the personal experiences of my company's legal career counseling clients who had ventured outside of mainstream law.

Some 20 years have now passed, and law-related careers for attorneys have become widely accepted by employers outside of the legal community, and gradually within certain legal community circles as well. And more good news: at least 200 additional *law-related* job titles can easily be added to the original list! In fact, JD-preferred positions have become ubiquitous, and are found everywhere…even in mainstream legal venues. See for yourself how many opportunities exist outside the mainstream. And visit Appendix D (*What Can You Do With a Law Degree? 800+ Options*) for a list of the most popular current law-related careers:

JD-preferred positions at law firms. Large law firms are evolving to where they now look more like businesses than collegial collections of partners and worker bees. Consequently, they have restructured themselves so that a whole new group of professionals now work for them in support positions. However, because they are law firms, they tend to favor hiring their professional support personnel who also understand their work. That gives a distinct advantage to attorneys who also happen to bring something else to the table.

The kind of large law firm jobs available include the following:

- Law firm marketing is an increasingly important function as competition for corporate clients heats up. In addition to an overall Marketing Director, large law firms increasingly employ marketing staff that focus on only one or two practice groups.
- Law firm administration has also made significant inroads into the law firm community. Many law firm administrators have both a JD and MBA or a JD and significant management experience.
- Professional development is now an important feature of every major law firm and an important recruiting enticement. In addition to a professional development director, many law firms have expanded their professional development staffs to include trainers.
- Recruiting has always been somewhat "professionalized" in law firms. Approximately 50 percent of chief law firm recruiters have a JD.
- Other law firm positions with a JD-preferred orientation include Pro Bono Coordinators and a wide variety of positions with law firm subsidiaries. Major law firms have established subsidiaries that focus on lobbying, litigation support, insurance matters, and many other topical areas. The professionals who work directly for these subsidiaries often have a JD.

Medium-size law firms are also moving in the same direction as their larger competitors, no surprise because they are subject to the same pressures causing large law firms to move in this direction. Firms of this size are usually more amenable to considering entry-level attorneys who have the requisite business skills or background necessary to perform these functions.

JD-preferred positions at corporations. While obtaining a job with a corporate in-house counsel office is a major stretch for an entry-level attorney, finding employment in one of the increasing number of corporate law-related positions is not. The JD-preferred recruiting and hiring philosophy is alive and well, and thriving in corporate America thanks to the increasing complexity of corporate existence and increasing scrutiny by both the federal and state governments.

The most important law-related positions include the following:

- Regulatory compliance is the poster child for fast-growing corporate JD-preferred career opportunities. This function used to be a component of the corporate in-house counsel office. Now it has become too important, too wide-ranging and consisting of too many responsibilities to be subsumed within a legal office. Regulatory compliance is now a separate operational office within almost all Fortune 1000 corporations and many other smaller companies. In some large companies, there are even separate offices that handle specific compliance areas.

- Risk management is also a rapidly growing corporate function. It is sometimes combined with the ethics function or with regulatory compliance, although increasingly the risk management office stands on its own.
- Every corporation of any significant size has a Contracting or Procurement Office. Many are conducive to entry-level attorneys, whose legal education more than qualifies them for contracting positions.
- Some corporations have a separate tax department. One of my company's major clients staffed its tax department with more than 30 attorneys.
- Privacy matters have become a major concern and headache for many corporations. Healthcare providers have had to comply with the Health Insurance Portability and Accountability Act's (HIPAA), Pub. L. 104–191 rigorous privacy mandates for 15 years and, with the push toward digitizing of medical records, recently given additional impetus by the Patient Protection and Affordable Care Act, Pub. L. 111–148, healthcare privacy has become big business.

Financial services is the other major area where legislation and increased government scrutiny has caused companies to focus attention on privacy. Increasingly, financial industry participants are establishing separate privacy offices.

JD-preferred positions in specific industries. In addition to law-related careers that apply to many industries, certain business sectors are home to law-related positions unique only to them. Selected examples include the following:

- A prime example is the Landman profession found in the oil and gas industry. Landmen are often hired directly out of law school, based on their legal education alone, which the industry considers a big advantage. One of the most attractive features of this job is that you are not desk-bound all day every day. The landman goes out to negotiate mineral leasing rights with landowners, then documents these transactions, so that his or her oil or gas company can explore for and develop these resources. The small size of most gas companies and recent discoveries of vast domestic gas deposits (as I write this, 70,000 gas wells are being drilled in the Marcellus Formation stretching from Central New York into West Virginia) make this a particularly favorable time to look for landman jobs. To a lesser extent, landmen put together "economic mining units" for the coal industry.

- Insurance claims managers and other claims personnel are another specialty area where attorneys are found in significant numbers. Insurance companies, in addition, are major employers of attorneys in a variety of JD-preferred positions, such as Litigation Managers, Environmental Underwriters, Professional Liability Underwriters, Document Compliance Specialists, Advanced Marketing Consultants, and Health Care Policy Analysts.

Attorneys fit into many employment sectors outside mainstream legal practice.

- The Financial services industry generates a variety of JD-preferred positions for which many entry-level attorneys with the requisite background or courses may compete. Representative job titles include: Bank International Trade Specialist, Bankruptcy Analyst, Community Investment Act Director, Estate and Financial Planner, Fiduciary Administrator, Investment Banking Officer, Legal Advertising/Sales Literature Manager, Legal Product Manager, Probate Manager and Trust Officer.

JD-preferred positions in government. The U.S. government offers more than 150 law-related job titles in which attorneys work. With few exceptions, these are open to new law school graduates. JD-preferred positions are found in every one of the close to 150 federal departments and agencies. When contemplating a federal legal or law-related career, it is very important to keep the following guideline in mind: the U.S. government is not a monolith. Just because an agency might happen to be the lead agency regarding a particular government function, that does not automatically mean that it is the only agency tasked with that function. Government is, if anything, wide-ranging in its scope and incredibly duplicative in its legal and regulatory functions.

Examples of this duplication abound in almost any conceivable arena of government interest. For example:

- The Environmental Protection Agency (EPA) is hardly the only federal organization with vast environmental responsibilities. The Departments of Defense, Energy, Interior and Justice, along with the Nuclear Regulatory Commission, Tennessee Valley Authority, and U.S. Army

Corps of Engineers, to name a few, also have far-reaching environmental interests and missions.

- The Equal Employment Opportunity Commission (EEOC) is one of many federal departments and agencies concerned with employment discrimination. Several other federal agencies focus almost exclusively on employment matters, including the Merit Systems Protection Board, the Office of Special Counsel, and the Office of Personnel Management (OPM). In addition, every single federal organization has its own offices (plural in almost every case) that deal with this issue, and lawyers engaged in employment law in all of its ramifications are present in either attorney or JD-preferred positions in almost all of them.
- Even something as presumably narrow as the federal interest in education is not the exclusive preserve of the Department of Education. The Defense Department administers a huge, global school system for military dependents and has a bureaucracy to match. Fourteen other agencies also have a piece of the education pie.
- If you think that the Department of Agriculture is where all of the issues involving farms and farm products gravitate, you would be off by nine agencies.

The most popular federal law-related job titles are listed below, along with their major federal employers:

- Adjudications Officer—U.S. Customs and Immigration Services (USCIS).
- Alternative Dispute Resolution Specialist—Library of Congress, Department of Defense, Federal Communications Commission, Department of Agriculture, Department of Justice, Department of Air Force, Federal Deposit Insurance Corporation (FDIC), Federal Energy Regulatory Commission, Federal Labor Relations Authority (FLRA), General Services Administration (GSA), Department of Health and Human Services (HHS), Department of Interior and the National Aeronautics and Space Administration (NASA).
- Analyst in Social Legislation-Congressional Research Service, the Centers for Medicare and Medicaid Services, Department of the Army, Justice, Department of Veterans Affairs, Government Accountability Office (GAO) and Department of Education.
- Application Adjudicator—USCIS.
- Asylum Officer—USCIS.
- Bankruptcy Examiner/Analyst—United States Trustee Offices nationwide.

- Civil Rights Analyst—Commission on Civil Rights and Department of Education.
- Compliance Specialist—Financial Crimes Enforcement Network, Internal Revenue Service and EPA.
- Contract Officer—Army, Air Force, DLA, Navy, Department of Homeland Security (DHS), GSA, NASA, Department of Transportation, HHS, Agriculture, Veterans Affairs, Interior, Energy, Justice, Treasury, Defense, EPA, Commerce, Department of Housing and Urban Development (HUD), Department of State, Small Business Administration (SBA), Labor, Education and U.S. Agency for International Development.
- Competition Advocate—Departments of Defense, Army, Navy, and Air Force, GSA, DHS and NASA.
- Copyright Examiner—Library of Congress
- Employee Benefits Law Specialist—Employee Benefits Security Administration (EBSA).
- Environmental Protection Specialist—EPA, Army, DLA, Navy, Air Force, Interior, Energy, Transportation and HUD.
- Equal Employment Opportunity Officer—Army, Navy, Treasury, HHS, Interior, Agriculture, Air Force, Transportation, Veterans Affairs and Justice.
- Equal Opportunity Compliance Specialist—Labor, HUD, Education, HHS, Transportation, Agriculture and EEOC.
- Equal Opportunity Assistance Manager—Army, Labor, Navy, Treasury, Interior, HHS, HUD, DLA, Air Force, Agriculture and Justice.
- Ethics Program Specialist—Office of Government Ethics, Justice, Interior, State, FDIC, GAO and U.S. Postal Service.
- Foreign Law Specialist—Library of Congress.
- Futures Trading Investigator—Commodity Futures Trading Commission.
- GAO Analyst—GAO.
- General Claims Examiner—Defense, OPM, Agriculture, Treasury, Army, Navy, Education, Air Force and State.
- Hearings and Appeals Officers—Treasury, Agriculture, Justice, Veterans Affairs and Interior.
- Import Compliance Specialist—U.S. International Trade Administration.
- International Trade Specialist—Commerce, Office of the United States Trade Representative, Trade and Development Agency and International Trade Commission.
- Investigator (Pension)—EBSA.
- Labor Management Relations Examiner—National Labor Relations Board (NLRB).

- Labor Relations Specialist—Treasury, Army, Navy, Air Force, HHS, Tennessee Valley Authority (TVA), NLRB, Department of Transportation, Federal Labor Relations Authority (FLRA) and Department of Homeland Security (DHS). (Note: The Department of Labor is *not* a major employer of Labor Relations Specialists).
- Land Law Examiner—Interior and Agriculture.
- Legal Instruments Examiner—Justice, Commerce, Treasury, Interior, Transportation, Agriculture, Veterans Affairs, Army, SBA and HHS.
- Legislative Assistant—Member offices in the Senate and House of Representatives.
- Legislative/Regulatory Analyst—Army, FDIC, Air Force, Treasury, HHS, TVA, Navy, Justice, Transportation, Interior and HUD.
- Mediator—Federal Mediation and Conciliation Service, EEOC, U.S. Postal Service, Air Force.
- Patent Adviser—Army, Agriculture, HHS, Air Force and NASA.
- Patent Examiner—U.S. Patent and Trademark Office.
- Pension Law Specialist—Labor, Pension Benefit Guaranty Corporation, IRS and Social Security Administration.
- Political Risk Insurance Analyst—Overseas Private Investment Corporation.
- Privacy Officer—DHS, Defense, HHS and Treasury.
- Program Integrity Specialist—Defense, Navy, Air Force, DHS, GSA and NASA.
- Refugee Officer—USCIS.
- Tax Law Specialist—IRS.
- Technology Transfer/Licensing Specialist—Energy, National Institutes of Health, National Institute of Standards and Technology, EPA and National Technology Transfer Center.

JD-preferred positions in the court system. The federal court system is also a good place to look for law-related positions. Several thousand attorneys besides Supreme Court justices, Court of Appeals and District Court judges, Bankruptcy Court judges and United States Magistrate Judges work in support positions in the federal courts. In addition to working as judicial law clerks, career law clerks, "elbow" law clerks and staff attorneys, lawyers work as clerks and deputy clerks of court, circuit and district executives, legal research specialists, and in other law-related positions.

JD-preferred positions in the quasi-government. You should also not overlook the quasi-federal sector, which consists of organizations that either have a federal charter (such as the Federal Home Loan Mortgage Association—Freddie Mac—or the Federal National Mortgage Association—Fannie Mae); fall under the classification of Self-Regulatory Organizations (SROs), such as the Financial Industry Regulatory Authority, New York Stock Exchange, Municipal Securities Rulemaking Board, or Public Company Accounting Oversight Board; or the Federal Reserve Banks and Federal Home Loan Banks. These institutions all employ attorneys in both legal and law-related positions.

JD-preferred positions in state and local government. State and local governments also employ a great many attorneys in JD-preferred positions. Many of these mirror the law-related job titles at the federal level; others are unique to the states or municipalities. Special districts are governmental and quasi-governmental units established to perform specific functions, usually for a region that cuts across state and/or municipal boundaries. There are approximately 12,000 such entities nationwide and most of them offer JD-preferred positions. Some of the better known special districts include: the East Bay Municipal Utility District (East Bay MUD), the Port Authority of New York and New Jersey, and the Washington Metropolitan Airports Authority.

JD-preferred positions in nonprofits. Not-for-profit corporations abound in the United States. Four examples make the point about their employment of attorneys in JD-preferred positions:

Trade and Professional Associations

These membership organizations are almost always set up as nonprofit corporations. Their mission is to serve the interests of their membership. Trade associations are usually industry-specific, such as the American Forest Products Association, American Petroleum Institute, and Electronics Industry Association. Professional associations are comprised of individuals who practice the same profession, such as the American Bar Association, American Association of Health Attorneys, and American Psychological Association. However, some trade associations also accept individual members and some professional associations countenance organizational members. The largest associations have memberships numbering in the hundreds of thousands.

> **Recruiting and hiring for JD-preferred positions thrives in corporate America.**

More attorneys work for associations in JD-preferred positions than in pure attorney jobs. While only approximately 10 percent of the estimated 30,000 U.S. associations have an in-house counsel office, the vast majority of them have a government affairs or government relations office, often employ-ing attorneys as lobbyists, legislative and regulatory analysts, and in other positions that favor a legal background. Professional associations in particular often have an ethics or professional responsibility staff populated by attorneys whose job it is to keep the association's members up-to-date on professional ethics and respond to requests for ethics opinions.

Colleges and Universities

Among nonprofits, the academic sector employs more attorneys in JD-preferred positions than any other type of employer. A generation ago, only a handful of America's 4,300 colleges and universities had their own in-house legal office. Today, very few do not. As their counsel offices' responsi-bilities expanded, they often found that it made sense to establish other legal and quasi-legal offices outside of the general counsel office to handle very specific problems with a legal component. These "satellite" offices expanded rapidly and today it is not uncommon to find multiple campus offices with attorneys working in either legal or JD-preferred positions. Some of the larger institutions have all of the following offices with law-related responsibilities while others—large and small—have a selection of them:

- Contract and Grants Management
- Development
- Disabled Student Affairs
- Employee Relations
- Environmental Affairs
- Equal Employment Opportunity and Affirmative Action
- Ethics
- Government Affairs
- International Student Affairs
- Judicial Affairs
- Labor Relations
- Legislative Affairs
- Ombudsman
- Real Estate
- Regulatory Compliance
- Risk Management
- Sponsored Research
- Technology Transfer and Licensing

Another major impetus to the hiring of even more attorneys for JD-preferred positions on campus is the Higher Education Opportunity Act of 2008 (HEOA), Pub. L. 110–315, which contained sweeping new regulatory mandates that require colleges and universities to report to the U.S. government on more than 300 new topics subject to federal scrutiny, such as tuition and fee information, tuition cost reduction initiatives, textbook prices by individual course, transfer-of-credit policies, file sharing, binge drinking, meningitis outbreaks, missing persons, fire safety, voter registration, drug violations, fatalities, student sanctions and technology disposal, among many others.

This law is so complex that it is still in the process of being implemented by the U.S. Department of Education. By the middle of 2011, academic institutions had hired several thousand individuals, many of them attorneys, for new campus compliance positions necessary to cope with HEOA's demands.

Hospitals

Just over half of the 5,800 U.S. hospitals are nonprofit community institutions (the rest are either for-profit corporations or federal, state or local government hospitals). Like academic institutions, hospitals have found that their functions and activities have become increasingly "legalized." Their response has been similar to that of academe. The last two decades has witnessed the rise of in-house counsel offices and the trailing separation out of hospital legal offices of responsibilities that have intensified to such an extent that it is thought that a special function-specific office is necessary to manage the function and protect the hospital. The difference is that hospitals are much smaller institutions than colleges and universities. Consequently, the major players when it comes to hiring for JD-preferred positions are those hospitals with 200 or more beds. There are more than 1,600 such facilities, of which approximately 1,000 are nonprofits. The greater the number of beds, the more likely the institution will have a multiplicity of JD-preferred positions.

The variety of JD-preferred positions in hospitals is diverse and growing, thanks to these major developments:

- **An aging population that requires more healthcare services.** The 80 million baby boomers now moving into senior citizen status at a rate of 10,000 per day and are putting a tremendous strain on the healthcare delivery system.
- **Healthcare reform legislation.** Beginning in the 1990s with HIPAA and accelerating since, attempts at healthcare reform have proliferated at both the federal and state levels. Implementation of the Affordable Care Act

is well underway and will continue for the rest of this decade (provided it survives court challenges to its constitutionality). This law changes everything about healthcare and will compel providers to respond to increased government scrutiny by bolstering their professional support staffs.

- **New technologies.** Telemedicine, e-prescribing, treatment breakthroughs and new drugs and therapies are fraught with cutting-edge legal, regulatory, ethical, business and other issues yet to be resolved.

- **Skyrocketing healthcare costs.** Americans spend over $2 trillion a year on healthcare—almost 20 percent of the U.S. Gross Domestic Product, which is twice as much as any other nation. And what do we get for this largesse? A rank of 45th in life expectancy and 37th in a World Health Organization study on the performance of national health systems. Seventy-five cents of every healthcare dollar is spent on chronic disease treatment (four out of every five chronic diseases could be prevented because they result from smoking, consuming alcohol to excess, obesity, and lack of exercise). We only spend five percent of each healthcare dollar on prevention.

- One of the major reasons why healthcare costs are exploding is the corruption endemic to the system. The provider temptation to overprescribe and overbill is overwhelming. One small example: the U.S. population increased by 13 percent from 1992 to 2002. Prescription drug use increased by 57 percent for non-controlled drugs and 154 percent for controlled drugs. Outright fraud accounts for an additional expense estimated by some experts at more than $200 billion per year.

> **The U.S. Government offers more than 150 law-related job titles, many of which are open to new lawyers.**

The following are the most prevalent hospital JD-preferred positions:

- **Regulatory compliance.** Healthcare regulatory compliance involves audits of various departments and work processes, encompassing such issues as fraud and abuse, kickbacks, privacy, pricing, rebates, grants, payments to customers, licensing, accreditation, FDA regulations and marketing/sales/promotional practices. There is often an employee-training component that is part of the compliance function. Depending on the size of the institution, compliance officers may specialize in one or more specific compliance areas.

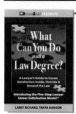

The New **What Can You Do with a Law Degree?**
Trade paper / 220 pages (September, 2012) , $30

America's leading expert on the psychology of lawyer behavior looks at career satisfaction for lawyers as never before. In this new 6th edition, Dr. Larry Richard introduces a unique, five-part career model that can help lawyers and new grads find long-term career satisfaction inside, outside and around the law.

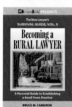

Becoming a Rural Lawyer
Trade paper / 148 pages (2013), $30

Rural lawyer Bruce Cameron, author of the popular blog *Rurallawyer.com*, can help you decide if you're meant to practice rural law, how to find the right small town to begin, what new lawyers must do to prepare, and what are the 8 myths of practicing rural law, and the 5 "hot" emerging areas of rural practice.

How to Litigate
Trade paper / 176 pages (2013), $30

A detailed and insightful work into the litigation process, and the psychological art of the lawsuit. Veteran defense lawyer Martin Grayson provides an accurate, big-picture perspective and specific tips for litigation success. Recommended for trial ad students and junior associates.

Solo By Choice 2011/2012
Trade paper / 306 pages (2011), $45

Now in its 2nd edition, *Solo by Choice* is an Amazon best-seller, and the go-to guide on how to start and maintain your own law practice. Recommended by law schools & bar associations for ex-associates and partners—and new grads—who want to be their own boss.

Small Firms, Big Opportunity
Trade paper / 254 pages (August, 2012), $30

Despite the gloomy job market, the percentage of grads getting hired at small law firms is actually rising! This new book, by two small firm insiders, discuss the 9 advantages to small firm practice, and when, where, how,—and why—new grads really need to explore the small firm market.

From Lemons to Lemonade in the New Legal Job Market
Trade paper / 254 pages (2012), $30

Law professor and law career expert Richard Hermann reveals legal job-finding strategies not taught in law school. Hermann's latest book demonstrates how your intangible attributes—more than grades, class rank, and honors—can impress prospective employers and get you hired!

☞ *Copies available from* **Amazon.com**

- **Risk management.** Risk managers investigate, analyze and evaluate actual and potential risk and liability exposures, and take steps to protect against them. They manage the organization's insurance programs and insurance financing. They may serve as liaisons with defense legal counsel and conduct educational programs for clinical and other personnel.
- **Ethics and bioethics.** Ethics and bioethics issues are inherent in healthcare. The ethical implications of interaction between healthcare providers (e.g., hospitals and physicians) and vendors (e.g., pharmaceutical and medical device companies) are huge. Providers wrestle daily with complicated self-referral rules. They deal with issues of patient confidentiality and informed consent. Stem cell research, end-of-life care, reproductive technologies, cloning, biomedical research, gene therapies, genetic testing, human subject research, human specimen repositories, "neuroethics" (e.g. brain imaging, pharmacological enhancement of cognitive function or emotion, brain-machine interface), laboratory animal care and use, and clinical trial ethical considerations are some of the major issues on the bioethics agenda.
- **Government relations.** Healthcare providers are increasingly subject to federal and state regulatory scrutiny. The number of investigations of hospitals and HMOs has increased exponentially in recent years. State licensing boards, insurance fraud bureaus, and Medicaid fraud control units are much more activist and aggressive than ever. Hospital government relations departments must monitor developments and advocate for their institutions.
- **Research integrity.** Major hospitals are increasing their research integrity efforts in response to closer scrutiny by grantor organizations of how research dollars are spent. The National Institutes of Health and the National Science Foundation, federal entities with fairly large research integrity staffs, scrutinize grantee activities very carefully. Hospital research integrity professionals monitor and investigate research misconduct, protection of human subjects, welfare of laboratory animals, conflicts of interest, data management practices, mentor and trainee responsibilities, collaborative research, authorship and publication, and peer review, and establish and administer research policies, codes and guidelines.
- **Patient rights.** Patients have certain legal rights, some guaranteed by federal law, such as the right to get a copy of their medical records and the right to keep them private. Many states have additional laws protecting patients, and hospitals often have a patient bill of rights.

Patient rights advocates investigate and resolve complaints from patients or their families about violations or abuses of their rights; educate them regarding their legal rights; advocate for those who are unable or afraid to register a complaint; and assist in negotiating a solution to a problem. Some may also represent clients in forums such as certification review hearings, administrative fair hearings and other dispute resolution processes.

- **Privacy.** This is currently a very "hot" profession in the healthcare realm. Healthcare privacy officers assure compliance with the HIPAA Privacy Rule, which protects the privacy of individually identifiable health information, and the confidentiality provisions of the Patient Safety Rule, which protects identifiable information being used to analyze patient safety events and improve patient safety. Many states have also enacted privacy and security regulations, some more stringent than HIPAA. Technology has become a major healthcare privacy issue, thanks to the impetus from both the federal government and insurers to digitize medical records.

- **Ombudsman/mediation.** The Long Term Care Ombudsman Program—a creation of federal law—consists of 53 State Long Term Care Ombudsman Programs and their statewide networks of almost 600 local programs. The Program's primary mission is to handle nursing home and other long-term care facility residents' complaints and represent resident interests through individual and systemic advocacy. A growing number of states have ombudsman programs that advocate for state residents who have healthcare and/or health insurance issues. Some state programs also track and study trends in healthcare, comment on federal and state healthcare regulations and recommend changes to state healthcare policies. Certain states limit their ombudsman programs to managed care matters, helping people enrolled in a health plan with access, service and billing problems.

- **The 2005 Bankruptcy Abuse Prevention and Consumer Protection Act**, Pub. L. 109-8 mandates the establishment of a Patient Care Ombudsman when a bankruptcy involves a healthcare business. Healthcare providers may also have ombudsmen. A major impetus behind the creation of private sector programs is the hospital-accrediting Joint Commission's New Leadership Standard, which "requires hospitals to manage conflict between leadership groups to protect the quality and safety of care." Further, the Standard "creates an expectation that hospitals will develop and implement a process to manage conflict."

- **Contracts and procurement.** In addition to the many negotiations and documentation requirements of basic hospital purchasing, devising contractual relationships with physicians and physician groups is an increasing component of this work.
- **Labor relations.** Hospital employee unions and periodic renegotiation of collective bargaining agreements have become increasingly contentious.
- **Technology transfer.** Large hospitals that also conduct research are always interested in commercializing their employees' inventions and innovations. Technology transfer officers are the focal point for the development and transfer of advanced technologies, specifically the implementation of pertinent legislation, rules and regulations and the administration of activities relating to collaborative agreements, inventions, patents, royalties and associated matters. They advise and assist in the development and management of intellectual property, registration and management of patents, trademarks and copyrights, terms and negotiation of licensing and interpretation of laws, policies, rules and regulations especially those related to the implementation of technology transfer statutes and policies.

Land Trusts

Land trusts are nonprofit organizations that work to conserve land, natural habitats and species of flora and fauna. They do this through the acquisition of land or conservation easements, or by stewardship of land or easements owned by or under the control of individuals, governments or private organizations. Land trusts solicit donations of land, conservation easements or money to purchase land. There are currently more than 1,600 land trusts in the U.S., consisting of both national and regional organizations as well as local ones. The most prominent land trusts are the national organizations such as the American Farmland Trust, American Land Conservancy, Audubon Society, Conservation Fund, Great Outdoors Conservancy, Humane Society of the United States Wildlife Land Trust, National Park Trust, Nature Conservancy, Trust for Public Land, and Wilderness Land Trust.

JD-preferred land trust positions include:

- Director of land preservation
- Director of project review
- Executive director
- Land conservation coordinator
- Acquisition manager
- Land steward

International Organizations

More than 200 international organizations employ American lawyers in either attorney or law-related positions. See Appendix F for a selection of international organizations (and their divisions and sections with JD-preferred positions) of which the United States is a member, which renders American attorneys eligible to work for them. The wide variety of JD-preferred positions in international organizations is best exemplified by the large number of law-related job titles found in the United Nations system:

- Advisor—Intellectual Property Rights
- Analysis and Reporting Officer
- Analyst
- Board of Inquiry Officer
- Chief of Staff
- Child Protection Officer
- Civil Affairs Officer
- Claims Officer
- Community Security and Arms Control Deputy Programme Manager (Policy)
- Conduct and Discipline Officer
- Consultant: Constitutional Law
- Contract Management Officer
- Contracts Officer
- Coordination Officer
- Corrections Officer
- (Deputy) Head of Rule of Law
- Director of Legal Affairs (JD required)
- Disarmament, Demobilization and Reintegration Officer
- Drug Control and Crime Prevention Officer
- Gender Officer
- General Services Officer
- Head of (Peacekeeping Operations) Field Office
- Human Rights Officer
- Information Analyst
- Judicial Affairs Officer (JD required)
- Judgment Coordinator (JD required)
- Legal Consultant (Administrative Law)
- Liaison Officer
- Policy Advisor—Local Governance
- Policy Advisor—Public Administration Reform and Anti-Corruption

- Policy Advisor—Rule of Law and Access to Justice
- Political Affairs Officer
- Political Affairs/Report Writing Officer
- Procurement Officer
- Programme Planning Officer
- Protection Officer
- Protocol Officer
- Recovery, Return and Reintegration Officer
- Representative of the High Commissioner for Human Rights
- Research Officer
- Rule of Law Project Manager
- Secretary to a Commission
- Security Coordination Officer
- Special Adviser
- Special Assistant
- Team Leader—Governance and Human Rights
- Terrorism Prevention Officer
- UN Office on Drugs and Crime Representative

As indicated earlier in this book, approximately one-fourth of all of the Risk Managers in the U.S. are attorneys. The U.S. government's Contract Officer work force numbers 37,000, of which more than 7,000 are attorneys. A large number of Regulatory Compliance professionals also happen to be lawyers. Many of the thousands of Landmen who negotiate and supervise real estate acquisitions and mineral leases for oil and gas companies are attorneys. The list goes on and on.

WORKING OUTSIDE THE LEGAL MAINSTREAM: PRO & CON

Like almost everything else in life, there is both good news and bad news associated with working outside the legal mainstream:

The Pro:

Greater civility. Few professions these days are as contentious as law. Whether you are involved in litigation, transactional work, regulatory law or another practice, there is almost always an opposing counsel competing with you for a victory. Much of law is a zero-sum game in which, for every winner there must be a loser. This is rarely the case in a law-related field.

Geographic flexibility. Unlike law, few JD-preferred careers are limited geographically by the interposition of state bar admission requirements. Those few that have a regulatory scheme similar to law are often easily transportable across state borders because there is far less complexity involved in their reciprocity standards.

Licensing requirements. The rigorous licensing requirements applicable to lawyers do not exist in most law-related professions.

Your JD is a big advantage. Law-related professionals who also have a law degree are highly respected, more so than their professional colleagues who do not have a JD.

Job security. Certain JD-preferred careers come equipped with much more job security than exists in today's law firm and corporate in-house environments. The demand for Compliance professionals, for example, is very great. When they leave a job, it is often because they have been recruited and/ or enticed by higher compensation and other attractions. Risk Managers in many milieus come as close to becoming indispensable as it is possible to be because it is their responsibility to know everything there is to know about their organization.

Less stress. Law is among the most stressful of professions. Few law-related careers can make this claim.

Work/life balance. The 40-hour week (or less) is standard among most law-related careers. Not so the law.

No billable hour requirements. This is closely related to less stress and work/life balance. This bane of law firm practice does not exist outside the mainstream.

No more lawyer jokes.

The Con:

Reduced earning potential. Most JD-preferred careers lack the earning potential of mainstream law. There are, however, some exceptions. For example, compliance professionals who work in the financial services industry have excellent earning potential. Moreover, not all mainstream attorney jobs come with high compensation.

Less marketability. The fungibility of a law degree is unique among the professions. Once you have moved into a law-related career, you will have limited those options to some extent. After a few years, you will likely be "typecast" by prospective employers as a Contract Administrator, Risk Manager, Pension Specialist, etc., which might make it more difficult to change careers.

Reporting to individuals with less education. This is a problem for some, but not all, attorneys who move out of the mainstream. You will likely report to and be supervised by professionals who lack your educational attainments.

Less prestige. If your ego is tied up with having attended law school, been awarded a JD, passed a bar exam, and being licensed to practice as an attorney, this might be a problem for you.

Stigmatization by some mainstream attorneys. This was a much bigger issue 20 years ago when knowledge that there were a great many law-related options available to lawyers was a new concept. Over time it has become less of an issue, although it is still prevalent in certain quarters and among certain attorneys.

Possible difficulty returning to mainstream practice. This is related to the stigmatization problem that some JD-preferred attorneys face should they seek to return to a mainstream practice environment. Some attorneys find that prospective mainstream legal employers regard them as less-than-committed attorneys because they tested the non-mainstream waters.

CHAPTER 3

Law Jobs Aren't Always
Where You Think They Are

This chapter explores the largely untapped hidden legal job market which, if fully understood and exploited by entry-level attorneys, law students and law school career services offices, can prove to be an immensely interesting job-hunting option. We will: (1) examine the general characteristics of "hidden" legal job market opportunities, (2) discuss the strategies that you can employ to uncover and compete for these positions, and (3) focus on specific hidden legal job opportunities in law firms, corporations, government, nonprofits, and in law-related arenas, respectively.

If you're able to navigate this hidden legal job market, you will have a significant competitive advantage over job seekers who don't know such possibilities exist, who neglect to incorporate them into their job-hunting and career-transition strategies, or who don't understand them.

The most obvious advantage: much less competition for you.

Profiling the Hidden Legal Job Market

The simplest definition of the hidden legal job market is that it consists of job opportunities that: (1) are not advertised, or more precisely, not advertised through traditional means, or (2) not readily known to job seekers or their advisors. This means that you have to dig a little deeper and more creatively to discover the opportunities that might be out there for you.

Recruiters, career specialists, and personnel professionals repeatedly cite the following claim:

"Over 80 percent of all job opportunities are not advertised. They are filled through networking. What you see on the Internet and in the newspapers is only the tip of the iceberg." There is a kernel of truth to this statement, but it is a different kernel than what the "experts" proclaim.

If you ask where this 80 percent figure comes from, you get a blank stare. It is one of those oft-repeated maxims that probably date back to the early days when the first human resources professional recruited the first job candidate for the first job. The only survey that has ever attempted to ascertain how positions are filled came up with a much lower number than 80 percent. In fact, 56 percent of the surveyed positions were filled through networking. This pre-Internet survey did not seek to determine the proportion of jobs that are advertised, nor whether what you see published is, in fact, only the tip of the iceberg.

The truth is that no one really has any clear idea how many jobs go unadvertised, or how deep the iceberg itself extends beneath the surface. While unadvertised jobs are probably not as massive as the statement alleges, they do exist in significant numbers. Moreover, they are not the only component of the hidden legal job market.

Why Are Jobs "Hidden"?

Employers do not usually conceal the fact that they are hiring. In most cases, that would be counterintuitive and self-defeating. Just because YOU don't know that recruiting efforts are underway does not mean that the human resources department is on vacation. There are valid reasons why a job may not be advertised—or may not yet be advertised.

The most frequent such reasons are:

- Some employers do not want to be compelled to review—and perhaps feel obligated to respond to—a ton of resumes from marginally qualified candidates. Consequently, they prefer to begin the recruitment process "quietly" by tapping into their existing networks. That could mean asking current employees to recommend possible applicants, or going outside the organization to ask trusted advisors, acquaintances, or professional colleagues.
- The hiring organization is growing so rapidly that it simply has no time to advertise its openings. This is true of many high-technology companies, consulting firms, and even some law firms in hot fields during good economic times.
- The organization promotes a current employee and has not yet gotten around to recruiting a replacement for the newly-created vacancy.
- Many employers retain the resumes they receive (both solicited and unsolicited) for a fixed period of time, and then turn to this resume bank or database when a similar position actually arises. They can then contact possible candidates without spending any additional time or money on advertising.

Identifying Hidden Opportunities

The strategies discussed below apply regardless of employment sector (e.g., law firm, corporation, nonprofit, government, international):

- **Network.** Communicating with persons within an employing organization or who have close contacts in the organization, or with individuals who have diverse connections to organizations in which you might be interested, is still one of the best ways to identify jobs that are not advertised. It is also the best way to become seriously considered for any position—advertised or unadvertised—particularly if your intermediary endorses your candidacy and is well respected within the employing organization.

  Fellow alumni of your undergraduate and law schools are among the best support groups and information resources about the hidden job market. Alums are fair game wherever and however you locate them, whether through an alumni directory, by contacting your schools' alumni affairs offices and/or career placement offices, identifying them in a database or commercial directory, or by joining the local chapter of the alumni association where you live or where you intend to relocate (which, in most cases, you can even do at long distance). They are likely to know about job possibilities that you will not have heard about. In addition, they are likely to be more amenable to unsolicited contacts by strangers who are fellow alums since they share the "old school tie" with you. Alums are by no means the only networking resource at your disposal. For an extensive list of possible contacts that a typical law grad might consider, see Chapter 16 (*Prepare Your Contacts Roadmap*).

  > **Your fellow alumni are among the best information resources about the hidden job market.**

- **Join or start support groups.** Support groups of fellow job applicants who are not competing for the same positions as you can be very useful. They provide a forum in which non-competing job seekers can meet in order to share job leads and career insights with each other. For example, attorneys seeking positions in certain geographic areas can advise and perhaps assist colleagues seeking positions in other geographic areas, sharing information, ideas, and potential networking contacts in order to leverage their job searches. While supporting your support group colleagues, you are also developing a network of professional colleagues for the future. This can be very important, given that the legal job market is becoming increasingly unsettled. A recent survey found that attorneys who left law school since 1995 change jobs every 3.8 years on average.

- **Invoke industry and professional contacts.** People who work in industries or employment sectors that interest you will often be "in the loop" concerning job opportunities. Attendance at professional meetings, seminars and conferences can put you in touch with these insiders. For example, if you aspire to a healthcare legal position, attending meetings of the local chapter of the American Health Lawyers Association (www. healthlawyers.org) will put you in direct contact with precisely the knowledgeable and influential people you need to know.

    You should also read industry and professional trade publications, which will help you monitor new developments, initiatives and projects that could create job opportunities. Trade publications such as *Oil and Gas Journal* (www.ogj.com) can alert you to industry trends, major transactions, large new government and private sector contracts, the names and backgrounds of major energy industry players, and much more. This kind of information is invaluable to any energy industry job seeker.

    The energy industry and its leading trade publication is only one of thousands of like possibilities. Every industry trade and professional association publishes materials that can be tremendous sources of information for aspiring job seekers. Since most of them have very accessible Web sites and post many of their publications online, you have a wealth of inside information at your fingertips. Staying in touch with local Chambers of Commerce, Boards of Trade, and economic development agencies in order to obtain early intelligence about companies relocating to, or expanding within, your geographic area of interest, is another activity that you can employ in order to track the hidden job market. Very few people, for example, are aware that public utilities have extensive business attraction programs that seek to entice businesses to relocate to their service areas. These organizations are repositories of early intelligence about what is—and will be—happening in their communities.

- **Analyze trends.** Keeping up with both macro and micro economic, demographic, political and societal trends—internationally, domestically, and locally—can give your hidden legal job market strategy a big boost. Say, for example, that you want to identify rapidly growing companies. Chapter 14 (*Enhance Your Law Credential*) discusses some of the major trends that have legal employment implications.

- **Examine promotion and new-hire announcements.** Internal promotions usually mean two jobs: one for the person being promoted and another for the one taking his or her place, sometimes at an entry-level (often, there is a "cascade" effect on moves up the organization ladder, until at the bottom of the pecking order, an entry-level position opens up). Promotion and new-hire announcements often appear in a "People" or similar feature column in the local newspapers, business journals, legal trade publications, and industry or sector trade publications, as well as on their Web sites. Your interest should be in the position the person promoted or new hire left rather than the one that is the focus of the media attention. If the person is leaving a job you are qualified to perform, send your resume to the organization before it can get around to formally seeking a successor.

  Press releases issued by employer public relations offices are widely available online. They are often about new hires. Identifying where a new hire previously worked is immensely valuable information for the hidden job market sleuth. Press releases also provide a steady stream of information about new business initiatives, acquisitions, spinoffs, divestitures, etc., all of which could be important for your career.

  Companies are not the only employers that issue press releases. Government agencies have massive public relations arms that publish a steady stream of such releases, often announcing promotions, new program initiatives, and projected budgets for the next fiscal year. All of these have an impact on agency hiring. Even law firms, now that they are compelled to promote their services like other businesses, issue numerous press releases and put them on their Web sites.

- **Join state, local, and specialty bar association sections and committees.** Monitoring the growth of these membership organizations can help you determine growth areas of the law, as well as provide you with organizations that you might want to join for both their intelligence and networking potential. For example, employment law sections of state bars have tripled their membership rolls in the last 10 years, as workplace disputes have escalated.

Where to Find Hidden Job Intelligence

Sources of information about the hidden job market are many and varied. Some of the most valuable, generic information sources are discussed below. Others will be examined later in this chapter.

Legal journals—both print and online—can be important sources of information about new jobs. Commercial legal journals in particular (as opposed to state and local bar association publications) often go into depth about positive and negative developments at law firms, corporate in-house counsel offices, and government law offices. They also focus a lot of attention on the comings and goings of lawyers who work for these organizations, thereby giving you a "heads up" concerning possible openings. Trade and professional association publications and Web sites, while having to be a bit more circumspect than their commercial trade publication counterparts when discussing the ups-and-downs of companies and people that constitute their associations' memberships, still contain a great deal of useful information about where their industries are going and what might happen when they get there in terms of job opportunities.

To cite only one example, the **Business Software Alliance** (www.bsa. org), an advocacy organization representing the world software industry in 65 countries, is currently focusing a lot of attention on the growing epidemic of software piracy and on what can be done about it, primarily from a legal standpoint. The Alliance's initiatives and research reports imply that there is an increasing number of jobs being created in both the public and private sectors that focus on anti-piracy matters and that the kind of "soft" intellectual property expertise necessary to work in this field can be readily acquired by any lawyer without a scientific, engineering, or technical background.

Investment newsletters often contain gems such as new product initiatives, company plans for the near-term and long-term, potential acquisition and divestiture activity, the impact of new and proposed legislation and/or government regulations on particular industries and specific employers, etc. Most investment newsletters charge an annual subscription fee. Some are available in the business sections of public libraries.

Government Annual Performance Plans and Strategic Plans are relatively recent additions to the massive volume of public sector information that can be mined for hidden job opportunities. For example, a recent U.S. Department of Justice Annual Performance Plan indicated that the Department wanted to increase the number of attorney positions devoted to prosecuting terrorist activities from 416 to 523 nationwide in the ensuing fiscal year. That kind of advance notice of hiring intentions can be invaluable to a job-seeker who wants to plan ahead and position oneself to take advantage of a promising opportunity. It means that you can proceed to be a proactive job hunter and get your credentials before the hiring organization before it issues a vacancy announcement, an initiative that may also impress the hiring officials with your foresight.

"Hidden" Legal Jobs in Law Firms

(Yes, even law firms have a variety of hidden legal job opportunities):

A. Hidden legal jobs in expanding existing practice areas. Law firms always prefer to find a way to earn more revenue out of an established practice than to have to craft an entirely new one. Sometimes a government policy initiative can have major implications for lawyers' livelihoods. For example:

- One of the big issues in Washington in 2003 was the proposal to eliminate the double taxation of stock dividends. A major tax policy shift like this one would likely have a significant impact on both tax and securities practice. It sounds rather simple, but the proposal itself was quite complex. The Internet was filled with articles and analyses of the proposal that pointed out the numerous issues that both public companies and investors would have to consider. The Spring 2003 issue of *CFO Magazine* called the proposal, "*The Tax Attorneys and Accountants Full Employment Act.*" Had you focused only on traditional legal job and career Web sites, you would not have even known that this was in the works. This example impacted primarily the larger law firms with corporate clients. The following example, however, is one to which everyone else in the law firm community (medium-size and small firms as well as sole practitioners) could relate to and benefit from.

- The Internal Revenue Service (www.irs.gov) undertakes and publishes a large number of statistical studies every year of virtually every facet of its activities. One of the most revealing bits of information from recent IRS studies is the fact that the number of tax controversies—disputes between the IRS and taxpayers, both corporate and individual—is escalating rapidly (up almost 35 percent in three years), and the rate of increase is accelerating, particularly with respect to high-income individuals. In times of economic and federal budgetary stress, enforcement efforts increase substantially, which is good news for tax controversy practices, many of which are solo and small firm activities. Moreover, as state budgets sink deeper into the crisis spawned by the Great Recession, state revenue departments are following the IRS lead and going after perceived under-payers and non-filers much more aggressively than at any time in the past.

    Tax controversy practice, heretofore something of a quiet "backwater," is emerging as a growth opportunity and a specialty that is by no means glutted (yet) with practitioners.

B. Hidden legal jobs in rapidly changing practice areas. Many traditional legal practice areas are rapidly evolving, presenting attorneys with new and exciting opportunities in which to find a niche and make a mark. Dramatic advances in technology, for example, are outpacing the ability of legislators and regulators to keep up-to-date. A few examples:

- **Securities and bank regulators** are confounded by their inability to regulate capital flows and transfers. Major financial market players and even individuals can move trillions of dollars around the world at the press of a computer key, rendering irrelevant any controls that national and international governing bodies thus far have been able to devise. Consequently, government enforcers continue to commit more resources to resolving this problem, which in turn prompts potential regulated entities to do the same from a defensive standpoint.
- **Telecommunications technology** has advanced with startling speed, creating new consumer products, services, and complexities that traditional regulatory schemes never contemplated and are finding difficult to oversee. Like the problem of regulating international capital flows, the telecommunications revolution spawns legal job opportunities on both sides of the regulatory divide.
- **Healthcare** has been profoundly affected by technology. Telemedicine, the ability to treat patients—and even perform surgery—at very long distance presents regulators with serious issues concerning the licensing of healthcare professionals (e.g., should a Colorado-licensed physician be permitted, via telemedicine technology, to treat a fallen skier on a Utah mountaintop when the physician is not licensed in Utah?), professional liability, etc. The ability of infectious diseases to move around the world limited only by the speed of air travel, has brought into sharp focus the dated nature of healthcare regulation at the borders and even impacts on seemingly distant, unrelated practice areas such as immigration law. Each of these developments presents big problems for regulators, which always mean major opportunities for savvy attorneys seeking to enter a dynamic practice area.

  JOB ALERT: Both sides of the regulatory ledger need fresh legal blood in order to cope with what is coming.

C. Hidden legal jobs in new practice area initiatives. Business realities are forcing law firms to anticipate trends and become much more aggressive opportunity seekers. Anticipating the enactment of the landmark legislation (the Sarbanes-Oxley Act) in 2002 responding to the corporate and accounting scandals that dominated the news, many law firms had already positioned themselves to market their newly minted "corporate governance" practices to clients by the time the new law was enacted.

The complacent days when law firms could rely on a handful of major, continuing clients and their recurring legal requirements are gone. Law firms now have to behave like any other business, be agile enough to respond instantly to changing market conditions, and then reposition, expand and market their services aggressively.

Law firms pay management consultants big bucks to alert them to the emergence of new practice areas. You can do the same thing for yourself. The skill involved in this kind of prognostication is not difficult to acquire. All it takes is keeping abreast of the news and doing some trends analysis of your own. It did not take a rocket scientist to discern that there would inevitably be a government regulatory and enforcement reaction to the excesses of Enron, WorldCom, Tyco, Adelphia, Arthur Andersen, etc., and that the additional regulatory "overlay" would create opportunities for attorneys. In more recent years, that Wall Street's shenanigans leading up to the collapse of the housing market and disappearance of credit would generate a political and policy reaction on Capitol Hill was eminently predictable.

D. Hidden legal jobs in "spin-off" practice areas. One of the most interesting developments in law firm practice in recent years is the division of traditional practice areas into subspecialties. "Executive Compensation" spinning off from "Employee Benefits" is one example. Another is what is happening to Intellectual Property (IP) practice, especially to "soft" IP—trademarks and copyrights:

Trademark and Copyright Law were, for years, fairly low-key areas of IP practice. Not anymore. Now they have become much more interesting—sexy even—as IP owners must cope with a flood of issues generated by the leapfrogging of technology over traditional soft IP practice. Read any IP trade publication or visit any major law firm website, click on "practice areas," then on "intellectual property," and what do you see? The practice is no longer broken down into just three subspecialties: patent, trademark, and copyright. Today you are just as likely to see subspecialties such as:

- Brand management
- Anti-piracy and counterfeiting

- Advertising and marketing
- Royalty securitization
- Intellectual property asset management

E. Hidden legal jobs in areas that major law firms think important. It is a good idea to take a look around and see where attorneys are flocking. This is an indicator of where the future lies. There are a number of very easy-to-implement analyses you can execute:

- State and local bar association section and committee membership can be very enlightening.
- What are the section and committee membership numbers and trends? Which ones are attracting the most attention?
- What new sections and committees have been added lately?
- Contacting bar staff should get you the answers.

Membership in state bar sections on Alternative Dispute Resolution, Employment Law, Cyber Law, Corporate Governance, Entertainment and Sports Law, Intellectual Property, and Health Law, for example, have been growing impressively. Trusts and Estates sections and committees have seen their memberships decline. New sections and committees addressing Terrorism, Mass Disaster Response, Elder Law, and Privacy, to name a few, have been popping up all over the country.

F. Hidden legal jobs in specialty bar associations. Which ones are growing? Which ones are new? How are they doing in terms of number of members? The American Corporate Counsel Association, the American Health Lawyers Association, the American Immigration Lawyers Association, the Association of Attorney-Mediators, the International Masters of Gaming Law, the Internet Bar Association, the National Association of College and University Attorneys, the National Employment Lawyers Association, and the Food and Drug Law Institute, for example, are doing very well.

Specialty bars now encompass organizations such as the American Association of Attorney-Certified Public Accountants, the Cyberlaw Association, the Cyberspace Bar Association, the National School Boards Association's Council of School Attorneys, and the Sports Lawyers Association, all of which have emerged in recent years as important harbingers of practice area growth.

Don't discount a specialty bar association's membership roster just because it does not include law firm practitioners. The important point is detecting expansion. The dramatic growth in membership in the National Association of College and University Attorneys over the last decade is an important indicator not only of employment growth among attorneys in academe, but also of opportunities for law firms to land educational institutions as clients.

G. Hidden legal jobs in law firm newsletters, "white papers" & other publications and presentations. Law firms have become mini-publishing and Internet broadcasting companies. Naturally, they do this for business development purposes, focusing on areas that they think will generate business and paying clients. A quick scan of what the law firms are writing and broadcasting about tells you what they think the major issues of the day are—and/or will be in the very near future. Thus, they are a strong indicator of where the law firm jobs are likely to be…or not to be.

In March, 2011, I conducted a survey of what 10 randomly selected major law firms with multiple domestic offices were writing, webcasting, podcasting, and presenting seminars about, and it can tell you a great deal about where law firms believe their businesses are heading. The survey results below reflect the most frequently cited topics, followed by the number of total events and publications about each topic:

- Banking and Finance Law and Regulation—78
- Government & Public Policy—46
- Securities Law & Regulation—35
- Technology and New Media—25
- Energy & Infrastructure—23
- Health Law & Insurance Regulation—20
- Doing Business in China—15
- Intellectual Property—15
- Private Equity—14
- Compliance—14
- Transportation—14
- Labor & Employment Law—8
- White Collar Criminal Defense—8
- Bankruptcy, Restructuring and Corporate Turnaround—6
- Environmental Law—6
- Tax—6
- Doing Business in the European Union—6
- Executive Compensation—4
- Privacy—4

- Advertising—4
- Food & Drug Law—3
- Mergers & Acquisitions—3
- Doing Business in Brazil—3
- Real Estate Law—3
- Outsourcing—2
- Government Contracting—2
- Islamic Finance—2
- Doing Business in India—1
- Alternative Dispute Resolution—1
- Doing Business in Mexico—1
- Pensions—1
- Maritime Law—1
- E-Discovery—1
- Doing Business in Russia—1
- Antitrust—1

What you can learn from this list is illuminating.

Keep in mind that this survey was national in scope, and that law firm emphasis on particular issues can vary with geographic location. For example, Wall Street law firms are disproportionately oriented toward corporate finance, investing, and transactions; Washington, DC firms focus considerable attention on government regulation and contracting; Miami firms look to Latin America; and Seattle firms are geared more toward Asia and high technology.

Not surprisingly, law firms believe that there is a great deal of business to be generated by financial regulatory reform (securities law and regulation could easily be subsumed under this topic, making it even more prominent on the list), government and public policy, energy, high technology and health law. Internationally, they believe that China and the European Union are where their focus should be.

You can also learn a great deal about practice areas that might give you second thoughts about proceeding with them: antitrust and pensions, for example (although my strong sense is that, as time goes on, you will see pensions go way up the list, given the looming bubble of severely underfunded retirement plans). E-discovery, which receives a lot of legal media ink, is not very attractive, which is surprising at first glance, but fairly rational if you think about it. Its incredibly weak position on the list might be due to the realization that something so technology-based may soon not require much human intervention in order to function effectively. Moreover, it is important to be aware of practice areas that did not make the list, such as estate planning (understandable given that only the very wealthy now really have to be concerned about generational transfers).

Finally, the list could be an indicator of emerging issues that are only now becoming interesting, thanks to external events. As this is being written, for example, the Middle East is in turmoil, beset by popular revolutions demanding greater political freedom and better living standards (reminiscent of 1848 in Europe).

> **JOB ALERT:** A savvy analyzer of the list above might want to delve into Islamic Finance as a promising practice area.

H. Hidden legal jobs in boutique law firms. The creation (and disappearance) of boutique law firms (firms that specialize in only one, or a handful of related, practice areas) is also an excellent indicator of where the action is among law firms in general. One place to look for this phenomenon in all of both its positive and negative manifestations is Washington, DC. The nation's capital is the Mecca of boutique law firms for obvious reasons (nothing generates legal business like federal action). In the 1970s, for example, telecommunications and energy boutiques proliferated in Washington. Then, Ronald Reagan was elected president, *deregulation* became Washington's mantra of the moment, and both practices came to a screeching halt. The telecom and energy boutiques closed up shop and left town or disappeared. In the mid-1990s, Congress passed the Telecommunications Reform Act, and the boutiques were resurrected. Similarly, electricity deregulation, increased global energy demand and corresponding rising fossil fuel prices, and a so-far modest push for energy independence and alternative energy development are prompting a return of energy practices.

> **The financial services industry employs a substantial number of lawyers to help launch new financial products.**

The rise, demise, and resurrection of telecom boutiques and energy practices were eminently predictable. All one had to do was be aware of what was going on in the world, administration public policy debates, Congress, the Federal Communications Commission, the Department of Energy and the Federal Energy Regulatory Commission… and plan accordingly.

I. Hidden legal jobs in the skills suddenly in demand. Contrary to conventional wisdom, lawyering skills are not static. In the past quarter-century, attorneys have been dragged kicking and screaming into the computer age, forced to learn Internet skills and certain software and cloud computing programs, not to mention learning a whole new workplace language. Practicing without resort to e-mail, computerized legal research, spreadsheets or PowerPoint is inconceivable today. It probably will not be too long before practitioners will find it equally inconceivable to practice without being at ease with videoconference depositions and voice recognition software. Those who are "first past the post" in learning how to utilize these technologies will clearly be ahead of the competition and have a distinct advantage in job-seeking.

J. Hidden legal jobs in law firm "ancillary businesses". More than 100 major law firms (and a growing number of smaller firms) have established ancillary businesses (many of which are consulting subsidiaries) in order to compete more effectively with CPA and management consulting firms that have been taking away market share from law firms. Ancillary businesses are the law firms' way of striking back, while also establishing potential new profit centers.

The term "ancillary business" was invented by law firms in order to circumvent bar regulator proscriptions on co-mingling law and other businesses, regulations that have largely gone unenforced by bar regulators.

Such subsidiaries are intended to be "one-stop shops" where a client can get an array of professional services—most often law-related services—in addition to legal services. Law firm ancillary businesses are often run by attorneys and are closely linked to the parent law firm, but with plenty of disclaimers about not giving legal advice, etc. The idea is twofold in purpose: (1) to earn more revenue from existing clients, and (2) to secure new clients who might also then engage the firm for their legal requirements.

Ancillary businesses are usually wholly owned subsidiaries of law firms. They can also be joint ventures or partnering arrangements between law firms and other professional service providers. They run the gamut of activities from very logical offshoots of lawyering, such as litigation consulting (with a view to incorporating an appreciation of the business issues involved in preparing cases for trial), document management for litigation support, and alternative dispute resolution services, to areas that are farther afield, such as insurance planning and recovery for policyholders, insurance claims analysis and valuation, risk management services, employee relations consulting, diversity recruiting and retention, government relations and lobbying, public affairs consulting, crisis communications, medical records consulting, business performance enhancement, governmental permitting, electronic compliance, corporate training programs on a vast array of topics (including online tutorials in a variety of legal topics), and many other fields of opportunity.

There is no accurate, up-to-date list of law firm ancillary businesses. However, a methodical examination of law firm Web sites can yield a lot of targeted information about law firm entrepreneurial efforts in the ancillary business arena.

> **JOB ALERT:** Ancillary businesses also hire attorneys, but attorneys with skills and backgrounds that are not necessarily those sought when a traditional law firm is hiring first-year associates. In terms of academic achievement, the bar is lower if you are able to supplement your legal background with something additional. For example, if you have experience working for a trade or professional association, you might be a strong candidate for a position with a law firm subsidiary that provides governmental relations services. If you are a nurse-attorney, you would be in serious consideration for a position with a law firm subsidiary that provides healthcare risk management consulting advice.

Consulting firms that advise law firms on business development believe that ancillary business ventures will snowball in the next several years and will expand into other professional service areas heretofore largely untapped, such as literary agencies, sports marketing, corporate human resources, and intellectual asset management.

K. Hidden legal jobs in specialization trends. The hidden job market is not limited to large, mid-size, or small law firms.

It also exists among sole practitioners, but takes somewhat different forms. Obviously, it would be very difficult for a sole practitioner to have an ancillary business (in addition to certain issues that might arise under the Unauthorized Practice of Law provisions of state Codes of Professional Conduct). However, it is not difficult for sole practitioners to specialize in one or more legal practice areas… and to market themselves as specialists.

Lawyers have traditionally regarded themselves as generalists able to handle any problem a client brought to them. However, as law has become more complex and intruded into virtually every facet of human activity, specialization has become almost a necessity.

Historically, state Rules of Professional Conduct prohibited attorneys from promoting themselves as specialists, with the exception of patent practitioners and admiralty lawyers (and occasionally trademark attorneys). But in the face of both the increasing complexity of the law and public demand for special competencies, state professional regulators have been dragged (often kicking and screaming) toward an acknowledgement that regulated specialization—and the advertising thereof—in some form has to be permitted. Thus was born the certification of legal specialists. A majority of states sponsor certification plans for legal specialists in specifically identified practice areas.

JOB ALERT: The hidden job opportunity embedded in getting yourself certified as a legal specialist is (1) the paltry number of certified specialists nationwide (estimated to be less than five percent of the attorney population), and (2) expanded marketing and advertising clout. You can determine the hot specialty areas in any jurisdiction that has a board of legal specialization or a comparable body by contacting it and asking for a specialist count. A few states (Minnesota, for example) post very good and detailed information on specialization (see the Minnesota State Board of Legal Certification's website at www.blc.state.mn.us).

Hidden Legal Jobs in Corporations

While major corporations employ a great many attorneys, legal employment levels among Fortune 500 companies' in-house counsel offices have largely been static for a generation. The real engines of corporate legal hiring in recent years have been (1) JD-preferred positions, and (2) smaller companies. In some corporations, the general counsel's office may not even be the largest corporate unit employing lawyers.

Virtually every major company has attorneys performing its ethics function, usually in an ethics office independent of the in-house counsel office. The Sarbanes-Oxley Act increased the prominence of the corporate ethics function, and compelled virtually every publicly-traded corporation that did not yet have one to establish an ethics office.

Many companies have discrete compliance/regulatory affairs offices that make sure that the organization is cognizant of, and in conformance with, the flood of Federal and state regulations that affect corporate activities.

A growing number of corporations have risk management offices that attempt to evaluate financial and other risks companies face and minimize them through insurance purchases and other risk-avoidance measures. Attorneys are taught to evaluate and temper risk every day, and the risk management industry recognizes that: approximately 20 percent of the risk managers in the U.S. have law degrees.

Perhaps the most interesting corporate legal hiring trend is the "embedding" of lawyers in diverse company divisions so that on-the-spot, immediate advice and counsel can be available to assess whether the corporation is doing anything "wrong." In other words, setting up satellite general counsel offices throughout the company.

Corporate tax departments are increasingly separate entities, thanks to the escalating complexity of the Internal Revenue Code and its state counterparts. The legal issues affecting human resources departments in some companies are so diverse, complex, wide-ranging, and vexing that there is a trend toward hosting their own legal counsel to handle employee grievances and charges of management misconduct, including sexual harassment, etc.

Industry-specific legal niches. While the opportunities discussed above are, in a general corporate sense, the most common manifestations of the proliferation of company legal functions, they by no means address every type of legal function found in corporate America. Specific industries and employment sectors often structure their own particular legal employment response to the unique circumstances of their corporate purposes and missions.

Manufacturing. Manufacturing firms with labor problems almost always have distinct and sometimes quite elaborate labor relations departments staffed with attorneys. Job titles include attorney, labor relations specialist ,and others with labor as part of the job title.

Spin-offs and divestitures. Corporate mergers and acquisitions adversely affect many attorneys. The classic example: Megacorp buys Minicorp and lets all of the latter's legal staff go. However, there is a far less well-publicized corporate reorganization phenomenon going on that presents great opportunity for attorneys: spin-offs and divestitures—the opposite of mergers and acquisitions. Twenty-first century companies have to be agile in order to survive in a rapidly evolving, global economy. Consequently, the shedding of unprofitable and underperforming corporate units is a growing occurrence. The reasons behind the growth in divestitures and spin-offs are many:

- A company may wish to exit a particular market.
- It may feel that it needs to sell a component in order to raise cash to grow the remaining portions of the business.
- It may sell a subsidiary in order to raise money to finance an acquisition.
- It may decide to concentrate on its core business and divest itself of anything that does not"fit"that core strategy.
- It may want to shed an underperforming division.
- Government antitrust or other regulators may force a divestiture.

Astute attorneys seeking opportunities in divestitures also have to be agile since such transactions normally occur in a much shorter time-frame than acquisitions. An excellent means of identifying and anticipating divestitures and spinoffs is to monitor merger and acquisition activity, which is frequently a precursor to such shedding. You can monitor spinoff activity at Web sites such as www.spinoffprofiles.com and http://stockspinoffblog.com.

When the major CPA firms first came under pressure from the Securities and Exchange Commission in the late 1990s regarding their provision of both auditing and simultaneous consulting services to corporate clients, their very public response was to spin-off their consulting arms into independent entities. They continued to provide consulting services, but probably bought some additional time by touting their divestiture activity. In every case, the spinoff resulted in additional opportunities for attorneys, including recent law grads.

Emerging companies. The discussion so far has focused on established companies as sources of hidden legal jobs. But they are not the only corporations that offer legal opportunities.

Keeping track of new companies that come on the scene and blossom is also a very valuable way to carve out a possible place for you to exercise your newly-acquired legal talents. Venture capital firms always announce their seed, "mezzanine", and other investments publicly, through press releases on their Web sites, in industry trade journals, and in the business sections of general circulation newspapers. *These announcements are advance notices of likely hiring activity, once the fortunate recipient gets the money.*

University technology transfer offices license faculty inventions and research, incubate nascent companies designed to commercialize university patents, and structure new businesses (e.g., joint ventures with faculty members; partnership arrangements and strategic alliances with outside companies), and announce these initiatives on their Web sites. Center your efforts here on major universities and those with a prominent research reputation, such as Harvard, MIT, Stanford and Johns Hopkins.

> **Management consulting firms have a track record of hiring entry-level attorneys.**

MIT laboratories, for example, have spawned hundreds of companies, including some that became huge success stories, such as 3Com Corporation, Cirrus Logic, Inc., Lotus Development Corporation, Open Market, Inc., RSA Data Security, Inc., and Akamai Technologies, Inc.

Just in the week that I am writing this chapter, the following research likely to soon be commercialized has been announced:

- Medical College of Wisconsin researchers are working on incorporating whole-genome sequencing into routine clinical tests at low cost, which has enormous implications for diagnosing rare inherited childhood diseases. An unidentified insurance company said that it would cover sequencing costs if they can be demonstrated to be cheaper than traditional diagnostic tests.

- Practical applications of smart computing is a current focus of the Linguistics Section of Brandeis University's Department of Computer Science. The objective is to enable consumers to find out more open-ended data without confusing their cybersources. To do that, computers have to be able to have a sense of time, understand the relationship of words within a sentence, be aware of synonyms, grasp common idioms, and be aware of social cues. Brandeis researchers are engaged in teaching smart computers to think more like the human brain. In "computerese," they are attempting to build an algorithm that will make it possible for computers to understand the hidden meaning of a narrative by applying math principles to language. Computational linguistics is a growth industry with vast potential in such areas as developing communication and language software for the Web, specific industries, government, cataloging and retrieving photographs and other images that do not include text, and performing complex archival tasks and translation.
- A startup company launched by University of Illinois researchers is commercializing technology that involves an inflatable catheter covered with "stretchy" sensors designed to make cardiac procedures shorter and safer. The underlying technology senses temperature and electrical activity, which could also lead to better monitoring during other types of surgery, potentially reducing the number of complications. The device has succeeded in animal tests designed to mimic atrial fibrillation, which affects more than two million Americans and 15 percent of all stroke victims.

Universities are by no means the only source of exciting innovation with vast commercial potential.

Corporations in the aggregate undertake far more research and development than universities. They outnumber university research departments and they have the profit motive to spur them on to new discoveries. Many of our most exciting and profitable scientific advances derive from small companies. Here are several examples, also from the week in which this is being written:

- A "gastric pacemaker" implant that could be an alternative to gastric bypass surgery. This is a far less radical alternative to stomach stapling or stomach bypass surgery for the morbidly obese, and is already being sold in Europe. The device senses when a person is eating and generates a premature feeling of fullness by stimulating nerves that curl around the stomach. The implant was developed by a Mountain View, California company called Intrapace. In clinical trials, the device led to an average weight loss of 22 percent after one year, with some patients losing as much as 38 percent of their body weight.

- A retinal prosthesis—a.k.a. "bionic eye"—has received clinical and commercial approval in Europe after more than 20 years of research and development. People blinded by degenerative eye disease will be able to get an implant that can partially restore their vision. The device was developed by a California company called Second Sight. Several million people in the United States suffer from degenerative retinal diseases such as retinitis pigmentosa. The device, the "Argus II," will cost around $115,000. Second Sight hopes to receive FDA approval by 2012.

Hidden Legal Jobs in Banking and Financial Services

Banks and other financial services institutions often offer trust and/or wealth management services and employ attorneys (often very recent graduates) to fill those roles. Since the enactment of the Graham-Leach-Bliley Act of 1999—which knocked down the firewall between commercial banking, investment banking, and other financial activities—the opportunities for attorneys in this market sector have increased, as banks and their competitors have established subsidiary businesses. The Dodd-Frank Wall Street Reform and Consumer Protection Act is generating a great many corporate opportunities for attorneys.

Hidden Legal Jobs in CPA Firms

CPA firms (such as the "Big Four"—KPMG, PricewaterhouseCoopers, Ernst & Young, and Deloitte Touche) have large legal staffs at both their headquarters and numerous field locations. A number of CPA firms even have more than one type of office performing legal functions. All have their own in-house counsel offices which have traditionally been interesting first stops for recent law grads with some "value-added" credentials in addition to their law degrees (e.g., concentration or strong performance in tax courses while in law school, an LLM in tax, or; initial steps along the multi-part CPA examination path). Several also have national tax offices that monitor tax activity in Congress, the Treasury Department and the IRS, and advise field employees on the constantly changing Federal tax laws and regulations.

Hidden Legal Jobs in Insurance

The insurance industry is another good example of hidden opportunities for entry-level attorneys. A number of my entry-level legal career transition clients went to work for insurance companies in a variety of roles, including litigation management (dealing with outside counsel, strategizing cases, coverage decisions, etc.), claims administration (especially directors and officers liability, professional malpractice, environmental liability, HIPAA matters, and disability concerns), and even underwriting (especially environmental and professional liability underwriting). There are also hidden opportunities at the insurance agency level, where attorneys are perceived as valuable contributors to closing group sales. A recurring model goes like this: the insurance agent markets policies to a large employer, elicits interest, and then calls upon the resident sales team attorney ("advanced marketing consultant" is a frequently employed moniker) to explain the legal and tax considerations to the prospective client and to advise and assist in negotiating the transaction and closing the deal.

Hidden Legal Jobs in Management Consulting Firms

Management consulting firms also have a growing number and variety of practice groups and teams that employ attorneys as consultants, and have a track record of hiring entry-level attorneys who also have a background in one of their areas of need. Among the most prevalent practices are Corporate Governance, Litigation Management, Regulatory Compliance, Tax Compliance, Procurement, Human Resources, Corporate Recovery, and Real Estate. In addition, CPA firms that provide consulting services in addition to their auditing function also have comparable practice groups. These five major industries—financial services, insurance, manufacturing, accounting and consulting—are representative of hidden legal job opportunities that can be found throughout corporate America.

Hidden Legal Jobs in New Product Announcements

Companies get a lot of mileage out of announcing the development of new products. If these are destined to be winners in the marketplace, it is likely that significant hiring activity, including legal hiring activity, will follow. Every new product could represent an opportunity. Some may have very obvious legal or regulatory implications that often result in a need for additional legal talent, particularly those that come out of highly regulated industries, such as pharmaceuticals and financial services, where innovative products are the lifeblood of continuing growth and profits. If you are a good trends analyst, you should be able to spot these implications before your competition.

The financial service sector generates new products all the time, essential in order to compete effectively and to satisfy the hunger among investors for new and exotic investment vehicles, whether it be a new equities index, a creative mutual fund that permits spreading the risk among companies that have emerged as the subject of sectorial investing interest (see, e.g., national funeral home franchises, thoroughbred racing stables, or something as off-the-wall as the Pentagon's 2002 floating of the rather tasteless idea of a futures market in terrorist attacks!), or complex debt instruments that even the people selling them do not understand, such as Collateralized Debt Obligations (CDOs) and Credit Default Swaps.

Despite the trouble that these latter two complex investment vehicles caused us so recently, they are still being created today notwithstanding so-called financial regulatory reform. Moreover, regardless of any reform efforts, smart Wall Streeters and their "quants" will also be able to come up with creative investment instruments that circumvent any government attempts to regulate them.

The financial services industry employs a substantial number of lawyers (many of them neophytes) in nontraditional roles where they craft and review the documentation necessary to launch new financial products, and to advertise them without running afoul of the securities laws and regulations. Naturally, these positions are usually located in the major money centers, e.g., New York, Boston, Chicago, San Francisco. More such positions are being created in response to the recent revival of regulatory scrutiny of these companies and their products by federal and state enforcement and compliance agencies. When searching for these positions, look for search terms such as "Legal Document" in order to identify matching job titles.

Hidden Legal Jobs in Planned Business Expansions

Very few businesses expand without adding more employees, lawyers included. Often, legal staff expansion trails behind basic business expansion by a few months, which is actually an advantage since it enables the legal job seeker with top-flight anticipatory skills to get his or her foot in the door before an actual job advertisement hits the streets.

As I point out often in this book, entry-level attorneys who can anticipate job opportunities gain a huge advantage because they can apply before a job ad with restrictive experience requirements or other limiting language hits the streets. Chambers of commerce, boards of trade, industrial and economic development agencies, business attraction agencies and utilities are either actively involved in these initiatives or monitor them, or both. This makes communication with them a very important hidden job market identification strategy.

Hidden Legal Jobs in Government Commercialization Initiatives

Government R&D initiatives also result in new companies and thus new opportunities for legal employment. The following selected items or the technologies that made them possible were invented or developed for the National Aeronautics and Space Administration (NASA) space program, resulting in multi-billion dollar industries and the creation of millions of jobs, including many legal positions:

- "Blue Blocker" sunglasses
- Cable television
- Cellular phones and beepers
- Compact disks
- Digital watches and thermometers
- Electronic ignitions
- Fiber optics
- GPS navigation systems
- Halogen lights
- Juice boxes
- Kevlar
- Laser scanners
- Magnetic Resonance Imaging (MRI) scanners
- Pocket calculators
- Satellite telephones
- Sports domes

NASA documents its technology commercialization projects on its website (www.nasa.gov), as do many other U.S. government agencies, including:

- Agricultural Research Service (www.ars.usda.gov)
- Centers for Disease Control and Prevention (www.cdc.gov)
- Defense Advanced Research and Projects Agency (www.darpa.mil)
- Defense Technical Information Center (www.dtic.mil)
- Department of Energy (www.doe.gov)
- Department of Homeland Security (www.dhs.gov)
- Department of Transportation (www.dot.gov)
- Environmental Protection Agency (www.epa.gov)
- Federal Communications Commission (www.fcc.gov)
- National Imagery and Mapping Agency (www.nima.mil)

- National Institute of Standards and Technology (www.nist.gov)
- National Institutes of Health (www.nih.gov)
- National Oceanic and Atmospheric Administration (www.noaa.gov)
- National Science Foundation (www.nsf.gov)
- National Telecommunications and Information Administration (www.ntia.doc.gov)
- National Technical Information Service (www.ntis.gov)
- U.S. Geological Survey (www.usgs.gov)
- U.S. Patent and Trademark Office (www.uspto.gov)

You can also monitor Government policy and commercialization initiatives likely to have a major impact on business by following the activities and research reports of the White House Office of Science and Technology Policy (www.ostp.gov), the Government Accountability Office (www.gao.gov), the Congressional Research Service (www.loc.gov/crsinfo/whatscrs.html), and the National Technology Transfer Center (www.nttc.edu). The U.S. Government also has 315 research laboratories that have their own technology commercialization programs. You can monitor many of these laboratories at www.federallabs.org.

The Public Sector

The public sector, especially the U.S. government, offers a large number of hidden legal job opportunities. The number of legal positions in the U.S. government dwarfs those of any other employer anywhere. At any given time, the U.S. government is seeking to fill a substantial number of attorney job vacancies, and is almost always creating new ones. This is true even in times of purported budget cuts.

How the government hires attorneys. In order to understand where the federal government's hidden jobs are and how to identify them, you first have to understand how the government hires lawyers. A key concept is whether the position carries with it the title "attorney."

Federal attorney positions are exempt from normal civil service rules. That means that federal agencies and their many legal offices (over 3,000 nationwide and abroad) have a lot of leeway when hiring lawyers.

Unlike almost every other government profession, there is no uniformity among federal law offices in how they recruit and hire attorneys. That means that you cannot assume that the government is a monolith and that the hiring procedures at the Office of Chief Counsel at the Department of

Transportation's Federal Highway Administration, for example, are also followed by the Justice Department's Civil Division, or even by the parallel and equivalent Office of Chief Counsel at the Transportation Department's Federal Aviation Administration. One office may want one type of application document; another office may require a different one. One office may want to see a narrative statement responding to specific "ranking factors;" another office may request only a resume. One legal office may delegate its initial candidate evaluation to its agency's human resources office; another may do it internally. In contrast, the tens of thousands of law-related (JD-preferred) federal positions, in contrast, are subject to the full panoply of civil service rules.

Unadvertised Jobs. U.S. government attorney jobs are not required to be publicly advertised. While most are advertised, many are not. The only ways to scope out these opportunities are either (1) receiving "inside information" from someone, or (2) anticipating where legal hiring is likely to occur. What this means is that a federal legal job candidate has to be both reactive and proactive. The reactive approach means that you have to keep your eyes open for job opportunities that are advertised on www.usajobs.gov. A proactive strategy means taking affirmative steps to alert federal employers to your credentials. For additional discussion, see Chapter 17.

Monitoring crisis management (major legislation & government reorganizations). In the first decade of the 21st century, the U.S. government has had to respond to a series of major crises:

- The aftermath of the 2000 presidential election prompted action to overhaul electoral mechanics. A new federal agency, the Election Assistance Commission, was established to funnel funds to state and local election administrations to upgrade voting equipment. The sudden focus on this perennial "backwater" forced the more than 3,000 election administration offices nationwide to engage legal talent and stimulated scrutiny of electoral processes, resulting in a steady rise in challenges to them.
- Following the September 11, 2001 terrorist attacks, Congress acted quickly to enact legislation with profound legal and law-related hiring implications that often went far beyond the obvious in creating job opportunities for lawyers in both the public and private sectors:
  ✓ The USA Patriot Act, Pub. L. 107-56, imposed new compliance requirements on insurance companies and certain financial services firms.

✓ The Aviation and Transportation Security Act, Pub. L. 107-71, created the new Transportation Security Administration (TSA), a far-reaching new bureaucracy with 40,000+ employees, including many attorneys in more than 30 law offices nationwide.

✓ The Bioterrorism Act, Pub. L. 107-188, imposed new duties and mandates on "first responder" organizations all over the country, all requiring sorting out by attorneys.

✓ The Homeland Security Act, Pub. L. 107-296, created the largest new federal agency in over 50 years, transferred 22 existing agencies into the new Department of Homeland Security, and established several new legal offices within the Department. In addition, billions of dollars of new federal contracts awarded by DHS and many other agencies with national security responsibilities fueled thousands of private sector projects requiring legal input.

- Congress acted rapidly in response to the corporate accounting and reporting scandals of 2001–2002. The Sarbanes-Oxley Act had vast implications for publicly traded corporations, accounting and auditing firms, attorney regulation, securities brokers and dealers, and other professional groups and their regulators, as well as the Securities and Exchange Commission, the Department of Justice, the U.S. Sentencing Commission, the Department of Labor, the Pension Benefit Guaranty Corporation, plus the Self-Regulatory Organizations (such as the Financial industry Regulatory Authority and the New York Stock Exchange). The Act also created a new Public Company Accounting Oversight Board. All of these actions generated new public sector opportunities for attorneys, as well as a much greater number of private sector attorney and law-related jobs needed to meet the new legal mandates.

- The U.S. invasions of Afghanistan and Iraq were also legal job generating events. The military service Judge Advocate Generals' Corps staffed up to their highest levels in history (now numbering more than 6,000 attorneys). Contract and procurement positions in defense industries saw increased demand. The huge increase in the number of veterans seeking disability benefits was accompanied by a surge in claims, which in turn prompted Congress to repeal a 150-year old restriction on attorneys' fees for representing veterans in such cases.

- Hurricane Katrina not only precipitated a humanitarian and political tsunami, it also disrupted the New Orleans and Southern Louisiana legal community (a portion of which has still not recovered) while creating a significant number of legal positions in both the public and private sectors.

- The Great Recession both negatively and positively affected attorney and law-related employment: real estate attorneys whose practices focused on commercial and residential development and closings were deeply affected by the screeching halt in those endeavors. Conversely, the "distress" side of the real estate business has exploded and attorneys positioned to take advantage of that surge have thrived. Financial regulatory reform means thousands of new attorney and JD-preferred jobs in banks, thrifts, insurance companies and other financial services firms, as well as new jobs in regulatory agencies at the federal and state levels. In addition, law firms have scrambled to form new practice groups to take advantage of the regulatory compliance complexities of the wide-ranging Dodd-Frank Act.

- Healthcare reform has also prompted law firms with existing health law practices to expand them and firms without such a practice to develop one. Insurers are hiring attorneys for both legal and law-related positions to help them implement and administer the new regimes under which they will have to operate. Healthcare provider organizations also need massive legal assistance to help them navigate through this confusing legislation into the Great Unknown.

- Rising energy costs and thus-far half-hearted and disjointed government moves toward energy independence have created new opportunities for attorneys in such industries as coal, natural gas, nuclear, wind, wave, solar, biomass and other "exotica."

- The 2010 BP oil spill was devastating to a region that has already suffered far more than its share of devastation, but like so many catastrophes, has been good news for lawyers seeking damages on behalf of their clients.

- Congress' and state legislatures' sudden concern about out-of-control spending is likely to have an adverse effect on public sector legal employment, although taking all of these crises into aggregate consideration, it is likely that the net public sector legal employment impact will be positive.

This one decade was marked by 10 major crises affecting every aspect of our lives and requiring massive legal resources to manage and from which the nation had to recover. We can only shudder to think what the next decade will generate. The only sure thing is that we can expect more such disruptions in the next decade. And never forget that chance favors the prepared.

The Nonprofit Sector

"Nonprofit" is a term that encompasses both a wide variety of organizational types and a multitude of organizations. Almost 1.5 million nonprofits are registered with the Internal Revenue Service, with the largest numbers categorized as Charitable/Religious, Social Welfare, Labor/Agricultural, Business Leagues, Social/Recreational Clubs, Benevolent Life Insurance Associations, Credit Unions, and Veterans Organizations. In addition, there are Academic Institutions, Legal Services Organizations, Foundations, Healthcare Provider Organizations, and Non-Governmental Organizations, to name select categories that employ attorneys in a variety of different capacities.

Despite the perennial funding and fundraising woes of many nonprofits, it continues to be an immensely popular "business" model. The number of nonprofits has grown by more than one-third in the last decade. Perhaps the most important feature of nonprofit organizations is that they are corporations. Consequently, they share many of the structural features of their for-profit counterparts. Lawyers who work for nonprofit in-house counsel offices have many of the same responsibilities as their for-profit brethren. Moreover, their employers have to deal with many of the same issues, meaning that they structure their "hidden" legal functions in much the same way. Thus, you can find attorneys working outside the in-house counsel office in offices such as Compliance, Ethics, Risk Management, Government Affairs, and occasionally even Tax.

The nonprofits that employ the most attorneys follow:

Foundations and other charitable organizations. More than 50,000 U.S. foundations and other charitable organizations award grants to organizations that use the money for what the grantors deem worthy projects. Foundations employ lawyers for their in-house counsel offices, as well as for grant administration, compliance, and to be in charge of legal and law-related projects. The Foundation Center (www.fdncenter.org) is the best repository of information about foundations, grants, grantees, IRS Form 990 annual nonprofit filings, etc.

Trade and professional associations. It is estimated that there are more than 35,000 trade and professional associations in the U.S., a number that is growing steadily. It seems that if two or more individuals or organizations share a common interest, an association representing that interest cannot be far behind. The Washington, DC area is home to approximately one-third of all U.S. associations. Most of the remainder are headquartered in our largest cities—New York, LA, Chicago, and Houston.

Only a few thousand associations have their own in-house counsel offices, but almost all of them have government affairs offices that are at the epicenter of most associations' core missions—lobbying legislators and regulators on behalf of their members and reporting to their members on legislative and regulatory initiatives that might affect them. Professional associations often also provide advice on ethics matters to their members and frequently have attorneys on staff serving as their ethics officers. In addition, association executive jobs are often held by attorneys.

The American Society of Association Executives (www.asaenet.org) maintains an online Gateway to Associations that lists and links to its member organizations.

Academic Institution Administration

The 4,200+ colleges and universities in the U.S. almost all now have their own general counsel office. In addition, many academic institutions hire attorneys for a rich variety of law-related campus positions in other offices, such as:

- Compliance
- Contracts and Grants Management
- Development (Planned Giving, Charitable Giving)
- Disabled Student Affairs
- Environmental Management
- Ethics
- Government Affairs
- Human Resources (for equal employment opportunity and affirmative action matters and labor relations)
- International Students
- Ombudsman
- Privacy
- Real Estate
- Risk Management
- Student Judicial Affairs
- Technology Transfer and Intellectual Property Asset Management

Compliance has become so important a campus function that the recent trend is toward having specialized offices to deal with different compliance matters, such as athletics, sponsored research, government regulatory reporting, security, grants and contracts, health information privacy, etc.

Nonprofit Healthcare Provider Organizations

More than 5,000 healthcare nonprofits operate in an increasingly complex and rapidly changing regulatory environment. Thus, they have a growing demand for legal talent for both in-house counsel and law-related offices. Close to 1,000 nonprofit hospitals are large enough (200+ beds) to maintain a general counsel office. In addition, these larger institutions may also have compliance, risk management, ethics, patient advocacy, privacy, contracting and other offices where attorneys work.

Non-Governmental Organizations (NGOs)

NGOs are primarily international in scope, meaning that they operate abroad. The emerging market economies and national democracies of the past two decades have stimulated the development of NGO rule-of-law programs that employ attorneys to advise and assist developing nations in establishing legal frameworks. Attorneys both work directly for NGOs and are engaged as contractors, subcontractors and consultants.

CHAPTER 4

Leapfrog the Competition

A true story.

"Jacob K" came to me for career counseling advice because he believed his legal career was at a dead-end before it even began. He had been forced to work his way through law school in non-law-related jobs, including driving a cab at night and on weekends. And if he wanted to keep his job during the school year, he had to work days during his two summers between law school semesters, making a summer legal position out of the question.

Jacob had even less legal experience than the typical graduating law student, but our career counseling discussions yielded one very interesting nugget of information:

The owner of Jacob's cab fleet, having discovered that one of his drivers was a law student, began sending him to the local taxicab commission to handle matters that required personal communication with that regulatory body. Those matters sometimes involved the periodic auctions that the commission held in order to distribute "hackers' licenses" required to place a taxicab in service. Hackers' licenses were very valuable because they were limited in number and, consequently, bidding for them brought in a great deal of money to the commission. Jacob became quite knowledgeable about the auction process and thoroughly enjoyed the legal and administrative nuances of these encounters.

Jacob's periodic success in securing additional licenses for his boss's expanding cab business earned him several nice bonuses. But his frenetic schedule made it difficult to earn top grades, and he graduated in the lower middle of his class. He attributed his inability to get a job offer during his 3L year to his mediocre law school performance along with his lack of any legal experience.

I pointed out that at least three U.S. government agencies were authorized to auction certain rights to the public and, due to pending legislation or public necessity, were likely to need some immediate expertise in this area:

- The **Department of Interior** was under pressure to expand and accelerate its auctions for outer continental shelf oil and gas leases, due to rapidly rising domestic demand for petroleum products;
- The **Federal Deposit Insurance Corporation** was authorized by law to auction off the assets of failed banks over which they had assumed control, and a rash of bank failures was expected due to the economic downturn;
- The **Federal Communications Commission** was asking Congress for renewed authority to conduct auctions for portions of the broadcast spectrum.

I suggested that Jacob tailor his resume to these organizations, elaborating in the document about his hackers' license auction knowledge and experience (which had gone unmentioned in his resume up to this point).

> **Follow company and industry activities in the Wall Street Journal to learn where legal and law-related jobs may occur in the near-term.**

We examined the legal positions for which these three agencies were currently recruiting and found that two involved auctions; neither, however, was an entry-level job. Nevertheless, I urged Jacob to apply for them, arguing that (1) his specialized experience was unlikely to be matched by any other candidate, and (2) U.S. government offices had almost unlimited flexibility when it came to hiring lawyers, not being bound by the customary competitive civil service laws.

Things turned out very well.

Jacob, the law student/cabbie, received invitations to interview with two of the agencies, and received and accepted a job offer from one of them!

His background enabled him to leap right into the auction legal environment and his agency promoted him rapidly over the next several years. He reported that one agency's interviewer told him she was discounting his law school performance because of his having to work his way through school.

Jacob's lack of conventional legal experience proved to be no hindrance to his employability for a highly specialized position for which he was uniquely qualified.

If you re-read Chapter 3 about trends analysis, you will see how performing such analysis enabled Jacob and I to anticipate where certain legal jobs might soon crystallize. Trends analysis is certainly one way—and reasonably effective—to guide you to where you should be looking for legal positions because it indicates demand. But it is hardly the only way. There are a variety of means at your disposal that permit you to foresee where there is likely to be legal hiring activity in both the public and private sectors.

Government Job Opportunities: Hiding in Plain Sight

Let's look first at the advance notice of legal hiring intentions that comes out of government:

Agency testimony before Congressional Appropriations Subcommittees. Every spring, U.S. government department and agency heads and/or other senior officials appear before congressional appropriations subcommittees to request funding for the forthcoming fiscal year (which runs from October 1st through September 30th). The hearings often become exercises in "drilling down" into the particulars of an agency's budget request. Sometimes this drill-down goes deep into the agency's personnel needs and itemizes them to the extent that the agency reveals exactly how many attorneys for legal and law-related positions it anticipates hiring, and for what purposes. For example, the following excerpts (paraphrased) are from the testimony of Commodity Futures Trading Commission (CFTC) Chairman Gary Gensler before the Senate Committee on Appropriations Subcommittee on Financial Services and General Government (http://appropriations.senate.gov/sc-financial.cfm) in April, 2010:

> Adequate legal staff is necessary to act swiftly to investigate and prosecute fraudulent acts, such as the rash of Ponzi schemes uncovered during the recent market downturn. Additional legal staff will enable the CFTC to conduct mandatory annual reviews of all contracts listed on exempt commercial markets (ECMs) to determine if they are significant price discovery contracts (SPDCs).
>
> Specifically, the funding will be allocated to increase staffing levels in the following CFTC divisions:
>
> Our goal for FY 2011 is to have an Enforcement staff of 200, including strategic plans to double the Enforcement staff in the Kansas City office. Note: approximately half of the Division's employees are attorneys.
>
> We need additional professional staff to actively monitor exchanges to ensure compliance with CFTC regulations; to keep a close eye for signs of manipulation or congestion in the marketplace, and decide how to best address market threats; and ensure that traders do not exceed federal position limits. The Commission seeks to increase staff from 139 in FY 2010 to 168 in FY 2011. Specifically, DMO requires additional economists, investigators, attorneys and statisticians.
>
> Additional resources to the Division of Clearing and Intermediary Oversight would allow the Commission to perform regular and direct examinations of registrants and more frequently assess compliance with Commission regulations.

The Commission proposes to bolster the Offices of the Chairman and the Commissioners from 35 staff in FY 2010 to 47 staff in FY 2011.

The CFTC also is working with Congress to bring comprehensive regulation to the over-the-counter derivatives marketplace. The Commission's budget request includes an additional $45,000,000 and 119 full-time equivalent employees for fiscal year 2011 to begin implementation of the Administration's comprehensive proposal for financial regulatory reform. The Commission's fiscal year 2012 total (current and proposed new authorities related to financial regulatory reform) staff requirement is estimated to be approximately 1,000 full-time equivalent employees. Specifically, the Commission's FY 2011 budget request for regulatory reform would be allocated as follows:

- 41 additional staff for Market Oversight;
- 30 additional staff for Clearing and Intermediary Oversight and Risk Surveillance;
- 18 additional staff for Enforcement; and
- Eight additional staff for General Counsel.

When you read such testimony, keep in mind that even if it does not drill all the way down to specific numbers of attorneys and law-related positions, you may find evidence of policy and regulatory initiatives that will alert you that additional lawyers might be required in order to implement these projects. In order to use this information, you also need to do your homework regarding the mission and activities of the CFTC (www.cftc.gov). You would learn that the CFTC is a "lawyer-laden" agency with numerous and far-flung legal and law-related responsibilities. You can keep tabs on such testimony by periodically checking both the Appropriations Committees' Web sites (Senate Committee on Appropriations, http://appropriations. senate.gov/; House Committee on Appropriations, http://appropriations. house.gov/) and department and agency Web sites to unearth information about federal legal hiring intentions.

There is no uniformity among agencies or within the appropriations subcommittees as to how—or even whether—they have this kind of information on their Web sites. If they do, it usually is presented as written testimony accompanying the agency representative's oral presentation, or in the transcript of the oral testimony itself. Sometimes, there may be a video of the testimony available on the subcommittee website.

Government annual performance plans and strategic plans. Annual Performance Plans are, as their name indicates, prepared and published on department and agency Web sites each year. Strategic Plans are prepared and published every 3–5 years. These relatively recent additions to the massive volume of public sector information can be mined for hidden job opportunities, and can be just as valuable as Appropriations subcommittee testimony. Annual Performance Plans and Strategic Plans are required, but are more hit-or-miss than Appropriations subcommittee testimony. For example, a recent U.S. Department of Justice Fiscal Year Annual Performance Plan indicated that the Department wanted to increase the number of attorney positions devoted to prosecuting terrorist activities from 416 to 523 nationwide in the next fiscal year. Another agency's comparable plan, however, said nothing at all about hiring plans.

Federal budget documents. A third means of obtaining advance notice of legal hiring intentions is to peruse the annual proposed Budget of the United States, best viewed at the U.S. Office of Management and Budget's website (www.omb.gov). Forget about immersing yourself in the actual budget documents themselves, which are dizzying collections of numerical data that will drive you crazy. Instead, examine each department and agency's Budget Appendix, which is primarily a textual document that explains why an agency is requesting the funds. This is where you will find information, if any, about legal hiring plans.

When you perform this kind of "advance notice" research, keep in mind that anything interesting you discover will be indicative not only of U.S. government hiring, but also of private sector legal recruiting as well. If the CFTC wants to hire more attorneys to provide closer scrutiny of the commodities markets and to bolster its enforcement activities, then it is inevitable that commodities exchanges and traders will also have to hire additional attorneys to handle the larger number of investigations and more intensive government scrutiny of their activities.

Corporate Job Opportunities: Hiding in Plain Sight

When you explore the universe of companies in an industry in which you are interested, don't limit yourself to examining only individual stocks. You will also want to scrutinize industry funds that focus on the industry. A look at green mutual funds reveals that these are also growing rapidly, both in terms of share prices and the amount of money flowing into them. What it means is that cleantech hiring is on the upswing... and attorneys are part of the hiring solution.

Companies whose shares are steadily increasing in value (for non-speculative reasons) usually have a consistent history of hiring new employees, including attorneys. This is particularly true of publicly-traded companies operating in highly regulated industries such as financial services. Your employer due diligence efforts need to identify target companies by (1) comparing their current share price to their price in the recent past, and (2) examining their underlying fundamentals as well as those of their industries. This will give you a sense of whether the share price rise is based on something solid.

Here is an example of how this might work:

As this is written, "green" stocks are doing quite well on Wall Street. They include solar, wind, biofuel, and nuclear energy producers, but also companies in the energy efficiency business as it affects transportation, buildings, and energy distribution and storage systems. Green stocks are consistently beating the averages lately after a very up-and-down history. A great many companies and investors see a bright future for clean technology. So-called "cleantech" companies are proliferating throughout the economy as technologies are refined and costs decline to make them more competitive with older energy industries.

Here is what the analysts at Bank of America recently declared: *In the context of the stock market, we believe cleantech offers more potential upside than most sectors.*"

The Obama Administration has committed several billions of dollars to wind, solar, and other green technologies. Solar energy is expected to grow by more than 600 percent by 2020, while wind energy facilities are expected to increase by almost 300 percent. Accelerating demand for alternative energy, combined with cost reductions and tax incentives, means that cleantech companies are positioned to grow rapidly in the coming decade. Between 2008 and 2010, cleantech capacity worldwide saw more investment than new fossil fuel capacity.

What Financial Publications Are You Reading?

Vibrant, growing companies tend to be in a hiring mode and, as they expand their businesses, the demand for legal professionals rises.

If you want to get a head start in identifying possible legal job opportunities in advance of their going public, one of the best ways is to become a consistent and careful reader of financial publications, including *The Wall Street Journal, Financial Times, Investor's Business Daily,* and *The Economist.* These publications, along with investment newsletters, contain a great deal of advance information about where the legal and law-related jobs are likely to be in the near-term based on their close study of companies and industries.

In addition, the business/financial sections of major dailies, and the online financial Web sites, report announcements of significant business financings. New financings usually predate major expansions and a corresponding need for additional employees at many levels. Scan your daily newspaper and online tables for quarterly earning reports that have increased their profits by more than five percent from the preceding year. This growth rate often presages a need for additional employees.

Some other suggestions:

Investment newsletters. Investment newsletters, particularly those that follow a specific industry in-depth, are excellent precursors of professional hiring activity. Their editors and reporters are often the first to hear about planned expansions and growth potential.

Monitor SARS Reports. SARS (Severe Acute Respiratory Syndrome) is best known to the public as a virulent disease. However, SARs is a "dual-purpose" abbreviation that can also refer to "Suspicious Activity Reports."

This kind of SAR is a report regarding suspicious or potentially suspicious activity filed with the Financial Crimes Enforcement Network (FinCEN), an obscure agency of the U.S. Treasury Department. SARs are required by the Bank Secrecy Act, Pub. L. 91-508, (codified as amended in scattered sections of 12 U.S.C., 15 U.S.C., and 31 U.S.C.), and its implementing regulations, 31 C.F.R. 103.11-103.77 (2010).

The purpose of SARs is to report known or suspected violations of law or suspicious activity observed by financial institutions subject to Bank Secrecy Act regulations. SARs often lead law enforcement organizations to launch financial fraud, money laundering, or terrorist financing investigations, as well as other criminal cases. SARs filings also enable FinCEN to identify emerging financial crime trends and behavior.

Many diverse financial industries must file SARs, including depository institutions (banks, savings and loans, bank holding companies, credit unions, non-bank subsidiaries of bank holding companies, U.S. branches and agencies of foreign banks, and Edge and Agreement corporations); money services businesses such as check cashing outfits and issuers, sellers and redeemers of money orders and travelers checks; securities firms; the futures industry; casinos; currency dealers and exchangers; and insurance companies. A proposal is in the works to add mutual fund operators to this list.

FinCEN requires a SARs report to be filed whenever the financial institution suspects: insider abuse by an employee; violations of law aggregating over $5,000 or more where a subject can be identified; violations of law aggregating over $25,000 or more regardless of a potential subject; transactions aggregating $5,000 or more that involve potential money laundering or violations of the Bank Secrecy Act; computer intrusion; or when a financial institution knows that a customer is operating as an unlicensed money services business. Many financial institutions file thousands of SARs each year. While SARs are confidential, FinCEN reports on the trends and patterns that they reveal.

SARs can be strong indicators of where legal jobs are going to be because they often lead to investigations and prosecutions by federal, state and local law enforcement, which involve attorneys representing government, financial institutions, corporations, and individuals who are the subject of a SARs report. If FinCEN detects a pattern of behavior, it is a good bet that financial institutions and law firms that fall within that behavioral category will bolster their legal hiring in anticipation of more vigorous government enforcement activity.

Also, the more SARs reports an institution is required to file, the more reliance by it on attorneys to investigate the suspicious activity and draft and review the SARs report prior to filing. Moreover, since the filing requirements include very short filing deadlines, attorneys get involved in the process early and often. The often dramatic increases in SARs filings and valuable information on their origins can be a solid indicator of near-term legal hiring activity, intelligence that you can use to frame your job search campaign.

The most recent FinCen SAR Activity Review, covering a six-month period, indicated the following:

- Suspected check fraud (including travelers' checks and counterfeit checks) increased significantly in every industry required to file SARs. Depository institution check fraud SARs were up 19 percent; counterfeit check SARs increased 36 percent; suspected travelers' check fraud zoomed up 76 percent; casino check fraud reports were up 18 percent; and securities and futures industry check fraud increased by 19 percent.
- Securities and futures industry overall SARs filings increased 29 percent over the same period for the previous year.
- Mail fraud filings increased by 52 percent, and wire fraud was up 56 percent. Foreign currency futures fraud and foreign currencies fraud reports skyrocketed up 2,600 percent and 300 percent, respectively.
- Suspected mortgage loan fraud rose just one percent from the corresponding period in the prior year, but remains at a historically high level following six consecutive years of double-digit growth.

FinCEN also recently released a separate report on insurance industry SARs reporting, indicating that filings almost doubled from the prior year, with most of the filing activity emanating from New York, California, New Jersey, Florida and Texas.

How to Use Advance Intelligence

The advance notice strategies discussed above can be invaluable to job-seekers who want to position themselves to take advantage of a promising opportunity before the rest of the legal job-hunting world jumps on it. Being able to apply for a legal position before it is announced and the formal recruiting process begins has seven major advantages:

- You can apply before anyone else even realizes that there is a job opportunity. It is impossible to overestimate the huge advantage this can give you.
- Applying in advance of any advertised job ad can help you overcome an experience gap. If you are able to apply for a position before it is advertised and is published replete with experience requirements, you can be considered for the job when the employer is most flexible with respect to the recruitment. You will be applying when there are, as yet, no experience requirements.
- If you inform the employer as to how you discovered the job opportunity, you accomplish two important things: (1) You will impress the employer with your creative approach to scoping out new job opportunities; and (2) you will imprint yourself in the employer's mind, making yourself memorable in the best possible way. Who would not want an employee with this kind of creative foresight, regardless of experience?
- You can submit a resume rather than an online application form. As you know, employers are flocking to online application forms instead of resumes. Online applications are, however, very restrictive of both the applicant and the employer. From the candidate's perspective, online applications make every applicant look the same. The opportunity to distinguish you from competitors in terms of presentation is gone. Legal employers complain that online applications do not allow them to differentiate candidates depending on how they organize their applications and elaborate on their results, outcomes, achievements, and accomplishments. Employers' ability to test organizational skills and logical thinking as reflected on a resume does not translate to an online template.

Your resume is far superior to an online application form because it is a document that is personal and distinctively "you." Your approach to your resume is uniquely your own, whereas an online application form reduces every applicant to a least common denominator. There is no possibility of distinguishing yourself in all of the formatting, structural and strategic ways that resumes permit. The only difference between candidates is the content of the application, and for many legal employers that is not enough.

Demonstrating your organizational skills and creativity are important personal traits that say a lot about you. If, for example, you want to liberate yourself from the typical reverse chronological presentation of your employment history, you cannot do that on an online application form. The lack of individuality in presentation often leaves legal employers just as frustrated as applicants.

In contrast, a traditional resume permits you to take an entirely different approach, one that presents you to maximum effect.

Bottom line: escaping from the strictures imposed by having to apply for jobs online, using an employer-provided template, is extremely important. Once a job ad is in play that instructs you to apply using an online form, you lose the flexibility that your much more personalized resume allows.

If you can apply *before* a job ad is published, you are in a much stronger position with respect to getting an interview and, ultimately, securing a job offer:

- **You can "outflank" the gatekeepers**. Applying before a formal recruitment begins permits you to send your application directly to the hiring official without having first to go through a Human Resources office or personnel specialist who might reject your application before the hiring official has an opportunity to evaluate you. Eliminating one or more levels of review reduces the possibility of rejection substantially.

- **You can avoid the risk of loss**. Online applications that go directly into a database upon receipt also present two additional problems: first, they can get lost in transmission. The federal government's online application system (www.USAjobs.gov) is now in its third iteration because, among other deficiencies, so many applications disappeared in the ether. Second, your application may be consigned forever to the database and never get retrieved if the key word(s) that are used to extract applications do not happen to appear in your application. Being able to submit a resume allows you to avoid all of those risks.

- **You can be considered for employment absent competition.** It will be a huge advantage to your candidacy for the hiring official to be able to examine your application in isolation from the likely barrage of applications prompted by publication of a job advertisement. The employer will be able to concentrate his or her attention on you in a vacuum, not distracted by countless competing applications. The benefits of being both "first past the post" and applying for a position that you know is coming but is not "there" yet cannot be overstated.

CHAPTER 5

The Upside of Small Town Law

When I was a 3L, my law school dean called me into his office and told me that he had recommended me to a 65-year old alumnus who practiced in a small town in New York State's Southern Tier, and who was looking for a successor to mentor. The Dean said that I "fit the profile" because I grew up in a similar small Western New York town. Intrigued, my wife and I headed out to what we thought was the ends of the Earth to spend the day with the attorney and his wife and scope out the opportunity.

From Wall Street to Main Street

The country practitioner lived in a stunning home with a fantastic view, on top of a hill that overlooked the small community. He and his wife both drove very expensive cars and it was obvious from their surroundings that he was doing exceptionally well in his pastoral milieu.

It turned out that he did not exactly fit my preconceived notion of a rural practitioner. And the tale of how he arrived in rural America is worth telling for its instructional value:

> He had been an equity partner in a major Wall Street law firm until age 50 when, like so many people at the midlife point, he began to wonder if the grind was still worth it, and if what he had been doing so successfully was "all there is." He spent several months researching the legal market throughout New York State with the intention of identifying underserved communities. He eventually zeroed in on little Alfred, NY in Allegheny County, the second poorest county in the state. But, as his research revealed, the county's dismal economy camouflaged the relative prosperity of the village which, in addition to having no lawyers, was home to two academic institutions, one a university, the other a state college. Out of Alfred's population of under 3,500, there were a disproportionate number of reasonably well-paid professors and college administrators. Within a year of relocating to Alfred, this very shrewd attorney

was outside counsel to both academic institutions, had established a thriving general practice, and was in the process of building a high-rise apartment building to supplement a chronic dearth of on-campus student housing.

Despite a very attractive job offer, as well as an offer to pay my wife's law school tuition at a law school an hour distant, we graciously declined in favor of legal life in the big city.

That Was Then...This is Now

Rural America isn't what it used to be. And that is mostly a good thing if you happen to be an attorney interested in a rural practice.

The transportation and telecommunications revolutions have homogenized our country to such an extent that the advantages and amenities—as well as some of the disadvantages—of metropolitan areas have crossed the divide and are seeping into less populated regions. Cable TV, the Internet, chain stores, good restaurants, multiplex cinemas, and the dispersion of high-culture entertainment even into remote locales (the small town where we have a second home has a huge concert shell that gets many of the same artists that appear in New York, Washington, Chicago and San Francisco, among them Willie Nelson, the Dave Matthews Band, and Yo Yo Ma). If you happen to be in a college town—and there are over 4,200 of those—you can find a great deal of good conversation and intellectual fodder to boot.

Taxes are often lower.

Crime rates do not come close to urban areas.

Living standards for professionals are quite high.

Work-life balance is virtually a given.

And guess what?

Rural America is still very much underserved by the legal community. Moreover, housing is affordable, commuting to and from work is a piece of cake, and schools have fewer problems than their urban counterparts, albeit drugs, sex and violence have also made their way into the youth population in rural areas. A recent survey of the top high schools in America included a solid representation of rural institutions.

The Beckoning of the Land

You are much more likely to see the inside of a courtroom much sooner in your career in the country than you will in the big city. You will also find that civility among opposing counsel still largely exists, if only because they see each other in court and across the negotiating table much more frequently, so there is a premium in acting mature, restrained and civil.

Another huge factor is the aging of the rural attorney population, a disproportionate number of whom are baby boomers on the cusp of retirement. Rural area practitioners are significantly older than their urban counterparts. Between 2011 and 2026, the retirement rolls will be overflowing with these lawyers.

Another attractive feature is the stability of a rural practice.

Change is slower, easier to accommodate, and much more predictable in a rustic setting. The population is nowhere near as transient as in metropolitan areas, and loyalty to service providers is paid a higher premium than in more urban settings. Rural areas also seem to spawn as much entrepreneurialism as you will find anywhere else. Small business startups are very common, and here again, complexity in launching and running a business in a federalist system requires considerable legal input. The increasing regulatory intrusiveness of government at all levels means an increasing demand for legal services.

While America's farm population has been suffering from attrition for 75 years, with no end in sight, farm families sit atop land whose values can exceed thousands of dollars an acre and whose mineral rights in this age of the drive for energy independence have enormous dollar potential. The natural gas industry in the gas-rich Appalachian region stretching from Central and Western New York down into Pennsylvania, Maryland and West Virginia anticipates drilling 70,000 wells in the next five years, and has increased its regional gas industry employment rolls by more than 50 percent.

> **Rural America isn't what it used to be, and that's a good thing if you happen to be an attorney interested in a rural practice.**

Making the Move

Law practice sales ads are now a fixture on Web sites such as Craigslist, for example. Many of these are aging small-town lawyers concerned about identifying and luring a competent replacement. To a much greater extent than in major cities, these rural practitioners are much more willing to mentor their putative successors during an overlap period and to introduce them around town, thanks to a love of and loyalty to their close-knit community.

It is far easier today to undertake location research than it was back when the Wall Street lawyer performed his due diligence on possible rural practice locations in Upstate New York. Web sites like the Avery Index (www.averyindex.com) can tell you essential information like the per capita attorney population of each state. As this is being written, the big winners for the lowest numbers are:

State	Number of Attorneys Per 10,000 Residents
North Dakota	4.4
Arkansas	5.3
South Dakota	5.8
Kansas	5.8
Idaho	6.1
Iowa	6.2
Wisconsin	6.8
New Mexico	6.9
Indiana	6.9
Kentucky	7.1

These are extremely attractive statistics if you contemplate a rural relocation and practice. Especially when compared to the Big Legal Kahuna—the District of Columbia—with its 276.7 lawyers per 10,000 residents. In Washington, DC, you can throw a stick out of your office window and be certain that it will bounce off of at least five attorneys before it hits the pavement.

When you look at the Avery Index numbers, you need to be sufficiently sophisticated to note that the distribution of per capita attorneys is going to be highly uneven from one part of a state to another. What that means is that rural areas that are part of very heavily populated states may nevertheless be attractive practice locations. You can drive for hundreds of miles through parts of California, Texas, New York, Florida, Pennsylvania, Ohio, Illinois, Michigan, and New England that are so bereft of cities and masses of humanity that you think that you are in the Dakotas, Arkansas or Kansas.

The costs of entry into solo practice have plummeted everywhere, thanks to the technology revolution, and are even lower in rural areas. Computerized legal research options have relegated hard copy law libraries to the dustbin of history along with quill fountain pens and reading the law in lieu of attending law school. With competition to Westlaw and Lexis, legal research is becoming less expensive at the same time that it is becoming more expansive. Word processing software means that you really do not need a secretary, certainly not when you are in an initial launch phase of your practice. Voicemail can serve as a bargain basement receptionist. A home office is an easy thing to establish and can serve you ably until you begin to generate cash flow. Moreover, zoning restrictions are much looser in rural America.

Alternatively, if you feel that an office is essential from the outset, rent is generally cheap, far less expensive than in urban areas.

I know an attorney in a rural locale who rents 3,000 square feet of space above the local bank (a great location for referral business from the first floor) for—are you ready for this?—$125 per month! His landlord has not raised his rent in this century. In contrast, 3,000 square feet in downtown Washington, DC is now going for more than $12,000 per month with an annual 3.5 percent escalator and real estate tax pass-through! This attorney's offices are as nicely appointed as any partner's office in a large law firm.

Marketing your practice in a small community is also easier and cheaper.

Rotary, Kiwanis, Elks, Moose and Lions clubs abound, and are always eager for new members and for speakers on topical matters. Local newspapers are often keen for new arrivals to interview and may even accord you op-ed page space in print and online for a legal advice column. Local bar associations are excellent referral agencies. Becoming active in the community can also pay off handsomely. A rural attorney I know even went so far as to join five churches. On Sunday morning, he made the rounds of services and positioned himself outside the church entrances at the end of Sunday services in order to meet, greet and hand out business cards to fellow parishioners. While that is admittedly extreme promotional behavior, it is probably also unnecessary in most rural locations. In summary, there is a lot to recommend to attorneys seeking something different from the conventional career route. America is full of small ponds conducive to the arrival of big and small legal fish.

> As a rural lawyer, you're likely to see the inside of a courtroom sooner in your career than in a big city practice.

If becoming a solo practitioner appeals to you, I recommend Carolyn Elefant's *Solo by Choice 2011–2012 Edition* and *Solo by Choice, The Companion Guide.*

CHAPTER 6

Teaching in Non-Traditional Environments

Many job options encompass much more than they appear to at first glance. Teaching law is no exception. Traditional law school teaching positions are growing slowly. U.S. law schools are a fairly mature industry, and relatively few new teaching jobs open up in any given year.

Moreover, the competition for law school teaching positions is intense. Thousands of highly qualified attorneys with stellar academic and practice backgrounds compete fiercely for the few hundred such positions that open up each year. Yet, hope springing eternal, several thousand aspirants show up at the annual Association of American Law Schools' (www.aals.org) Fall Faculty Recruitment Conference in Washington, DC.

The overwhelming majority of traditional law school teaching positions go to top graduates of the most distinguished law schools who then served in federal judicial or state supreme court clerkships. Many law teachers go directly from such clerkships to the classroom. Others spend a few years in private practice, generally with top law firms before entering the academic precincts. But that is hardly where law teaching options end.

The Expanding Universe of Teaching Opportunities

There are plenty of alternative law teaching opportunities that are available to attorneys—recent grads included—that do not require you to meet the highly selective criteria described above. I have grouped these together under the broad label of non-traditional law teaching positions. They include non-traditional teaching positions in the 200 American Bar Association-accredited law schools, the 50 or so law schools that are not ABA-approved, under-graduate and graduate programs in America's 4,000+ colleges and universities, paralegal programs that are not affiliated with a college or university, opportunities to teach law—in English—at foreign academic institutions, and teaching and training opportunities outside of an academic environment.

Non-traditional Teaching Positions in Law Schools

Law schools are slowly realizing that they have to offer a more diverse curriculum in order to keep pace with their competitors and also with new legal developments and changing practice paradigms. Consequently, they are now paying more attention to basic legal skills (research, analysis, writing, negotiations, transactions, litigation), and offering more clinics and special training programs. In fact, this has become so important to the future of law schools that the AALS June 2011 mid-year meeting was devoted exclusively to this topic.

Law schools now number among their faculties a growing number of teachers who do not fit neatly into traditional professorial teaching modes. The growth in law school teaching positions is almost all on the non-traditional side of the teaching ledger. Moreover, these positions are open to other than just individuals with "dream" resumes.

In addition to hiring for traditional tenure-track positions (assistant, associate, and full professors), law schools also hire non-tenure track teachers under titles such as instructor, lecturer, academic support instructor, clinical program director, legal research and writing program instructor, adjunct professor, and others. Non-tenure track positions have a lower qualifications bar that makes them easier to obtain. Depending on the institution's standards for promotion and tenure, they may become or lead to tenure-track positions.

Most legal writing program faculties (many of whom consist of recent law school graduates) are on short-term contracts of one, two or three years' duration. Compensation for non-traditional teaching positions (for which data is collected) at ABA law schools is approximately as follows:

Legal Writing Program Director	$100,000
Legal Writing Program Assistant Director	88,000
Legal Writing Instructor	62,000–68,000
Lecturer	44,000–85,000
Clinical Attorney/Instructor	38,000–63,000

In addition, a majority of ABA law schools offer their writing program instructors summer research grants averaging around $8,000.

Teaching in a Non-ABA Law School

Approximately 50 currently operating law schools are not approved by the ABA. The majority are either accredited by a state or by the Distance Education and Training Council, which accredits online academic institutions.

These institutions employ more than 1,500 faculty members, split between approximately one-third full-time faculty and two-thirds adjunct faculty. These schools typically pay substantially less than their ABA-accredited counterparts. However, adjunct faculty pay at these institutions normally exceeds what adjunct faculty earn for teaching in graduate or undergraduate programs in colleges and universities. The hiring criteria for teachers in these schools are, in the aggregate, less stringent than they are for comparable positions in ABA-approved law schools. However, there is a stronger preference among these institutions for attorneys with some experience.

Teaching Law in Colleges and Universities

Law teaching also takes place far beyond just law schools. In fact, there are now more positions teaching law outside of law schools than within them, and the gap in favor of non-law school positions is growing rapidly. These jobs do not require that you meet the same very rigorous qualifications criteria that you must to teach at the law school level.

Interest in law among undergraduate and graduate students is avid and growing. Law has infiltrated virtually every aspect of human endeavor, making knowledge of the law and legal processes central to many non-legal disciplines.

The largest growth in demand for law teachers is found in undergraduate and graduate programs in colleges and universities. In addition to teaching in undergraduate Legal Studies programs, opportunities abound in non-law academic departments such as accounting, business, criminal justice, economics, environmental, history, insurance, international relations, labor relations, paralegal programs, real estate, tax, and many other disciplines.

You do not have to have a Ph.D., or graduate from a top-15 law school, or have served on a law review, or worked as a federal judicial clerk, or have earned superior class rank for the majority of such positions. One thing you do want to have, however, is an understanding that academic job titles vary considerably from one institution to another. When you visit the Web sites that advertise such positions (see below), you need to go beyond the job titles and read the fine print.

Undergraduate Legal Studies Programs

One of the most interesting recent developments has been the formalization of"pre-law"studies into an actual undergraduate major, most commonly called Legal Studies. While Legal Studies programs vary by institution, they usually have the following elements in common:

- A focus on basic legal knowledge, skills, and ethical principles.
- Courses that address the legal organization, functions, and processes of the U.S., legal ethics, legal analysis, legal drafting and writing, legal research, and computer competence in the legal environment.

Legal Studies has proven so popular that, in less than 15 years, the number of institutions offering this (or a comparable) major has grown exponentially, from a handful to over 3,000, according to the College Board (www.collegeboard.com). Legal Studies program instructors are almost always attorneys. It is a liberal arts major in most of the institutions that offer it. If the university is also home to a law school, the Legal Studies program often works closely with the law school faculty in terms of course design and supervision.

Other College and University Law Programs

As indicated above, there is also a strong market for attorneys in other, more traditional undergraduate and graduate departments. The following list is representative of undergraduate, graduate, and professional schools, departments, and programs employing JDs as teachers for their law course offerings:

- Accounting
- Anthropology
- Biotechnology
- Business
- Criminal Justice
- Journalism
- Economics
- Forensic Science
- History
- Industrial and Labor Relations
- International Studies
- Library Science
- Medical Schools
- Political Science
- Psychology
- Public Affairs
- Public Health
- Real Estate
- Social Work
- Sociology

Compensation varies widely among undergraduate, graduate, and professional institutions. Typical ranges for full-time teaching positions are $28,000–$86,000 for instructors; $34,000–$90,000 for lecturers; $40,000–$160,000 for assistant and associate professors; $50,000–$185,000 for full professors. These variances are the result of factors such as geographic location, size of the institution, and whether the institution is private or public, among other factors. Adjunct positions paid by the course may also be available.

Teaching in Paralegal Programs

The rapid expansion of paralegal certificate programs also means more teaching positions for lawyers. Attorneys from a practice background predominate in paralegal program faculties, but there are also positions for entry-level lawyers. The ABA (www.abanet.org/legalservices/paralegals/directory/allprograms.html) has approved 264 paralegal programs, all of which are associated with colleges and universities. There are several hundred additional paralegal certificate programs offered by other institutions. ABA-approved paralegal programs tend to pay their instructors somewhat better than unapproved programs, with salaries ranging from about $45,000 to $95,000. Non-ABA-approved program compensation varies widely. However, most non-ABA positions are for adjuncts who are paid by the course. Many attorneys who aspire to teach full-time get their foot in the door in one of these programs first, in order to "build" their resumes to compete for a full-time law teaching position.

Teaching Law Abroad

English has become the *lingua franca* of international business. This has given rise to a proliferation of law and law-related course and degree offerings in English by foreign academic institutions. There has been a corresponding increase in demand by these institutions for U.S.-educated individuals as teachers. Most opportunities for teaching law outside the United States are found in the English-speaking common law countries (Canada, the United Kingdom, Australia, New Zealand), countries where English is a primary second language (India, South Africa, other former and present Commonwealth nations, and the Philippines), and also by countries that are—or aspire to be—international business centers (e.g., Belgium, the Netherlands). There are also programs that teach in English in the Caribbean, Scandinavia, Continental Europe, the Middle East, Asia, Africa, and even Fiji. More than 180 institutions worldwide offer such programs in English.

> **The largest growth in demand for law teachers is found in undergraduate and graduate programs.**

Foreign academic institutions have historically compensated faculty at levels below their American counterparts. However, much depends on the exchange rate between the local currency and the U.S. dollar. Consequently, there are now some institutions that, because they pay their faculty in local currencies and due to a weak dollar, exceed U.S. academic pay scales.

U.S. Government Legal Training Program Providers

The U.S. Government does a large amount of legal and law-related training of its employees. Similar to private sector companies, there is a strong, across-the-board concentration on ethics training. The government also invests considerable resources in alternative dispute resolution instruction.

Enforcement organizations and government entities that have a role in criminal and civil penalty investigations and prosecutions focus attention on training in criminal procedure, evidence, investigations and administrative procedure.

The following is a selected list of federal offices that have significant legal and/or law-related training responsibilities:

- Administrative Office of the U.S. Courts (www.uscourts.gov)
- Equal Employment Opportunity Commission (www.eeoc.gov)
- Federal Defender Organizations Nationwide (www.fd.org)
- Federal Judicial Center (www.fjc.gov)
- Federal Labor Relations Authority (www.flra.gov)
- Federal Mediation and Conciliation Service (www.fmcs.gov)
- Federal Trade Commission (www.ftc.gov)
- Library of Congress—Congressional Research Service—American Law Division & Copyright Office (www.loc.gov)
- National Labor Relations Board, Office of General Counsel (www.nlrb.gov)
- National Mediation Board (www.nmb.gov)
- National Science Foundation (www.nsf.gov)
- Nuclear Regulatory Commission (www.nrc.gov)
- Office of Government Ethics (www.oge.gov)
- Office of Personnel Management, Office of General Counsel (www.opm.gov)
- Securities and Exchange Commission (www.sec.gov)
- U.S. Agency for International Development, Office of the General Counsel (www.usaid.gov)
- U.S. Court of Federal Claims, Office of Staff Attorneys (www.uscfc.uscourts.gov)
- U.S. Department of Commerce (www.commerce.gov)
- U.S. Army Corps of Engineers (www.usace.army.mil/Pages/default.aspx)
- U.S. Department of Health and Human Services—Food and Drug Administration (www.fda.gov)
- U.S. Department of Homeland Security—Federal Law Enforcement Training Center—Artesia Training Division (www.fletc.gov/training/programs/artesia-fletc/)
- U.S. Department of Homeland Security—Bureau of Immigration and Customs Enforcement—Office of the Principal Legal Advisor—Enforcement Law Division & Training Division (www.ice.gov)
- U.S. Department of Justice—Criminal Division—Office of Overseas

Prosecutorial Development, Assistance and Training & Training Center (www.justice.gov/criminal/opdat/)

- U.S. Department of Justice—Executive Office for U.S. Attorneys—Office of Legal Education (www.justice.gov/usao/eousa/ole/)
- U.S. Department of Justice—Office of the U.S. Attorney for the Eastern District of Calif.—Appeals and Training Unit (www.justice.gov/usao/cae/)
- U.S. Department of Justice—Federal Bureau of Prisons, Office of General Counsel—Discrimination Complaints and Ethics Branch & Legal Training and Review Branch (www.bop.gov)
- U.S. Department of Justice—U.S. Trustee Program—National Bankruptcy Training Institute (www.justice.gov/ust/)
- U.S. Department of Justice—Federal Bureau of Investigation, Office of the General Counsel—General Law and Legal Training Branch— Procurement Law Unit (www.fbi.gov)
- U.S. Department of State—Foreign Service Institute (http://fsitraining. state.gov/)
- U.S. Department of the Interior—Ethics Office (www.doi.gov/ethics/index.html)
- U.S. Department of Treasury—Office of Technical Assistance (www.treasuryota.us/)
- U.S. Sentencing Commission—Office of Education and Sentencing Practice (http://ftp.ussc.gov/training/about.htm)
- United States Congress—Office of Compliance (www.compliance.gov)
- United States Congress—Office of House Employment Counsel (http:// clerk.house.gov/about/offices.aspx).

Since the vast majority of U.S. government trainers are full-time federal employees, they are included in the standard Federal pay scales, with compensation ranging from approximately $55,000 to $155,500, depending upon experience. There are also Locality Pay (upward) adjustments depending upon where a position is located and the cost of living in that area. Pay scales for certain federal agencies (e.g., financial services regulatory agencies such as the Federal Reserve Board, Federal Deposit Insurance Corporation, and Securities and Exchange Commission) fall outside of this "General Schedule" and typically compensate employees at higher salary ranges. Federal legal and law-related training positions are often advertised on www.usajobs.gov.

State & Local Legal and Law-related Training Programs

Most states and some of the larger cities and counties also provide legal and/ or law-related training to their employees. Among the states and cities, there is an emphasis on trial and appellate practice training, primarily with respect to criminal practice.

The following is a sampling of state and local training programs that advertise positions for trainers:

- Office of the Arizona Attorney General, Policy, Training and Appeals Unit
- Office of the Colorado State Public Defender
- State of Connecticut Police Officer Standards and Training Council
- Office of the Attorney General for the District of Columbia, Child Support Services Division, Policy and Training Section
- Pro Bono Program, District of Columbia Bar
- Illinois State Board of Education, Training & Staff Development
- Office of the Iowa Attorney General, Office of the Prosecuting Attorneys Training Coordinator
- Louisiana Public Defender Board
- Office of the Maryland Public Defender, Training Division
- Massachusetts Committee for Public Counsel Services
- Superior Court of New Jersey, Human Resources Division
- North Carolina Department of Justice, Training and Standards Division
- Office of the Texas Attorney General, Child Support—Training Virginia Indigent Defense Commission
- Washington State Criminal Justice Training Commission
- Mohave County (AZ) Public Defender
- Office of the San Francisco (CA) District Attorney
- Prairie State (IL) Legal Services, Inc.

Opportunities are posted on state and local job Web sites. Compensation ranges all across the board and, like the federal government, is usually linked to the standard pay scales that apply to all or most employees in the jurisdiction. These salaries are typically lower than comparable positions in the U.S. government.

Law Firm Training Options

Law firms are in the process of "professionalizing" and formalizing internal training programs for their attorneys. Look for job titles such as the following:

- Training Manager
- Training Coordinator
- Professional Development Director

- Learning and Development Manager
- Legal Recruitment and Development Manager
- Manager of Lawyer Development and Diversity
- Director of Employment and Training

Law firm compensation for professional trainers has increased significantly in recent years as firms have seen tangible evidence of the difference a good training program can make in their bottom lines. Compensation varies, depending on the size of the firm (mindful that these types of positions are primarily found in the larger law firms), its geographic location (large city firms pay more than smaller city firms), and the perceived value of the training function (this is still evolving). Recent hires have been at levels ranging quite widely, from $60,000 to $200,000+. The higher the salary, the more likely it is that training is only one of several responsibilities within the firm (all of which generally fall under the title of "Professional Development").

Law Firm Subsidiary Training Opportunities

Corporate consulting subsidiaries of law firms are an emerging phenomenon, and are proliferating throughout the legal community.

The impetus behind such businesses is both financial and defensive. Financial because law firms find it easier to earn additional revenue from existing clients, as well as attract new clients by offering additional services; defensive because management consulting firms now offer "thinly-veiled" legal services to their clients and are perceived as a serious threat by law firms.

"Ancillary business" is the term of choice describing these ventures, a term devised to ward off scrutiny by bar regulators concerned about the impact of such initiatives on client confidentiality and proscriptions on revenue-sharing by firms and non-firms. So far, it appears to work.

These subsidiaries are usually creatures of the larger law firms. The key point, however, is that attorneys can often compete for these positions without being filtered out by virtue of where they went to law school, their class rank or where (or if) they are admitted to the bar. Candidates who bring the added value of a dual career to the table are also very competitive. The traditional hiring standards that apply to new associates and lateral attorneys generally are not applied to candidates for law firm subsidiary positions.

One of the hottest arenas into which law firm subsidiaries have ventured is legal and law-related training.

The following list of selected law firms with training subsidiaries illustrates the types of legal and/or law-related training offered:

- Baker & McKenzie—LawInContext—information and training on legal, tax, regulatory and compliance for multinational organizations.
- Buckingham, Doolittle & Burroughs—Seminars
- Budd Larner—Software Licensing Seminars
- Davis Wright Tremaine—Employer Services Customized Training Programs—Examples include: Managing Within the Law; Respectful Work Environment/Anti-Harassment/Sexual Harassment; Employees with Disabilities; Managing in a Drug-Free Work Environment; Maintaining a Discrimination-Free Work Environment; Responding to a Union Organizing Campaign; Managing In a Unionized Environment.
- Duane Morris—Wescott Professional Publications LLC
- Faegre & Benson—Legal Seminars
- Harris Beach—HB Solutions
- Hunton & Williams—ProWorkplace
- Kaufman & Canoles—Seminars on employment issues.
- Kilpatrick Townsend & Stockton—Seminars
- Lathrop & Gage—HROI LLC
- Liebert Cassidy Whitmore—Management Training Services—topics include discrimination, harassment, disability, discipline, investigations, the Family Medical Leave Act and the Fair Labor Standards Act.
- Littler Mendelson—Legal Learning Group
- Morgan, Lewis & Bockius—Morgan Lewis Resources
- Proskauer Rose—WeComply
- Seyfarth Shaw—Seyfarth Shaw At Work®—legal compliance training.

There is no central repository of information available about law firm subsidiaries. Moreover, there is precious little information concerning law firm subsidiaries at all. Compensation is generally on a par with management consulting firms that offer legal and law-related training to their clients and can range from $65,000–$200,000+.

Corporate Training Options

Corporations have been compelled to undertake a great deal of staff legal and law-related training, prompted by a number of government initiatives, including:

- The U.S. Sentencing Commission's Organizational Sentencing Guidelines, which both award and deduct "points" for good and bad behavior, respectively, when organizations—mainly corporations—come up for sentencing in criminal cases

- The compliance mandates of the Graham-Leach-Bliley (Financial Modernization) Act of 1999, Pub. L. 106-102
- The Sarbanes-Oxley Act of 2002, Pub. L. 107-204
- The Consumer Protection and Wall Street Reform Act (Dodd-Frank Act), Pub. L. 111-203; as well as
- Many other Federal and state laws and regulations.

The primary topical areas that receive the most focus from a corporate training perspective are ethics and compliance. The following selected companies and consulting firms offer corporate training in legal and law-related subjects:

- ADC Legal Systems, Inc.
- Altman Weil Pensa
- BISYS Education Services
- Booz Allen Hamilton
- Citigroup Inc.
- Google, Inc.
- Hildebrandt International
- Holt Learning
- JPMorgan Chase & Co.
- Metropolitan Life Insurance Co.
- Nationwide Mutual Insurance Company
- Nortel Networks Limited
- Office of Legal Compliance, Law and Corporate Affairs Division, Microsoft Corporation
- Practice Development Counsel
- The Hartford
- Thomson Legal & Regulatory Corporation/West Group

Salaries for corporate legal trainers are comparable to other professional positions in corporations. The same compensation variables that apply to corporate attorney positions also apply to trainers, namely:

- The larger the company, the higher the compensation.
- Publicly-traded companies generally pay better than privately-held corporations.
- Geographic location influences compensation, e.g., trainers located in large metropolitan areas are likely to make more money than their small city counterparts.

- Certain industries pay better than others, e.g., consulting firms, financial services companies (other than insurance).

Continuing Legal Education (CLE) Providers

Many organizations have jumped into the CLE arena, spurred largely by the online and distance education revolutions, as well as by the accelerating pace of change in the law and legal topical areas. These range from law schools and state, local and specialty bar associations to private sector companies and consulting firms. There are several hundred CLE providers now operating. Good lists of CLE providers can be found at: www.aclea.org and www.cpe-tracker.com/legal/provider.htm. Few CLE providers maintain a permanent, full-time staff of instructors. Rather, they engage law professors and practitioners for specific courses or presentations, and for the most part pay their faculties by the course or presentation.

> **Paralegal certificate programs are growing fast. It means more teaching positions, even for entry-level lawyers.**

Other Selected Legal and Law-Related Teaching & Training Options

This category includes public interest and advocacy organizations, as well as Non-Governmental Organizations (NGOs) and Self-Regulatory Organizations (SROs). A selected list follows:

- American Association of Retired Persons (AARP) (www.aarp.org)
- Equal Justice Works (www.equaljusticeworks.org)
- American Prosecutors Research Institute (APRI) (www.ndaa.org/apri)
- Council on Law Enforcement Education and Training (www.ok.gov/cleet/)
- Central European and Eurasian Law Initiative (CEELI), American Bar Association (http://apps.americanbar.org/rol/)
- National Center for State Courts, NCSC International (www.ncsc.org)
- Financial Industry Regulatory Authority (www.finra.org)
- Research Training and Compliance, Columbia University (www.columbia.edu/cu/compliance/index.html)
- Center for Legal Aid Education (www.legalaideducation.org)

For more information:

- Education Law Association (http://educationlaw.org)
- Society of American Law Teachers (www.saltlaw.org)

- Chronicle of Higher Education (www.chronicle.com)
- Higher Education Jobs (www.higheredjobs.com)
- Academic360 (www.academic360.com)
- The Adjunct Advocate (www.adjunctnation.com)
- Journal of Legal Education (www.law.georgetown.edu/jle/)
- Inside Higher Ed (http://insidehighered.com)
- Legal Writing Institute (www.lwionline.org)
- Times Higher Education Supplement (www.timeshighereducation.co.uk)
- Academy of Legal Studies in Business (www.alsb.org)
- National Minority Faculty Identification Program (www.southwestern.edu/natfacid/)
- National Federation of Paralegal Associations (www.paralegals.org)
- American Association for Paralegal Education (www.aafpe.org)
- Directory of Paralegal Schools in the United States (www.paralegalschools.com)
- National Association for Law Placement (www.nalp.org)
- Association of Legal Administrators (www.alanet.org)

SECTION TWO
GETTING STARTED

CHAPTER 7

Doing Nothing is Not an Option

Whenever an attorney job candidate I interviewed for my company presented a resume that did not address a lengthy time period between law school graduation and our interview, I posed this question: *"What have you been doing since you graduated from law school, other than studying for the bar examination?"* If the response was: *"Nothing. I've been looking for work full-time,"* I almost always concluded that the candidate would *not* be a desirable employee.

While job-hunting is often called a full-time job in itself, it really is not. You can both seek employment and do something else simultaneously without jeopardizing your job search. After all, lawyering is often much more than a full-time job. Just ask any major law firm associate about his or her "normal" 80+ hour weeks. If you are just job-hunting, period, you are sending a negative message to prospective employers. Employers want to see initiative. Moreover, doing something while job-hunting is a very effective way of overcoming a perceived experience gap. The array of possibilities open to you to gain experience are vast.

Here are some of the things that my legal career counseling clients who were fresh out of law school and jobless for an extended period of time did to "fill-in-the-blanks."

ADR Certification and Opportunities

Getting certified as an Alternative Dispute Resolution (ADR) professional can be done easily, quickly and relatively cheaply. Most ADR certification programs take only about one week. Getting certified as a mediator is the first step toward gaining experience doing actual mediations. Certification programs are abundant, and there is a lot of good information about them online. In addition to general mediation, it is possible to enroll in a mediation program that focuses on a specific topical area, such as family mediation, healthcare mediation, employment mediation, international trade mediation, etc.

The following selected mediation programs have a strong track record:

- American Arbitration Association Programs (www.adr.org). Not all are open to the general attorney public.
- American Association of Health Attorneys (www.healthlawyers.org). Dispute Resolver Program.
- Association for Conflict Resolution (www.acrnet.org). Approved Family Mediation Training Programs.
- Boise State University (www.boisestate.edu). Certificate in Dispute Resolution
- Center for Legal Studies (www.legalstudies.com). Alternative Dispute Resolution Certificate (online option).
- Hamline University School of Law (www.hamline.edu/law). Certificate in Dispute Resolution; Certificate in Global Arbitration Law and Practice.
- Hawaii Pacific University (www.hpu.edu). Certificate in Mediation and Conflict (online).
- Institute for Conflict Resolution (www.icmadr.com). Commercial Mediation Certification (online); Commercial Arbitration Certification (online); Family Mediation Certification (online).
- Marquette University (www.marquette.edu). Graduate Certificate in Dispute Resolution.
- Marylhurst University (www.marylhurst.edu). Certificate in Conflict Resolution & Mediation (online).
- Mediation Matters (www.mediationmatters.com/training.html). Basic Mediation Training; Business and Employment Mediation Training; Divorce Mediation Training; Marital Property Mediation Training; Child Access Mediation Training.
- Mountain States Employers' Council (www.msec.org). Mediating Workplace Disputes.
- New York University (www.nyu.edu). Certificate in Conflict & Dispute Resolution.
- Northeastern University (www.cps.neu.edu/programs/certificates/). Conflict Resolution Studies Certificate.
- Northern Virginia Mediation Service (www.nvms.us). Virginia Mediator Certification.
- Southern Methodist University (www.smu.edu). Dispute Resolution Graduate Certificate Program.
- World Trade Organization (www.wto.org). Dispute Settlement System Training Module.

If you have a choice between an onsite or online program, you are best advised to choose the former. Mediation is a very people-intensive, face-to-face undertaking, and you are likely to see that mirrored in the role-playing that is central to most ADR training programs. If an onsite program is impossible, then online ADR training is acceptable.

Once you have obtained your ADR certification, there are a large and growing number of organizations for which you can volunteer in order to gain experience. Chief among these are state and local courts. The National Center for State Courts (www.ncsc.org) has identified more than 1,300 court-connected ADR programs at state and local levels throughout the country. They consist of programs for small claims, probate, juvenile, family, criminal, civil and appellate matters. In most jurisdictions, cases are referred to ADR by judges, and most mediators are volunteers.

Private organizations also maintain ADR programs and sometimes provide training to their members interested in serving as mediators. Two of the most prominent and widespread are those of the Financial Industry Regulatory Authority (www.finra.org) and the American Association of Health Attorneys (www.healthlawyers.org).

Assigned Counsel

An assigned counsel is an attorney appointed by a court to represent an indigent person. Unlike ADR referral programs, which almost always rely on volunteer attorneys, assigned counsel appointments are paid assignments. In New York State, for example, assigned counsel is paid $75/hour for Family Court cases and felonies, and $60/hour for misdemeanors and lesser charges. This is an excellent way to both gain some experience and fill in a gap in your resume. State indigent defense systems are all over the map when it comes to organization and funding. In New York, for example, the system is a county one, with no state administration. In contrast, neighboring New Jersey has a statewide public defender system with trial and appellate attorneys throughout the state. However, when caseloads expand beyond the New Jersey Public Defender's ability to handle them, private attorneys are hired on a contract basis to deal with the overage. For more information about this opportunity, see www.nacdl.org.

Volunteering

The Great Recession has put a severe crimp on legal services and legal aid programs that rely for their funding on a combination of government appropriations, grants, and private contributions. Legal assistance programs are always under severe budgetary strain, even in good economic times. Consequently, they always need volunteer attorneys to help them cope with their caseloads. Moreover, in times of economic crisis, their caseloads increase as more and more families and individuals fall below the poverty line. The federal Legal Services Corporation (www.lsc.gov) funds 136 independent nonprofit legal aid programs with more than 900 offices that provide legal assistance to low-income individuals and families throughout the country. In addition, many states also maintain and fund civil legal aid programs for their residents. These are often funded by a combination of state appropriations and the interest earned by attorney trust accounts. Overall, there are several thousand legal aid programs that have volunteer opportunities for attorneys available.

> **Becoming an "assigned counsel" is an excellent way to gain experience and fill in a gap in your resume.**

Instant Solo Practices

It has never been easier to open a solo law practice. Both the barriers to, and costs of, entry are lower than ever before, thanks to computers and the Internet. In addition, virtually every state bar association can provide you with thousands of dollars' worth of free law office management consulting advice through their law practice management programs.

Certain practice areas are extremely attractive at present and represent excellent opportunities for young lawyers seeking both experience and a resume filler while they pursue full-time jobs. Social Security Disability Income (SSDI) claimant representation, for example, is at an historical peak in terms of demand. The system has been overwhelmed in recent years with applicants for benefits. In 2010, approximately 3.2 million people applied for SSDI benefits. Every expert who studies the SSDI system expects the number to increase every year.

The SSDI Administrative Law Judge hearing backlog now numbers more than 700,000. Moreover, a large number of Administrative Law Judges who hear and decide SSDI cases are retiring.

What makes SSDI practice almost irresistibly appealing is that (1) there is no opposing counsel, (2) the federal government collects your fee for you, (2) case preparation is very straightforward and simple, (4) you will learn a great deal about both administrative litigation and the nexus between medicine and law, (5) you will position yourself to handle other administrative cases and appear in other administrative hearings conducted under the Administrative Procedure Act, 5 U.S.C. §§500 et seq., such as the growing field of Medicare Appeals, and (6) opportunities to market yourself to prospective clients are abundant and easy to exploit, e.g., leaving your business card and brochure with local Social Security offices, legal services agencies, vocational rehabilitation offices and disability organizations.

For a comprehensive examination of solo practice, get a copy of Carolyn Elefant's *Solo By Choice 2011/2012 Edition*, and *Solo By Choice, The Companion Guide*.

Contract Lawyering

This has become a fall-back of last resort for unemployed lawyers. And given the high number of experienced attorneys who lost, and continue to lose, their jobs during the Great Recession, contract lawyering is not quite the safety net that it used to be. It has actually become somewhat competitive in certain cities, such as New York, San Francisco, Los Angeles, Miami and Washington, DC. Nevertheless, it is still a possibility if nothing else pans out. The biggest problem with contract lawyering, aside from the numbing nature of much of the work (and the low pay), is that it is likely to be more time-consuming than any of the other options discussed in this chapter. And you will still need some time (and energy) to hunt for a job. Do not give prospective employers a reason to reject you because they think that you are lazy or unmotivated. Demonstrating initiative and the need to keep your legal skills fresh can count for a lot with employers.

CHAPTER 8

Understand the Hierarchy
of Employer Needs

I haven't yet encountered a legal career counseling client who thought to put themselves in an employer's shoes so that they might "think like an employer" in a hiring mode. But once I point this out to my clients, their legal job campaign picks up.

If you are currently looking for that first law job, the key question you need to ask yourself is this: "*If I am the employer, what do I want to see in a candidate?*" Do this and you will make your job search much more focused and, ultimately, more successful. You won't be flying blind; instead, you will be able to see the road ahead of you clearly.

This is especially true for entry-level attorneys.

With a tip of the hat to psychologist Abraham Maslow and his now-famous 1943 paper in which he outlined his "Hierarchy of Needs," I developed a comparable hierarchy for legal employers after years of feedback from hundreds of such employers. I knew I was onto something important that would benefit my career counseling clients when I capped off this legal employer feedback survey with this question: "*What are the most important traits you look for in an attorney applying for a job with your organization?*"

Over and over, the same six traits—I call them the Big Six—appeared high up in the majority of employer responses. Frankly, I expected academic achievement to be the leading trait sought by legal employers. To my surprise, though, academic achievement was often Number 3 on the list! But before discussing the Big Six, and several other important attributes, it is important that you not get too hung up on precise definitions of some of these characteristics. There is invariably going to be some overlap between traits such as "Productivity," "Work Ethic" and "Meeting Deadlines," for example. Remember, the words chosen to describe the traits were the legal employers', not mine. Moreover, employer preferences and idiosyncrasies need to be considered if and when you consult the Hierarchy of Legal Employer Needs to devise your own personal job-hunting strategy.

The Big Six

The six candidate traits that dominated the concerns of legal employers separated themselves from the rest of the hierarchy by a good distance, both in terms of the number of times they were mentioned and the emphasis employers placed upon them. They're listed here in order of frequency of appearance in the employer survey responses and feedback:

1. Likeability. Employers only hire people that they like. Nothing matters more than *likeability* in arriving at a final decision to make a job offer. If your future boss does not like you, all of your other attributes count for nothing. The reason this attribute is Number 1 on almost every employer's list is simple: if you are going to be spending 40+ hours a week interacting closely with someone, you want it to be someone with whom you feel comfortable, someone you like. So how do employers determine if a job candidate is likeable? Interestingly, it is not only a matter of personality. If it were, then there is probably very little that you can do to change your personality. However, you can have an important impact on your "likeability quotient."

From what employers tell me, likeability begins with the candidate punching all of the proper tickets. That means submitting a resume or job application that is both logically organized and, above all, responsive to what the employer is seeking, and—very important—lacking any off-putting language or devices such as the ones I discuss in Chapter 18 (*Extenuate and Mitigate Your Resume Weaknesses*) and Chapter 11 (*How to Dissect a Job Ad*). If you submit a resume or application that passes the "reader-friendly" test, you are well on your way to getting the opportunity to lock in your likeability. "Reader-friendly" is the key concept. At best, you want the employer to come away from reading your job application materials feeling "warm and fuzzy" about you. At worst, feeling neutral, which may result in cutting you some slack and giving you another chance at the interview. Chapter 22 (*Understand the Cosmetics of Legal Job Hunting*) and Chapter 18 suggest some of the positive things you can do to get to reader-friendly territory.

A reader-friendly application is the platform upon which every likeability determination rests. If the first impression of you is of someone who "doesn't get it," it will not matter what you do to build upon the platform. In

> **What's the leading trait sought by legal employers? It's likeability not academic achievement!**

fact, you probably will be summarily rejected before you get the chance to demonstrate what how likeable you are.

This is a delicate stage in the hiring process. In addition to making a positive impression, your primary objective here is not to make a negative one where you have annoyed or irritated the employer. If your application survives this stage, then you will probably have the opportunity to demonstrate in a job interview how likeable you are.

The job interview then becomes the critical element in your likeability campaign. Here again, there are a few proper tickets to be punched. Call this Platform #2. If ably constructed, you will then have the opportunity to seal the likeability deal. Some job interview basics:

- The way you present yourself when you walk in the door is vital. You need to be well-dressed and well-groomed; that is, professionally presentable. All other factors being equal, surveys reveal that the better-dressed and groomed candidate gets the job offer. Employers tend to jump to immediate conclusions about candidates upon first impression and it becomes very difficult to alter that first impression if it is a negative one.
- A firm but not crushing handshake. This is not a wrestling match.
- Employers like job candidates to ask them great questions (see Chapter 17, *Differentiate Yourself from the Competition*). They tend to react negatively to a candidate who, when asked if s/he has any questions for the employer, responds with something like this: *"No, I think you have answered all of the questions I might have had."* A response like that is such a turn-off that you might as well have said, *"This job does not really interest me. Thank you for your time."*

If platform #2 is solidly constructed, then comes the final likeability determination, which is, unfortunately, not as easily defined as the more tangible elements of platforms #1 and #2. Surveyed employers were all over the map when it came to asking them what makes a candidate likeable in the final analysis. Nevertheless, here is what I distill from the totality of employer responses. Likeable legal job candidates...

- listen attentively and with interest.
- radiate self-confidence
- look the interviewer in the eye without making it a staring contest.
- smile, but only at appropriate times.
- sit up and look comfortable.

- act polite and respectful.
- manifest energy and enthusiasm without going overboard.
- don't interrupt.
- don't "fawn."
- don't fidget.

Every employer has a somewhat different litany of likeability traits, so this list is by no means absolutely determinative. However, if you are able to demonstrate these qualities on top of the two prior platforms, you will probably pass the likeability test. One final point: psychologists who have examined what it means to be likeable in this context sometimes claim that if you mimic the posture, gestures and breathing patterns of your interviewer, you will win the likeability battle. Take that for what it might be worth. It may be true, but if the other likeability components are not present, I question whether mimicry by itself gets you there.

2. Fitness. "Fit" is really a very simple concept. It has nothing to do with being in good physical condition, although studies indicate that individuals who present as physically fit have a decided advantage in job interviews. What it means in the job-hunting context is the following: "*Will this candidate fit into our organization?*" Fit in this sense means aligning with the organization; not being obviously out of place or being a square peg in a round hole. Fit has three elements:

- You must be compatible with the position offered;
- Your temperament must match that of existing employees; and
- Your personality must blend in well with other members of the organization.

Similar to likeability, fit is assessed first by examination of your resume and any other written application materials, then again during job interviews, and finally by the employer posing "fit" questions to your references. Key fitness questions that employers pose to candidates and their references include the following:

- **Tell me about yourself**. An open-ended, deceptively simple question, it is often a killer for candidates who either say too much or say the wrong thing. While a little personal background information is acceptable, don't go overboard. Get to talking about your professional self quickly.

- **Are you a team player?** *"Yes"* is not responsive. Give specific examples of your collaborative work.
- **What experience relevant to this position have you had?** Again, specific examples of your relevant experience are sought. Make sure that you do not go off on a tangent and present experiences that it would be a stretch to call relevant. If you have not had directly related experience, cite ones that contain elements transferable to the offered position.
- **What do you know about our organization?** Do your research prior to the interview.
- **Why do you want to work here?** Your response to this question can be either a game-breaker or a deal-sealer. It's an open invitation to demonstrate that you fit within the organization. If, after all of this, the employer has any concerns about your fit, you probably will not get a job offer.

> **"Why do you want to work here?" How you answer that interview question could be a game-breaker or a deal-sealer.**

3. *Intelligence.* Academic achievement, as I mentioned earlier, is only one indicator of intelligence, and of only one kind of intelligence. And while law school performance was at one time almost always good enough to get your first job, it is invariably not the case anymore. An increasing number of sophisticated employers have experienced the occasional disconnect between great grades and success as a practitioner, as well as the opposite, the mid-dling law school grad who becomes a stellar performer. There are all sorts of ways to demonstrate your intelligence…even in the absence of superior law school performance. Example: the way you structure your resume can be a sign of intelligence. The logic that supports your resume structure and format can go far toward demonstrating intelligence. A resume addendum is another way to manifest intelligence. Asking great questions at the job interview is another indicator of superior intelligence. Or, accompanying your writing sample with an explanatory cover sheet also works in your favor with respect to this point. For additional discussion of this trait, see Chapter 19 (*Emphasize Your Intangibles*).

4. *Being a quick study.* This attribute is highly valued by employers because time is money. If you're an individual who comes up the learning curve quickly, you will earn a great deal of credit for that. You will cut client bills at a time when this has become a major issue for every law firm. But you don't have to wait for a job interview in order to imprint this trait on a prospective employer. You can do so via your resume, elaborate on it in your resume addendum (see Chapter 19), and discuss it with specific examples in a cover letter or transmittal email. Despite the formal mentoring programs that many law firms and some other legal employers have in place, quick learners are highly prized.

5. *Writing ability.* This is one of the easiest of the Big Six to demonstrate from the outset. Just remember that every document—every document!—you prepare and deliver to a prospective employer is, in fact, a writing sample. Take the time to do your very best to craft application documents that are logical, impressive, and correct when it comes to grammar, tense, syntax, agreement, parallel construction, etc. Always have a second set of eyes that you trust look over your documents before you submit them. When the time comes to submit your actual writing sample(s), make sure that you provide a cover sheet that puts the document in context for the employer.

6. *Persuasive ability.* I was surprised to find that persuasive ability occupied only the sixth position in the Big Six hierarchy because, when you strip away everything else, persuasive ability remains as the characteristic that separates a top-flight attorney from the legal masses. It is the core essence of effective law practice; it distinguishes winners from losers. What this means for you is that results and outcomes count for much more than mere job descriptions. It also means that you can use your resume as your initial mechanism to persuade an employer that you possess persuasive ability. Discussing your duties and responsibilities in prior positions that you have held or in other milieus, such as volunteer or community activities, is a very effective way to get the point across. Again, adding a "Highlights Addendum" to your resume can go a long way toward confirming the capability (see sample in Chapter 19).

. Unfortunately, the rest of the Hierarchy of Legal Employer Needs does not lend itself to the same precise positioning of the Big Six. Still, what follows are the additional characteristics that many employers do deem important. And the more of them you are able to demonstrate, the better off you will be when competing for a position. The following employer needs are presented in alphabetical order because my survey and empirical feedback from employers did not reveal a clear hierarchical order.

- Accountability
- Analytical ability
- Attention to detail
- Business bottom-line/budget consciousness

- Client skills
- Flexibility
- Follow-through
- Goal-oriented
- Initiative
- Leadership or leadership potential
- Leading by example
- Meeting deadlines
- Organizational skills
- Problem-anticipation ability
- Problem-solving ability
- Productivity
- Stability
- Well-roundedness
- Work ethic

A candidate who possesses all of the traits that comprise the Employer Hierarchy of Needs is an extreme rarity, so do not be discouraged if you do not have them all. Employers know how unusual it is to find such a candidate. Moreover, even if you possess only a few of these attributes, the fact that you understand the hierarchy and can respond to it in your application documents and during a job interview makes you competitive and attractive to employers, and even puts you closer to an equal footing with candidates who might have more experience.

CHAPTER 9

Shop Where There is Demand

A colleague of mine practices equine law.

No, she does not live in Kentucky or Virginia's "hunt country". Instead, she lives and works as a sole practitioner in a very unlikely place for an equine lawyer—Boston, Massachusetts. It happens that "old-money" Bostonians own horses, and Boston is full of such folks. And these days, horses and their owners generate a good number of legal issues. There are very few equine lawyers in Boston, so she finds herself in a good position. If she had gone to Kentucky and hung out a shingle as a sole practitioner focusing on equine law, she would likely have had a very rough time of it.

If you are interested in a law practice area that overflows with competitive candidates—in other words, where supply far exceeds demand—then you will find that the experience requirements in a job ad are likely to be absolute. After all, why should a legal employer cut you any slack when s/he has an abundance of qualified candidates with the requisite experience beating down the door to apply for the job? Not likely to happen.

Often, however, a little bit of supply-demand analysis can point you in the right (geographic) direction.

Take international trade law and litigation, for example.

Aspiring to an international trade law/litigation practice in Washington, DC might be difficult when you have hundreds, if not several thousand, international trade lawyers plying their wares before the Commerce Department's International Trade Administration (ITA), the U.S. International Trade Commission (USITC), the Export-Import Bank, the Overseas Private Investment Corporation, the Office of the United States Trade Representative, or any of the other agencies that play a role in international trade and investment. In fact, examining the dockets of just the two international trade litigation agencies—the ITA and USITC—would reveal that the number of cases before them has been static for more than a decade. So, while the practice has not grown, the number of international trade litigators has increased, making the competition for clients all that much more intense.

Conclusion: Washington DC might not be the best place to launch an international trade law/litigation practice. But as surprising as it might be, DC is by far *not* the only place in the U.S. where international trade litigation is conducted.

Today, an attorney could locate almost anywhere and practice international trade litigation. The reason is that the third judicial body that hears international trade law cases, the U.S. Court of International Trade, headquartered in New York City, is authorized to conduct trials anywhere in the U.S. and does, for the convenience of the parties. Judges of the court may be assigned by the Chief Judge to preside at trials in any U.S. Courthouse anywhere. Moreover, the International Trade Court is equipped to hear oral arguments and conduct conferences with parties outside of New York City.

The combination of globalization and a rash of smaller companies that are becoming involved in exporting and importing mean that international trade law is spreading out into the "provinces." It is not uncommon anymore for a small manufacturing company in the rural Midwest to be an exporter. And for that company to be represented by a local attorney who must come up to speed on the law and regulations governing exporting.

> **The FDIC has an almost 25-year record of hiring entry-level attorneys, especially during times of banking crises.**

An additional factor in your favor is the vast expansion of two concepts: Foreign Trade Zones (FTZs) and (for want of a better term) Technology Councils and Corridors. FTZs are defined areas set aside to provide special customs procedures to U.S. companies engaged in international trade activities. Items can be processed duty-free in FTZs if they are then exported after processing, and duty payments are deferred on items until they exit the FTZ for sale in the U.S. As of this writing, there are approximately 275 FTZs in the U.S. There is at least one in every state. Attorneys located near an FTZ also have an opportunity to cultivate foreign clients engaged in international trade.

Technology Councils and Corridors are consortia of high technology companies that are often located in special areas established by states and municipalities in order to offer tax, regulatory, job training and other concessions for the purpose of encouraging job creation. Examples include: the Arizona Technology Council, Austin Technology Council, Ben Franklin (Central and Northern Pennsylvania) Technology Partners, Florida High Tech Corridor, Metroplex (Dallas-Fort Worth) Technology Business Council, Northern Virginia Technology Council, Research Triangle Park (North Carolina), Silicon Valley and Colorado's Convergence Corridor.

These two expanding concepts are very good news for aspiring international trade lawyers with little or no experience, but who are sophisticated enough to perform this kind of research and whose job search campaigns are driven by the results.

Locational Analysis

You can do similar "locational analysis" for virtually any practice area. Doing so is not only important to your initial decision about what to practice and where to practice it, but also for your long-term economic and career "health."

Locational analysis means much more than merely determining where a particular kind of law is practiced. It also has to take in a considerable amount of unrelated information, such as population growth trends, business-friendliness, attorney-practice area "saturation," local perceptions, and more. Then you need to synthesize what you have learned and apply it to your particular situation.

What follows is another example of the creative way in which locational analysis can make a career difference:

My legal career counseling company undertook a great deal of outplacement work on behalf of the U.S. government.

One such assignment consisted of 135 attorneys being laid off by a federal agency whose workload had declined abruptly and steeply as a result of the bursting of the dot.com bubble in 2000. It was our job to help these lawyers secure re-employment elsewhere. Most of them were very young, two years or less out of law school (some with only a few months on the job), inexperienced in any other practice area than the one that had suffered so much that they were let go. Moreover, the impact of their agency's decline in work was reflected in a comparable decline in the private sector. It looked to us to be a very difficult job helping these folks move on.

What we discovered was entirely unanticipated.

The more distant from Washington, DC, the more attractive these unemployed lawyers were in the eyes of potential employers. Even more astonishing was that, although very few of our candidates had attended top-tier law schools, and even fewer had excelled academically, they were attractive to legal search firms, a.k.a., headhunters, despite the fact that headhunters virtually always handle only attorneys from top law schools with stellar grades and law review backgrounds, and with at least several years of superior experience in large law firms.

Here's what we found:

In picking the brains of several headhunters who had taken on our candidates and successfully placed them, we found that the candidates' limited experience and expertise was perceived quite differently in Des Moines, Cincinnati, Albuquerque, and Boise, places where even a few months of intensive exposure to the practice area in a federal regulatory agency exceeded what virtually any local candidate could bring to the table.

What this experience taught us was that *value* is a variable concept, and that how value is perceived can vary considerably with location.

This was a lesson that we subsequently incorporated into our legal career counseling practice that had broad application to many candidate practice preferences. We also discovered that it is possible to determine how different locations view candidate experience in "real time" rather than ex post facto via feedback from successful and unsuccessful legal job seekers. Communicating with local legal headhunters and law school career offices, demographic analyses, discussions with local attorneys and business professionals, etc., proved to be excellent information resources.

Employers *Unlikely* to Hire Entry-Level Attorneys

Attorneys are very bright people.

By the time you've achieved licensed attorney status, you have had to compete and successfully negotiate college admission, academic success, secure a decent LSAT score, gain admission to law school, graduate with a JD degree, and survive a bar examination. Along the way, you've picked up a great many techniques and strategies that can be applied to both job-hunting and career success, among them...

- Issue identification
- Analytical and writing skills
- Verbal competence
- Deductive reasoning
- Problem-solving
- And, considerable knowledge of human behavior.

Thus, you are more than capable of identifying employers who rarely, if ever, recruit and hire entry-level attorneys and, conversely, those employers who have a history of such hiring: The evidence is out there for any savvy attorney to see. Let's begin with the employers who are *not* likely to hire entry-level attorneys:

The Fortune 1000. America's largest corporations almost never hire a lawyer fresh out of law school. They uniformly prefer attorneys with several years of experience so that they can come into the company and hit the ground running without a lot of training and mentoring. Unlike large law firms, corporations as a rule do not have "learning curve" programs in place. Spending money on "luxuries" like this is not part of the corporate mind-set. In contrast to law firms that worship the billable hour and thus, can afford to hire a great many young attorneys whom they can "bill out" at high rates immediately (although that is gradually changing due to pressure from corporate clients), corporations are answerable to shareholders and quarterly earnings reports. Besides, corporate in-house counsel offices know that tens of thousands of lawyers at large law firms, where they have gained great experience, dream constantly about the supposed greener pastures available in corporate America. The supply will always exceed the demand, so why bother with "newbies."

The evidence for this is both direct and inferential. Numerous studies of corporate job creation and hiring patterns exist. A scan of legal headhunter ads will alert you instantly to the fact that only a tiny minority of them are corporate placements and that those few always seek experience. Discussions with any law school career office will underscore this corporate propensity for experience. Nevertheless, many recent law school graduates continue to deny—rather than play—the percentages and barrage companies with resumes.

In contrast, major law firms tend to hire entry-level attorneys but employ the following rigorous criteria:

- Attendance at a top law school (or if not, graduating at the top of the class)
- Law review, preferably on the basis of grades
- Recruiting entry-level lawyers only during the fall recruiting season

Despite these well-known parameters, I continue to encounter 3Ls and recent law school graduates who believe that these criteria do not apply to them. Some of them get angry at me when I tell them that they likely have little chance at these law firms and insist despite this reality to focus their job campaigns on these firms. Of course there are going to be exceptions to every rule or strong tendency. I have witnessed these exceptions myself. However, when you are looking for work, you are going to be much better off playing the percentages rather than deluding yourself and wasting your time, energy, money and self-esteem on a lottery ticket. It will get you employed quicker and with far less anxiety and elevated blood pressure along the way.

Employers With a History of Hiring Entry-Level Attorneys

Instead of trying to break down brick walls, why not pursue a legal job with an organization that has a history of hiring entry-level attorneys, such as:

The Federal Deposit Insurance Corporation. The FDIC, which moves from financial crisis to financial crisis with depressing regularity, has an almost 25-year record of hiring entry-level attorneys, especially during (1) banking crises when banks are failing right-and-left and must be liquidated by the agency, and (2) following financial "reform" legislation such as the Financial Modernization Act of 1999 (a.k.a. Graham-Leach-Bliley Act), Pub. L. 106-102, the Sarbanes-Oxley Act of 2002, Pub. L. 107-204, and the Dodd-Frank Wall Street Reform and Consumer Protection Act of 2010, Pub. L. 111-203. Each time a precipitating event occurred, the FDIC "staffed up" and hired entry-level attorneys, among others. A former FDIC General Counsel once told me that the agency preferred recent law school graduates because they came aboard with a clean slate and no bad habits, and thus could be trained more easily than experienced attorneys in the subtleties of bank takeovers, deposit insurance, regulation-writing, and the arcana of financial regulatory jargon, transactions and litigation.

Moreover, the FDIC had a history of hiring far beyond the top law schools and academic criteria that major law firms apply in their recruiting efforts. And even more interesting, the agency did not necessarily hire according to the calendar because financial crises do not predictably arise only during fall recruiting season and major legislation can come out of Congress at any time of year.

Mid-size and smaller law firms & small and start-up corporations. These employers are traditionally much more flexible in their hiring criteria than their larger brethren, and they will countenance entry-level lawyers on occasion. These employers almost always have to be more budget-conscious than their larger counterparts, and entry-level attorneys come relatively cheaply. They are also more easily blended into organizational cultures that are less diverse than those of larger organizations.

Colleges and universities. The academic arena almost always has what are usually called "Judicial Offices" whose personnel resolve disputes among students, faculty and administrators, and handle minor student disciplinary cases. These are relatively low-paying positions that experienced attorneys are unlikely to be able to afford to take because of financial obligations such as families and mortgages. Thus they are more conducive to younger attorneys (these are JD-preferred positions for the most part) with fewer financial burdens.

Legislative assistants in Congress. Several thousand legislative assistants work on Capitol Hill and in state legislatures. The positions are relatively low-paying, but ideal for young lawyers just beginning their careers. They can also be excellent "career builders," stepping-stones to good jobs after a few years in the halls of a legislative body.

These are just some of the examples that a little bit of sweat equity investment in employer research could turn up.

CHAPTER 10

Don't Take Job Ads at Face Value

Far too often, novice attorneys are deterred from applying for good jobs because a job ad that intrigues them asks for more experience or other qualifications than they possess.

I frequently witnessed that "deterrent effect" among my legal career counseling clients. They might have been seriously considered for these positions had they just bothered to apply for them. There is an almost universal misconception that attorneys without the requisite qualification requirements will apply when reading a job ad. The misconception is that an employer will reject out of hand any application that does not meet the requirements contained in the job ad. That may well be the case…but often it is not.

When you dissect a job ad (see Chapter 11), do so with the following premise in mind: the vast majority of job ads are written with the "ideal" candidate in mind.

Naturally, any employer wants to hire the best possible employee, one that can leap tall buildings at a single bound and is faster than a speeding bullet. Superman, however, is very difficult to find. These superior beings simply do not come calling very frequently. In fact, they almost never do. Employers know that they probably will not unearth Superman.

Mindful of the thinking behind most job ads, you the candidate should not necessarily be deterred from applying. You might just be the best candidate available. If you do not apply, you will never know. A couple of caveats, however: government jobs that state experience requirements are usually much more rigorous in applying them when sifting through applicants than other employers. The reasons for this are twofold:

- Civil service recruitment and hiring rules (which often specify certain experience requirements for specific positions at defined civil service grade levels), and
- Bureaucracy, where rigidity and precedent are mindsets that breed inflexibility.

But even these are not absolutes that should cause you to say, "*Oh, forget about it.*"

Do not cast a government vacancy announcement aside until you have slogged your way through its arcane and obfuscating language carefully. You will often find exceptions and offsets buried deep within these absurdly lengthy documents. In fact, there may be an exception whereby you can substitute education for experience. The position may be offered across a range of possible grade levels, each with differing experience requirements.

Another important possible exception is one that applies across-the-board in the U.S. government. Attorney vacancy announcements with the job classification series "0905," which you will see immediately following the job title at the top of the vacancy announcement, fall within what the government calls the "Excepted Service." This means that the customary civil service hiring rules do not apply. Employers seeking 0905 attorneys have plenary authority to use any hiring scheme they desire and thus, have almost unlimited flexibility when it comes to hiring attorneys for "attorney" jobs (an important concept because many government attorneys work in "law-related" positions that do not contain "attorney" in their job titles, all of which do fall under competitive civil service regulations).

This exception does not mean that you should apply for every job that you see offered by government regardless of the experience mandates in the vacancy announcement. You need to apply some common sense to your analysis. If the announcement calls for "10 years of experience litigating D'Oench Dhume Doctrine cases in U.S. District Courts, and you have never heard about this doctrine, do not waste your time applying for that job.

Certain other employers who mirror government and/or bureaucracy in some ways may also be rather rigid when it comes to imposing experience or other qualification requirements. As a rule, the larger the organization, the more likely such requirements will not cut candidates any slack. However, even here you can perform a fairly sophisticated analysis before you decide whether or not to apply for the job. If your application is going to go to the Human Resources department, then it is likely that "strict construction" of the requirements will apply. Personnel specialists who may be reviewing your application before it gets to the attorneys or other professional staff have little or no discretion when it comes to matching an application to the qualification requirements in the job ad. If, however, your application goes directly into the legal office (or other office where you would be working), there is likely to be more leeway in considering candidate qualifications.

If you happen to be totally unqualified for a position and would have difficulty even remotely meeting—or substituting something else for—the qualification requirements, applying for such a position may be too much of a stretch.

Other Circumstances When You Can Discount Experience Requirements

Most non-governmental employers are inclined to be more flexible when hiring attorneys than what their job ads would have you believe at first glance. Again, you will encounter this more in smaller organizations.

- If you have attractive attributes other than experience, these should be highlighted in your application (and, hopefully, in an interview).
- If you meet or exceed the other job ad requirements and lack only the requisite experience, it may be reasonable to submit an application.
- If you have experience gained from summer and semester jobs in another area that might be transferable to the experience sought, you might consider applying and pointing out how your experience would translate to the position offered.

Common sense needs to govern your assessment as to whether it is worth your while to apply. If too much experience is called for, you probably should not. There is no rule of thumb to apply to every job ad, but roughly speaking, I would dispense with any job that calls for more than three years of experience if you have none.

The Aura of the East

The East—that is, Asia—has always held a certain fascination for Westerners. But the aura of the East also holds true within the boundaries of the United States. Maybe because the East is where the country began its historical journey, and is also home to the largest population concentration, the financial center (New York) , the political and governing center (Washington, DC), and arguably the academic center (the Ivy League). This still persists despite 50 years of population movement from the East to the West and South.

I have seen this phenomenon manifest itself too many times with my counseling clients to discount it. A few real-life examples make the point:

- An Army JAG officer who graduated from a lower-ranking law school on the West Coast and then idled away his service time in the Pentagon fielding calls from military bases for advice on handling traffic violations, got three job offers from major California law firms when he was discharged from the Army. He was told by the firm from which he accepted a job offer that his working at the Pentagon intrigued them.

- A graduate of a middling law school in Washington, DC who could not get an interview with any major law firm in Washington was gobbled up by the largest firm in Mississippi.
- A trademark attorney whose one year of experience at the U.S. Patent and Trademark Office got him a job with the intellectual property office of one of the largest consumer products companies in the world, headquartered in the Midwest.
- An Ivy League law school graduate from the bottom of her class who was able to select from the top law firms in the Pacific Northwest.
- A recent graduate of a New York City, second-tier law school who worked for a Wall Street boutique firm as an unpaid volunteer while a law student who was hired by a St. Louis law firm that did securities work for major Midwestern corporations and was seeking an attorney with two years of experience.

This is not to say that this Eastern mystique always works. It does not. Much depends on what you are seeking and where you want to locate. The next chapter describes how to take apart a job ad and determine if competing for the position offered makes sense.

CHAPTER 11

How to Dissect a Job Ad

Every job advertisement and vacancy announcement is an admission by an employer that he or she has a problem that requires resolution. Your goal should be to position yourself in the employer's mind as the *solution* to that problem. Once you begin thinking of a job opportunity in these terms, you will be able to craft and submit a superior application.

To do that, it is critical that you correctly interpret the job ad; in fact, it is especially critical for an entry-level attorney who is competing against (1) other new law school grads, (2) law school grads of immediately preceding years who have been jobless or underemployed since law school due to the Great Recession, and (3) recently laid off lawyers with some experience. For these reasons, you have to go the extra mile to get seriously considered.

Step #1: The first step is to dissect the job ad, breaking it down into its component parts. Just divide a sheet of paper, or your computer screen, into three columns, labeling Column 1 "Job Ad Requirements," Column 2 "My Qualifications," and Column 3 "My Compensations."

Step #2: In the first column, list each of the ad's requirements and the preferred or desired qualifications.

Step #3: In the middle column, list your qualifications in response to each requirement. Note: I don't have to remind you that cold-blooded self-awareness and brutal honesty is required here.

Step #4: In the last column, you need to be at your creative best and come up with compensating background, experience, skills, talents and/or achievements that, while not perfectly matching the column one requirements, can wholly or partially bridge the gap between the first two columns.

Going through this dissection exercise is valuable in several respects:

- It helps you answer the question, "*Should I even apply for this job*?" If the gaps are too vast, the answer is probably "*No.*"
- It helps you become a realist and act accordingly. Your responses will keep you grounded.
- It encourages you to apply for a position despite not matching every requirement perfectly, thanks to your "bridge" information in Column 3.
- Most important, this job dissection exercise will make your job application highly responsive. This will guarantee that you are several steps ahead of many of your rivals for the position. As an employer of attorneys and a reader and evaluator of thousands of legal resumes and job applications, I can assure you that this level of responsiveness is certain to impress a prospective employer. Ripping apart job ads should be an essential component of any job search campaign. If you apply for a position without going through this analysis, you are highly likely to submit an application that rambles and risks summary rejection. For attorneys fresh out of law school, this is a non-starter of epic proportions!

> **Every job ad and vacancy announcement means an employer has a problem that needs resolution. You must position yourself as the solution to that problem.**

JOB AD "DISSECTION" TEMPLATE

The Job Ad Dissection Template is intended to make it easy for you to: (1) determine if you meet enough of a legal job ad's duties and qualification requirements to make it worth the effort to apply for the position, and (2) take apart a job ad so that you can be as responsive as possible if and when you apply.

Column One of the three-column template is reserved for a breakdown of what the job ad says about job responsibilities, required qualifications, and preferred or desired qualifications. Column Two is where you enter your responses to each of the elements of the job ad that you identified in Column One. Column Three is where you can enter your "compensation(s)" if you do not meet the qualifications, in other words, how you can bridge the "qualifications gap."

Sample Job Ad

The Federal Public Defender Office's Division of the Committee for Public Counsel Services is seeking an entry-level attorney for its Appeals Unit. The Appeals Unit provides legal representation and appellate advocacy for indigent clients in the United States Court of Appeals for the 9th Circuit. The cases handled by the Appeals Unit are primarily post-conviction criminal cases, usually involving clients convicted of serious felonies and sentenced to substantial periods of incarceration. Although the bulk of the work takes place on cases pending in the Circuit Court of Appeals, Appeals Unit attorneys occasionally represent their clients in trial court on motions for new trials, motions to revise and revoke sentences, and motions to correct or enlarge the appellate record.

Responsibilities: *Duties include representation of clients in interlocutory proceedings, on direct appeal, and in other related proceedings, including the following:* '

- *collecting and reviewing documentary evidence*
- *interviewing clients*
- *conducting legal research*
- *preparing appellants' and occasionally appellees' briefs, reply briefs, and applications for rehearing, for reconsideration, and for further appellate review*
- *arguing before the Court of Appeals and U.S. District Court*
- *at times conducting post-conviction investigation, including visiting crime scenes and locating and interviewing witnesses*
- *providing formal and informal assistance to Public Defender Division trial attorneys on trial court level cases*
- *providing training to Public Defender Division and Private Counsel Division staff*

Requirements. *Candidates must become a member of a state bar in good standing within six months of appointment, be able to work in a defense-oriented capacity, both independently and collaboratively, and be committed to working with a culturally diverse, low-income population. Candidates must possess very strong writing and oral advocacy skills. Candidates with access to an automobile preferred.*

Column One:

Responsibilities/Qualifications

- Client representation
- Appellate representation
- Collecting & reviewing documentary evidence
- Interviewing clients
- Conducting legal research
- Preparing appellants' and occasionally appellees' briefs, reply briefs, and applications for rehearing, for reconsideration, and for further appellate review
- Arguing before the Court of Appeals and U.S. District Court
- Conducting post-conviction investigation, including visiting crime scenes and locating and interviewing witnesses
- Providing formal and informal assistance to Public Defender Division trial attorneys on trial court level cases
- Providing training to Public Defender Division and Private Counsel Division staff

Required Qualifications

- State bar within 6 months of appointment
- Able to work within defense-oriented capacity
- Able to work independently
- Able to work collaboratively
- Committed to work with culturally-diverse, low-income population
- Strong writing skills
- Strong oral advocacy skills
- Preferred or Desired

Column Two:

My Qualifications

Column Three:

My Compensations

If you are permitted to accompany your legal job application with a cover letter or transmittal email, you also need to determine what to say in the limited space available (and it is limited; no employer wants to see a dissertation from you). I am not going to tell you how to write such a missive here. What I want to impart to you is how to filter the important points you need to address from the less important ones.

As a very rough rule of thumb, job ads and government or other vacancy announcements tend to lead with the most important requirements. And if they are ably and intelligently written, they will take you down their list in order of importance to them. What this means for you is that you absolutely have to address the "top-level" needs and pay less attention to lower-level employer requirements or preferences. Addressing these top-level needs does not mean that you admit, unequivocally, that you do not possess these employer requirements. Rather, this is where Column 3 of your dissection template enters the picture. You need to point out how you compensate for your "lack" without expressly stating the deficiency.

Of course, all of this presupposes that, after having dissected the job ad or vacancy announcement, you have nevertheless concluded that it is reasonable to apply for the position. When you are making that assessment, do not forget that there may be factors involved—such as a dearth of supply in the employer's location, or your intangible attributes—that come down on the side of applying for the job.

CHAPTER 12

The Legal Job Hunter's 13 Biggest Mistakes

The baker's dozen of legal job-hunting mistakes in this chapter are derived from my observations after (1) almost three decades of legal career advising, and (2) my conversations with, and feedback from, several thousand legal employers in every legal employment sector—private practice, corporate in-house counsel offices large and small, government at all levels, and non-profit entities ranging from the largest universities down to those that consist of a handful of public advocacy organizations.

The 13 "Biggest Mistakes" that follow are the ones that occur most often during a legal job campaign:

Mistake #1. Failing to Identify Likely Employers

Sending mass-mailed applications to hundreds of employers simply because they are there and happen to hire attorneys from time-to-time is a complete waste of time, money and energy. Targeting employers is the name of the game, played correctly. Submitting job applications to just 10 employers who you have thoroughly researched and who you have concluded are compatible with your career goals, values and expectations, will almost always reap greater rewards than mass mailing/emailing applications to 1,000 employers extracted from Martindale Hubbell or "identified" by a resume mailing service.

Mistake #2. Failing to Research Your Practice Area

If your passion is to practice Golf Law, do your research very carefully. Other than working for the Professional Golf Association (PGA), the Ladies PGA, the U.S. Golf Association or one of the few law firms with such a practice, you will find a huge vacuum out there in the working world. It is important that you thoroughly understand this before you commit yourself exclusively to a Golf Law practice. It is also crucial that you understand the trends in the economy and elsewhere that might affect a Golf Law practice. Estate tax attorneys whose bread and butter was small-to-medium size estates have suffered enormously over the past decade, as Congress has fiddled with the estate tax, which currently exempts estates of up to $5 million for married couples. This legislation eliminated 98 percent of the potential client pool. That Congress would do something about the estate tax was eminently predictable for a long time before the legislature acted. That the days of many estate tax attorneys were numbered should not have come as a surprise.

Mistake #3. Looking for Opportunity in Adversity

We hear this a lot, and often we hear it in a career counseling context. Sometimes this strategy even works. Much more often, it does not. There is a reason for adversity and, unless you understand exactly and in a very sophisticated way why a company, an industry or a product line encountered hard times, you best stay away from the potential "turnaround" situation.

Mistake #4. Not Searching ALL the Legal Job Ads

Not every legal job ad online or in the newspapers contains the words "*attorney, law* or *legal*." Whenever I ask lawyers what search terms they use, these are the Big Three. The growth in JD-preferred positions and other law-related positions means that you are doing yourself a serious disservice if you don't expand your searches to include search terms such as "compliance," "enforcement," "licensing," "contract," "regulatory" and many others.

Mistake #5. Writing Only One Resume

I have yet to meet a law student or attorney, entry-level or experienced, who could conduct a thorough job search relying on only one, "one-size-fits-all" resume. Different employers require targeted applications. Using the same resume for every job opportunity diminishes your chances of being invited to an interview.

Mistake #6. Cramming Everything On a Single Page

Resumes that overflow with type, lack acceptable margins, or employ tiny type fonts that are difficult to read send a negative message to an employer. They are intimidating, to say the least, and few employers look forward to slogging their way through such type-rich documents with enthusiasm.

Mistake #7. Failing to Proofread Your Application Documents

I find grammatical mistakes—typographical errors, misspellings, the wrong tense, the absence of parallel construction, etc.—in more than 50 percent of the attorney application documents I see. When I hired attorneys, an error of this kind meant automatic rejection, regardless of how impressive the candidate was otherwise. My concern is that if this person is going to represent my company in writing, then errors such as this are unacceptable. Most legal employers have the same attitude. The careless need not apply.

Mistake #8. Including Your Interests and Hobbies on Your Resume

Discovering that a candidate likes "reading, jogging, music, and sports" is not terribly illuminating to an employer. It is also a waste of resume space that might otherwise be used to make a marketing point about the candidate. Moreover, interests such as these activities hardly distinguish you from the rest of the world. Better to omit such information. As always, there are exceptions. If you discover that you share an avid interest with the individual who will see your resume and/or interview you, by all means mention it. If you were to apply for a judicial clerkship with Chief Justice Alan Page of the Minnesota Supreme Court, it would not hurt to mention that you were a nose tackle in high school and at State U. Chief Justice Page's prior career was as an all-pro defensive lineman for the Minnesota Vikings.

Mistake #9. Revealing Too Much About Yourself

Under most circumstances, you need to be very careful if your application materials reveal a political preference, religious affiliation, or some other feature of your life that might be viewed askance by a prospective employer. A highly accomplished client of mine was general counsel to a prominent business that was a wholly-owned subsidiary of a very controversial, non-mainstream church. Over time, my client suspected that he was being summarily rejected for every position to which he applied because of bias against the church. Once he omitted mention of the church and just listed the business, interviews began coming his way.

Mistake #10. Relying on Letters of Recommendation

Increasingly, I run across law students and entry-level attorneys who claim that they cannot come up with any references, but have several letters of recommendation that they intend to submit to prospective employers as a substitute. Letters of recommendation are a poor substitute. Employers want to talk, person-to-person, to your references. They tend to discount letters of recommendation because they generally all read the same, full of excessive praise and laudatory language. Worse, those that do not contain such immoderate language about you are perceived even more negatively. The only time you should rely on a letter of recommendation is if you simply cannot find anyone to serve as a professional reference.

Mistake #11. Including Personal References

The only time to proffer a personal reference is if it is specifically requested by the employer. This rarely happens. Employers want to see professional references—current or former employers, professors, opposing counsel in cases you might have argued as a special 3L admittee under the state bar rules in the state where you attended law school, judges or hearing officers before whom you have appeared.

Mistake #12. Sending Unrequested Materials with Your Resume

Employers dislike being inundated with paper (or its electronic equivalent). If they ask for a resume and cover letter, send them a resume and cover letter, period.

Mistake #13. Not Making Sure Your Application Gets There

One of the most stunning job search oversights in my opinion is the failure of legal job candidates to follow-up on their applications. The road to job search success is littered with the detritus of applications that never made it to the employer. While this was a fairly minor issue in the pre-Internet era when reliance on the U.S. Postal Service or an overnight service was quite reliable, it is a much bigger issue now, when applications often can and do get lost in the "ether." Call or email the employer to confirm that your application arrived.

And for good measure: there is one more job-hunting mistake: **Relocating without research**.

Often, legal job hunters assume that a geographic move is going to solve their career problems. It may, but before you pick up and move, do your due diligence regarding the new location and its legal opportunities. There is an immense amount of online information with which to compare geographic areas with respect to the number of attorneys per capita, cost of living, quality of life, client demographics, industries and much more. Did you know, for example, that an elder law attorney can do very well in places other than the obvious ones like Florida and Arizona? Military retirees, for example, tend to retire to places near military bases and veterans hospitals. Research also reveals that there are large military retiree populations in such non-obvious locations as Waco, Austin, College Station and San Angelo, Texas; Oklahoma City; Harrisburg and Carlisle, Pennsylvania; Madison, Wisconsin; Pittsburgh; New Orleans; and Syracuse.

CHAPTER 13

What Mobile Job Search Apps Can Do for You

How do you conduct a job search if you're desk-bound, and at risk taking time from work and using your employer's technology? And how do you conduct a job search if you work at home, and are distracted by family matters? Or if you can't search for work on a daily basis, and risk losing the competitive edge that reacting rapidly to new job opportunities can offer?

What can you do?

You can conduct a job search using the latest mobile job search apps.

The environment for job search apps is still pretty new and hectic, and—as we go to press—there are still no iPhone, Android or tablet apps specific to legal job seekers. But the general ability to search for jobs anytime, from anywhere nowadays—and to get your qualifications in front of a prospective employer before the competition—is already becoming the difference between success and failure.

Without a doubt, a new communications revolution is underway, and it has already begun to liberate job-seekers and employers from being tethered to one place at one time in order to execute all of the traditional activities that characterize job hunting and recruitment. In short, our contacts, connections, information, research, and documents can now come to us—and we to them—wherever we or they happen to be.

Of course, in an environment evolving on a daily basis, and where mobile apps selling for as little as 99 cents already number in the hundreds of thousands, there surely will be new and even more "emancipating" job search apps soon. Maybe next week, next month. In spite of rapidly shifting circumstances, though, we will do our best to call attention to some of the best mobile apps currently on the market for all the usual job-seeking activities: organizing, calendaring, and tracking your job search activities; research; resume preparation and transmission; networking; interviewing; and fast-breaking news you can use:

Mobile App Search Engines & App Blogs

Amazon App Store (www.amazon.com). User-reviewed apps available on Amazon's site in conjunction with Google's Android Market.

Android Market (https://market.android.com). Apps, books, and movies from Google's own app store.

AndroidZoom (www.androidzoom.com). A comprehensive search alternative for Android users. Apps may be downloaded by using links or scanning QR codes.

Blackberry App World (www.appworld.blackberry.com/webstore). The official Blackberry app store.

iPhone4Lawyers (www.iPhone4Lawyers.squarespace.com). Former Texas litigator Tom Mighell is a passionate blogger on all things related to productivity apps for the iPhone and iPad. Mighell is also the author of iPad in One Hour for Lawyers (ABA, 2011).

TabletLegal (www.tabletlegal.com). An iPad-for-lawyers blog authored by Oregon business attorney Josh Barrett.

The Droid Lawyer (www.thedroidlawyer.com). Oklahoma business lawyer Jeffrey Taylor has one of the few Android-oriented blogs for lawyers ("Tips & Techniques for Using an Android-Powered Device in Your Law Practice").

UCLA Law Library (http://libguides.law.ucla.edu/mobilelegalapps). The law school site lists a diverse selection of user-reviewed apps for all mobile platforms in such categories as legal research, bar exam study, productivity, and fun.

uQuery (www.uquery.com). A popular new social mobile search engine focused on the emerging market of mobile applications. Users can search among more than 200,000 iPhone, iPad, and iPod Touch applications.

USA.gov Mobile Apps (www.USA.gov). Information and downloadable links for a variety of mobile apps created by the federal government.

Smartphone & Tablet Apps

ABContacts. Manages and organizes contacts into dynamic groups based on various criteria; first name, last name, company, notes, job title, department, etc. Rates high with users.

AMightyRiver. An iPhone app that specializes in helping African-Americans find job opportunities.

Bento. A flexible organizational app with 25 database templates that you can use to organize your job search. Rates high with users.

Careerbuilder. An early mobile app with built-in geolocation capabilities that automatically determines which city you're in and lets you to find a job via keyword search. You can read job descriptions and salaries, save jobs to a list of favorites, and email job links. The app has the full functionality of Careerbuilder's Web site. The app gets mixed ratings from users; some say the app is prone to crashing.

Craigslist. *The New York Times* says Craigslist's own mobile app is not as user-friendly as three independent apps: CraigsPro+ , Craigslist Mobile (both on the iPhone), and Craigslist Notification on Android. Users especially liked CraigsPro+ for being intuitive, convenient and full of great features.

Evernote. At the present, this superb cloud-based app is one of the best organizers for your job campaign (and your entire life). Its organizational scope is all-encompassing. A great app for every legal job seeker. One of the *New York Times'* Top 10 Must-Have Apps.

HireADroid. This Android app searches through multiple job search engines, returns all of the results to you, and lets you apply for them. The search screen is intuitive and applies Boolean search logic ("AND", "OR" and "NOT"), a big advantage. Searches can be performed in 18 countries. You can save previous search queries so that you can perform the same search every day with a single click. When you drill down into a job result, you wind up on the employer's application page, which lets you either apply immediately or email the listing to yourself.

iJobs. Delivers millions of job listings to your iPhone. A keyword search allows you to search for a word in a title, description, salary, etc. There is also an auto-detect on your location, a zip code search, and an ability to automatically save your last search. You can add jobs to a favorites list and filter the results by category, company, title, industry, and employee type.

JobFinder. Collects jobs from multiple job Web sites. Specify locations that you're interested in, along with your other preferences, and JobFinder will remember them and use them whenever you use the app. JobFinder also organizes jobs into 73 categories, including Law, Government/Military, Insurance, etc.

LinkedIn. You can browse your LinkedIn connections and search for jobs, use an address book integration utility, and save your search history and results. Just like LinkedIn.com, you can search profiles and connect with professionals or friends. Mixed ratings from viewers on the app's functionality.

LinkUp Android Job App. This app pulls job listings directly from company Web sites, then sends you back to the company Web site if you want to apply. The "Advanced Mode" is a sophisticated search function that permits you to perform a radius search and company search.

Monster.com Jobs. Users can search and apply for jobs, access their

Monster account, save job searches, and email jobs to friends. Using location awareness, Monster Job Search will also find jobs near you and your current location. Mixed ratings from users.

Monster Android Job App. This app provides a very clean search screen by job title, skills, location. Clicking a button next to "location" collects your location from your phone and returns summary search results. Clicking on a job returns a detailed description. You can apply for a job by clicking the "Apply" button.

Notability. This is multi-featured note-taking app is especially useful to people who pull Web clips while traveling, need to type text notes, or record audio notes. Rates high with users.

NPR for iPad. NPR's magazine-style approach with its iPad app delivers hundreds of NPR live station and on-demand streams. This app can keep you in the know about current events that might impact your job search and career goals in more depth than other news sources.

PocketResume. This iPhone app produces a "good enough" resume quickly, but its best feature is making it easy to edit it on the fly in order to tailor it to particular employers that you discover while on the move. This app rates highly among users.

Priority Matrix. A time-management tool that lets you visually organize lists, agendas, and priorities by color and labels, set target dates, keep pro-and-con lists, and perform many other productivity tasks useful to a job search.

Real-Time Jobs. This app lets you search the 50+ million tweets-per-day for job openings, and permits you to "re-tweet your LinkedIn professional profile to prospective employers.

Reuters News Pro. Reuters News Pro delivers news and market data in a broad context. The app comes with numerous customizable categories, a personalized watch list for business news, and geographic-specific news views.

Save2PDF. This app is very useful if you want or need to edit documents, such as your resume, and create PDFs on the move. Rates high with users.

WordPress. WordPress is a major blogging platform, and the tablet version contains many of the desktop features that make it a world leader. Bloggers can create, save, publish, and schedule posts and pages.

The Future

Morgan Stanley predicts that by 2014, mobile Internet searches will exceed computer searches.

This has major implications for employers, recruiters and job candidates.

One of the most important of these implications is that mobility and "immediacy" will become increasingly significant to all three sides of the employment transaction. All three players will need to incorporate a mobile job search strategy into their employment, recruitment and job campaigns, respectively.

Many more job-search apps are likely to become available very soon, intensified by the overall dismal jobs recovery from the ongoing Great Recession, and the seeming inability of government and our other institutions to solve our chronic unemployment problem. As for legal job search apps, I expect them to remain on the back burner because the market is not large enough to warrant the cost of research and development given the low prices that developers can charge for apps. Still, mobility among both the employed and job seekers is on the increase, and is certain to stimulate additional app development.

While Google and Apple envision a future where everything online will be converted into smartphone and tablet apps, mobile job searches cannot yet replace the personal desktop "experience." This is especially the case if you want to create top-notch job-search documents.

So, for now, you are best advised to prepare these documents—resumes, cover letters, contacts roadmaps, etc.—as a Web app on your personal home desktop.

CHAPTER 14

Enhance Your Law Credential

One of the most predictable mantras from frustrated legal job seekers is this:

"I'm going to go back to law school and get an LL.M."

The thinking is that, now equipped with an LL.M., it will provide an easier career path. Of course, this is based on the assumption that the LL.M. will contribute to leveling the competitive playing field, and make a candidate more attractive to prospective employers. Which is true...to an extent, and with a lot of qualifiers.

I am often asked whether it makes sense to go back to law school for an LL.M. degree. My standard response is: "Well, it depends." I then relate the sad tale of one of my clients. He spent more than $50,000 to obtain an LL.M. in Environmental Law from a top-tier law school. When he graduated with the degree and began searching for an environmental position, several employers grilled him:

"Why did you go to _____ law school for your LL.M.? Didn't you realize that _____ is not a top school for an environmental LL.M.? Why didn't you go to either _____ law school or _____ law school?"

This fellow came to me for career counseling because he was upset at his lack of job market success after spending a fortune for an additional law degree that he thought would position him for a great job. When I asked him some of the same questions posed by the employers who rejected him, he said that he chose _____ School of Law because it was top-ranked and among the U.S. News & World Report's top 25. He said he hadn't known that the two schools the employers mentioned were home to the two top-rated environmental law LL.M. programs in the country.

My client was devastated. The credential for which he invested so much time, money, and effort was not much of a career-builder.

There Are More Credentials Than an LL.M.

Before we examine how to identify good programs that can give your career a real boost, you need to understand that LL.M.s are *not* the be-all and end-all of credential-boosting programs.

There is an entire range of certificate and comparable programs, as well as other degree programs.

Certificate programs offer an opportunity to obtain a credential—often a very strong one—with far less investment of time and money than for an LL.M. For example, for an investment of about $1,000 and a few months of your spare time, you can earn a prestigious Associate in Risk Management (ARM) credential, completing the three levels of courses and three examinations online at your convenience! Once you have an ARM credential to accompany your JD, you become a serious candidate for corporate risk management positions. Between 20–25 percent of U.S. risk managers possess a JD degree. U.S. law schools currently offer more than 30 certificate programs in more than 25 topic areas that are open to non-degree (JD or LL.M. candidates). What's more, a growing number of these programs are available online.

In addition to law school certificate programs, many non-law school academic institutions, as well as trade and professional associations and private companies, offer legal and law-related certificate programs, both onsite and online. *There are at least 400 such programs in approximately 60 practice areas that might be suitable for you, depending on your interests and career aspirations.* Take a few moments to look over Appendix C for some of the most popular such programs. Note: certificate programs warrant the same pre-enrollment scrutiny and due diligence as LL.M. programs.

Expand your research into credential-enhancing programs to include law-related ones. Depending upon your background and interests, and the state of the job market in your area, you may be better off in terms of enhancing your legal employability if you obtain a law-related graduate degree or a law-related professional certificate instead of an LL.M. There are, for example, superb law-related programs in 70 legal and law-related fields, among them Alternative Dispute Resolution, Compliance, Contracting, Risk Management, and Real Estate (again, see Appendix C).

Some Pros & Cons of an LL.M.

The failure to adequately research LL.M.'s or other credentialing programs—or to even perform the necessary due diligence before matriculating and handing over a very large check—is a classic case of something that I saw every day in my career counseling practice.

In the context of legal job-hunting, due diligence means scoping out a prospective employer, but it also applies to the scrutiny required before enrolling in any academic program. Especially an LL.M. program, which could set you back more than $50,000 and require two years to complete. Before you embark on an LL.M., or any other educational program that you hope will boost your legal career and help you compete more effectively, carefully consider the following observations:

An LL.M. can be a valuable addition to your credentials portfolio, but you have to go into it with eyes wide open in order to maximize its utility. Some economic cost-benefit analysis and opportunity-cost consideration is a good idea. The benefits of, and the opportunity afforded by earning, an LL.M. degree better be pretty fantastic if they are to outweigh the costs. In addition to tuition, and after factoring in fees, books, living expenses, you are probably looking at a total cost near $60,000 per academic year. And when you add lost wages for the duration of the program (assuming you are leaving a job to pursue the LL.M.), it becomes even more expensive.

Program Due Diligence

Mindful of the sad tale I related at the beginning of this chapter, you need to be very careful about where you decide to matriculate in an LL.M. program. Some LL.M. programs are generally deemed much superior to others in the same legal field. For example, if you contemplate an LL.M. in Taxation, you have a choice of more than 50 law schools. However, the Tax programs at New York University School of Law and Georgetown Law School are considered the top ones by the vast majority of the legal community. If you can get into one of these two programs, you will have enhanced your employability substantially.

Below are the due diligence requirements that can enable you to make an intelligent credentialing program selection:

Talk to individuals who have already earned the credential. Get their opinions as to whether the credential made a difference to their legal careers, employability, promotion potential and compensation.

Ask them:

How difficult was it to find suitable employment after completing the program?
How much help—and what kind of help—did you receive with respect to finding employment from the granting institution's career and/or program office?
If you had it to do over again, would you still pursue the credential—again?

Talk to employers of individuals who have recently earned the credential. Ask them:

Do you value the fact that your employee has the credential?
How does the credential benefit your organization?
Would you have hired the employee absent the credential?
Do you believe the credential is a career booster?
What is your opinion of the credential-granting organization?

Talk to current students. Ask them:

Is the program worth the time, effort, money, and career interruption?
What do they intend to do with their degree or certificate?
How much, and what is the nature of the, the career assistance they are receiving from the granting institution?

Talk to the career placement professionals and program directors at the sponsoring school or organization. This is the most important due diligence component of all. Ask them:

Where can I expect to work once I successfully complete the program?
What is the institution's track record when it comes to placing program graduates?
Where do recent graduates work and what career paths will be open to me?
What are the specifics of what you can do for me during and after completing the program.

If a school's placement and/or program officers stonewall you—that is, you're told that they do not maintain such information or statistics, or they assert privacy or confidentiality reasons for not sharing this information, or they become defensive, or if their answers are vague or otherwise unsatisfactory—say "thank you," pocket your check and/or loan application, and walk away. You have every right to know what you are buying.

> **LL.M's are not the be-all and end-all of credential-boosting programs. See Appendix C.**

Demographic Upheaval Creates LL.M. Opportunities

Another facet of your research should be "trends analysis," a careful examination of economic, demographic, political, societal, and other trends that might make your decision to pursue an LL.M.—as well as what kind of LL.M.—a very attractive proposition or, alternatively, a very dubious one.

Some of the trends worth considering include:

- The aging of the U.S. population is less a trend than a population bomb, one with profound implications for law practice and for many legal credential-boosting programs.
- Baby boomers are turning 65 years old at a rate of 10,000 every day, and between 2008 and 2026 almost 80 million people will "age up" to 65. Boomers have dramatically transformed American society and life at every stage of their life journey. Their dominant demographic presence has altered many facets of American life, including law, education, families, business, government and work. In the course of their journey, society has been compelled to alter many of its traditional ways of operating. As they age, Boomers will once again be a transformative generation.
- As of January 1, 2011, the U.S. population age 65 and older numbered an estimated 39.5 million. The 65+ age group has doubled in size in one generation, and the number of really old codgers—85 and older—is growing even more rapidly. By 2020, the peak "aging-up" year when Boomers hit their golden years with a vengeance, there will be 55 million seniors, more than 7 million of them 85 and older.

This is not just an age "wave". It's an "age tsunami," and it is destined to overwhelm our social insurance and healthcare systems. When contemplating the effects, you also have to include the tens of millions of potential legal clients who are members of the families of their aging relatives. Their legal needs are directly impacted by their Boomer relatives who are growing old, whether the issue is long-term care insurance and options, durable family powers of attorney, living wills, healthcare proxies, Do Not Resuscitate directives, wealth transfers, Medicaid eligibility, and many more.

LL.M. Opportunities in Elder Law

The legal impact of an aging population is profound. It has created entire new, viable and dynamic practice areas such as Elder Law, and it has instilled life and energy into practice areas that for years were quiet, uneventful backwaters, such as Pension Law, Employee Benefits Law, Social Security Law, and Medicare Appeals. Other practice areas impacted profoundly by the age tsunami include Health Law. Boomers are the most populous and wealthiest generation in U.S. history. This is still true despite the devastation wrought by the 401-K and IRA meltdowns prompted by Wall Street greed, rampant consumerism, and government indifference and ineptitude. That means that

Boomers have a lot of money to spend on getting their lives in legal order. What does this demographic upheaval mean for an LL.M.?

- First, an LL.M. in Elder Law, Pension & Benefits Law, Social Security Law, Health Law, Food and Drug Law, or even Real Estate Law might be a very good credential to have in your arsenal. There are currently five Elder Law LL.M. programs available, for example.
- Second, in the absence of LL.M. offerings in some of these topical areas, there is a proliferation of certificate and comparable programs that address these areas and are far less costly and time-consuming than LL.M. programs. See Appendix C for more about these kinds of programs.

LL.M. Opportunities in Family Law

Another demographic upheaval has to do with the massive changes that are going on with respect to the traditional family structure. Consider:

- The traditional family model—mother, father, children—now accounts for only about 25 percent of the nation's households.
- Incrementally, legal recognition is being extended to the other 75 percent: cohabiting families, single-parent families, blended families and stepfamilies (generally created by divorce and remarriage, where biologically unrelated children may live in the same household), grandparent-led families, families where the adults are gay or lesbian, commuter families, foster families, and group home families, to name the major variations.
- Sixty percent of all children spend some of their lives in single-parent families, 88 percent of which are headed by women.
- Eight percent of U.S. children live in households headed by their grandparents (a number that is growing rapidly).
- Two-parent gay and lesbian households are on the rise, as are single-parents who are gay or lesbian. Their children may have originally come from a heterosexual parent relationship, or may have been adopted or conceived by assisted reproductive technologies. One gay or lesbian parent may be the genetic parent and the other parent the adopting one.

Policy changes directed at this demographic change are unusual in that they have been fostered from the bottom up—by corporations and municipalities—rather than by legislation. Many private companies, municipalities and nonprofits have adopted domestic partner policies that give benefits and rights to unmarried heterosexual and same-sex couples. Some state governments have done the same. Courts throughout the U.S. are recognizing nontraditional family relationships and rights. Single-parent adoptions are no longer a rarity. Today, about one-third of all U.S. adoptions are by single parents, including a growing number of men.

The legal needs of nontraditional families are often different from those of the traditional family and represent a growing opportunity for attorneys, and Family Law is scrambling to play catch-up with these emerging family structures

Representation includes counseling clients on formalizing domestic partnerships, pursuing benefits, domestic and international adoption, alternative reproduction, financial matters, as well as all of the issues surrounding the end of relationships (including divorce when both partners are gay, lesbian, transgender, or bisexual). It includes such tasks as drafting partnership, co-parenting, donor, surrogacy, and dissolution agreements; the legal validation of same-sex marriages; alternative and assisted reproduction; non-traditional adoption proceedings (including the growing field of international adoptions); de facto parent status; custody of sperm donations; grandparent visitation rights and much more.

> **For more than a century, copyright law was the poor stepchild of IP practice. Thanks to the Internet and digital media, IP is an important practice area.**

An analysis of Census Bureau statistics is very encouraging for nontraditional family law credential seekers: more than 40 million nontraditional U.S. households; 30+ percent of American children are born out of wedlock; more than half of gay Boomers don't have a will; and exploding membership in the American Academy of Matrimonial Lawyers (membership increases in such interest groups is always a positive sign). While this phenomenon is still sufficiently new that it has not spawned any credentialing programs specifically about the topic of nontraditional family law, existing family law LL.M., certificate and comparable programs are gradually incorporating syllabi and materials addressing it. Nevertheless, job opportunities in this area are expanding.

Nontraditional family practice is dynamic. A lot of issues are yet to be resolved. This is good news for attorneys seeking such a practice.

Law vs. Technology

Technology always outpaces the ability of the law to keep up with it.

What this means for attorneys and law students seeking to augment their legal credentials by adding an LL.M. or certificate is that any practice area where a growing trend is evident is likely going to be very attractive.

Food and Drug Law, Telecommunications Law and Securities Law are perennially dynamic, always in flux, and thus invariably positive practice areas in which to seek a credential. Consider these examples:

- Drug-device combinations where a medical device does double duty by also dispensing a therapeutic drug suddenly appeared on the scene and took the Food and Drug Administration (FDA) by surprise. It has taken several years for the FDA to catch up with this new technology and begin to regulate its approval and monitor its use, safety and effectiveness.
- The Federal Communications Commission has, for years, been in the forefront of regulatory agencies challenged by new technologies that do not fit neatly into existing regulatory schemes. Currently, the Internet and its accompanying issues, such as "net neutrality," are vexing the agency and forcing it to scramble to keep pace with innovation and its unintended consequences and attendant abuses.
- The Securities and Exchange Commission is stymied by its inability to monitor or regulate the transfer of funds across borders. Every day trillions of dollars move across borders with the push of a keyboard key, and the principal U.S. regulator of capital movements has no approach for coping with this phenomenon.

Good News for Anti-Fraud Credentials

Like the dynamic tension between technology and law, a similar relationship exists between the ethics movement and the creative advance of fraudulent practices and malfeasance. The two have a history of moving in lockstep.

As fraud increases, government and the private sector react by instituting more attempts at ethics education and compliance and enforcement controls. This, in turn, prompts the defrauding community to devise creative avoidance mechanisms which then prompt the fraud fighters to impose more stringent controls. And so on.

As this is being written, the U.S. government has in place no fewer than seven distinct interagency and intergovernmental task forces focused on fraud, including oil and gas price manipulation fraud, Medicare fraud, procurement fraud, mortgage fraud, financial fraud, computer crimes, and Hurricane Katrina fraud. This is in addition to more than 70 federal agency Inspector General offices already tasked with identifying and fighting "fraud, waste, mismanagement and abuse," plus a number of other federal organizations whose primary function is fighting fraud.

And that's not all:

- State and local governments are not far behind in their anti-fraud efforts. Almost every state and many municipalities have insurance fraud and Medicaid fraud bureaus, among others.
- American corporations have also joined the anti-fraud effort. Virtually all of the Fortune 1000 corporations have an Ethics Office, thanks to the legislative and regulatory pressures emanating from Washington, led by the U.S. Sentencing Commission and its Organizational Sentencing Guidelines. Regulatory compliance is the fastest-growing corporate profession, according to the Bureau of Labor Statistics. This function is often combined with the corporate Ethics function.
- Insurance companies are establishing and expanding internal anti-fraud efforts. Statistics on the volume of insurance fraud are elusive. Cobbling together disparate analyses leads to a figure somewhere north of $350 billion. Every $2 of investment in combating insurance fraud returns more than $17 in recoupments.
- Colleges and universities are also part of the ethics mix, as are trade and professional organizations, the larger of which have independent ethics offices staffed by attorneys who advise members on ethics matters.
- Professional licensing organizations increasingly focus on ethics matters. State bars have been in the forefront of this movement for decades, and are staffed with ethics officers, bar counsel and client protection fund attorneys. Not to be outdone, other professional regulators, such as medical licensing agencies, are following the attorney model.
- Finally, the prolific escalation of international counterfeiting and piracy of products, patents, trademarks and copyrights—manifested by knock-offs—has given rise to laws like the Prioritizing Resources and Organization for Intellectual Property Act of 2008 (PRO-IP Act), Pub. L. 110-403, that enhance career opportunities for attorneys interested in an exotic anti-fraud practice.

Despite the Herculean efforts at investigation and prosecution by government and the private sector, fraud keeps growing and expanding into new arenas. The escalation of both fraudulent activity and efforts to combat it are unlikely to dissipate, as societies and economies become increasingly complex and do so at an accelerating rate.

The number of LL.M. and certificate programs addressing fraud is growing. This, too, is good news for attorneys seeking an anti-fraud credential. See Appendix C for selected programs.

Good News for Energy-Credentialing Programs

Oil-dependent economies (which means every national economy) are slowly coming to an end. The era when global oil supply kept pace with energy consumption is long over. Its end, first announced in the mid- and late-1970s when Middle Eastern nations turned off the oil spigot for political reasons, now looms larger and is a concern of the highest priority. The energy crisis—

> Once you have earned the added credential, make sure prospective employers both know about it and understand its value.

and we are clearly in a crisis situation—is now a constant, fueled by rising demand from rapidly growing economies like China, India, and Brazil. Rising demand means rising prices, and these will be facts of life for America and the world for many years to come. American politicians' days of hiding from this reality are numbered. Of necessity, a national "Energy Independence" policy and accompanying legislation and regulatory initiatives must be just around the corner. Companies and law firms are already anticipating this inevitability and positioning themselves for it. Energy practices are popping up and expanding nationwide, and increasingly encompass alternative and renewable energy sources.

All of which should be good news for attorneys considering an Energy Law credential. See Appendix C for a list of energy credentialing programs.

What an IP Credential Could Do For You

As of 2010, almost 80 percent of aggregate American corporate assets were intellectual property (IP) and intangible assets, up from 32 percent only 25 years ago. This stunning rise in IP assets and their increasing critical importance to the U.S. economy has prompted a corresponding rise in the number of IP professionals, and in the array of complex issues with which they must cope.

It is important to note that not all IP attorneys have a scientific or engineering background. IP encompasses much more than patent law. In fact, it is other issues that account for much of the recent growth in and prominence of IP. "Soft IP," i.e., trademarks, copyrights, intellectual asset management, technology transfer, and the flood of counterfeit and pirated products worldwide are the major issues responsible for the prodigious increase in IP's importance today.

Trademark filings with both the U.S. Patent and Trademark Office (PTO) and internationally pursuant to the Madrid Protocol are increasing, despite the devastation wrought by the Great Recession. Protecting trademarks and licensing them to outside organizations has become a very big business on university campuses. Even government gets into the act, with no fewer than

23 federal agencies outside of PTO with trademark legal practices.

Copyright law, for more than a century the poor stepchild of IP practice, has emerged from hibernation to become a critically important practice area, thanks to the Internet and digital media.

A recent example of Intellectual Asset Management (IAM) occurred when a British company acquired a large portion of a North American beverage business. The acquisition brought with it approximately 30,000 trademarks in various states of protection (with filings in more than 80 countries) and use. An IAM consulting firm was engaged to sort through these trademarks and perform the necessary steps to protect and maximize their value, a years-long process.

IAM consists of transforming and leveraging IP and other intangible assets (such as trade secrets, brands, business processes, and employee know-how) into strategic revenue-producing corporate assets. It encompasses identifying IP assets, taking whatever steps are necessary to fully protect them both domestically and internationally, analyzing them for their revenue-producing potential, marketing and licensing them to outside parties, and monitoring and managing these assets.

IAM is now very big business, both for companies and universities, and also for the growing number of consulting firms and law firms that offer this wide-ranging service.

Technology transfer, defined as the transfer of inventions, innovations and IP assets from one party to another, through licensing or other means for commercialization purposes, is widespread and expanding. Companies, universities and governments that want to maximize the revenue produced by their IP assets are heavily involved in technology transfer. As of this writing, 316 U.S. government laboratories engage in technology transfer activities while the number of academic institutions and corporations that do this number in the thousands.

Counterfeiting and piracy are rampant in places like China, India, and other Asian countries with lax IP laws and half-hearted enforcement mechanisms, making this a major headache for American business. One of my former clients, an attorney for a major trade association whose members' assets are almost 100 percent IP, makes an annual trip to Beijing where he strolls Tiananmen Square noting the pirated and counterfeit goods sold in hundreds of curbside kiosks that impinge on his association members' IP rights. He then presents his lists to the Chinese government IP regulators and files formal protests (although he has so far been able to accomplish very little to reduce the number of counterfeit and pirated products).

Congress enacted—and the President signed—the Prioritizing

Resources and Organization for Intellectual Property Act of 2008 ("PRO-IP Act"), Pub. L. 110-403, which increased criminal and civil penalties for trademark and copyright infringement, established an IP Enforcement Coordinator's Office in the Office of Management and Budget, and expanded the number of attorneys and other IP professionals serving in embassies and consulates abroad charged with monitoring IP violations and taking steps to reduce them and punish the violators (700 such positions exist as of this writing).

Taken together, the surge in IP prominence means a lot of opportunities for individuals who add an IP credential to their law degree. Numerous law schools, colleges and universities, trade and professional associations, and commercial vendors offer credential-enhancement programs in IP in general or some aspect of IP, such as Electronic Commerce, e-Discovery, Food and Drugs, Art and Museum Law, Technology Transfer, IP Licensing, and International IP matters. See Appendix C.

How to Find Credential-Boosting Programs

One of the most important areas you need to monitor, for the purpose of identifying and researching potential credential-boosting programs as well as for many other legal career-related purposes, is federal and state legislative and regulatory activity.

Three important benefits of such monitoring include:

Early warning of looming career crises. When Congress went about abolishing the Interstate Commerce Commission in 1995—an effort that took on a very serious mien for more than 18 months before the legislation became law—the handwriting was on the wall for a variety of legal practice niches that had provided certain attorneys with a very good income for decades. For example, lawyers who specialized in the trucking industry suddenly found their livelihoods jeopardized because of deregulation.

New societal directions and redirections. Congress often alerts the public to new policy directions and redirections. Its reaction to the corporate scandals of the first years of the 21st century, the need to do something about a broken healthcare system, and the financial meltdown of 2007–2008, manifested themselves in the Sarbanes-Oxley Act, Pub. L. 107-204, the Patient Protection and Affordable Care Act, Pub. L. 111-148, and the Dodd-Frank Wall Street Reform and Consumer Protection Act, Pub. L. 111-203, respectively, all of which generated thousands of new jobs for attorneys, some in entirely new practice areas. All three of these major legislative actions impacted powerfully on legal job opportunities. But that does not mean that you should restrict your legislative and regulatory monitoring only to "headline bills" and regulatory proposals with "star power." You need to look at everything. For example, the low-key and virtually unpublicized Higher Education Opportunity Act of 2008, Pub. L. 110-315, has had, and will continue to have, a monster impact on legal jobs on campus due to its imposition of more than 300 new regulatory compliance and reporting requirements on academic institutions.

New opportunities for you. Legislative and regulatory initiatives often alter the legal job market, both creating and eliminating attorney jobs. Even deregulatory initiatives sometimes create jobs.

A classic example is the Telecommunications Reform Act of 1996, Pub. L. 104-104, often pointed to as a centerpiece of deregulation. The Act in fact created a large number of new positions at the Federal Communications Commission which suddenly was tasked with reviewing hundreds of regulations in order to determine which ones to eliminate while simultaneously being required to issue a panoply of new regulations to implement deregulation. Sixteen years later, those positions still exist. Another facet of "legs and regs" reveals itself in what I call Hermann's Corollary to Newton's Third Law of Motion (for every action, there is an equal and opposite reaction). The Corollary reads as follows: "*For every government action, there is at least an equal (but usually much greater) private sector reaction.*" In practice, this means that a legislative or regulatory initiative that results in the hiring of one new federal attorney almost always results in the hiring of multiple private sector lawyers for each new government legal hire.

Before we leave this topic, let me say a quick word about regulations. With the Dodd-Frank Act looming and its recent history of lax regulation generating a tremendous amount of both political and media criticism, the Securities and Exchange Commission (SEC) moved ahead with its own spate of internal reforms even before any legislative mandates were imposed upon it. Six months before Dodd-Frank was enacted, the SEC established no fewer than five new offices in its Enforcement Division designed to combat some of the regulatory defects that emerged from the Wall Street collapses.

You will want to consider the impact of legislation and regulations on any credential-boosting program decision you face. Georgetown University, for example, offers a certificate program in legislative studies (see Appendix C).

Court decisions. Court decisions can also impact on your credentialing decisions. For example, one of the quietest backwaters of legal practice has always been Election and Campaign Finance Law. Only a handful of attorneys have ever been able to make this a full-time practice, and business is always down during the periods between elections. Now, thanks to the U.S. Supreme Court's decision in Citizens United v. Federal Election Commission, 130 S. Ct. 876 (2010), that is changing. Election and Campaign Finance Law is now an emerging practice area with a much better future than past.

Promoting Your Credential to Employers

Once you have earned the added credential, you need to make sure that prospective employers both know about it and understand its value.

You need to "maximize the boost."

Given that employers tend to read resumes with increasing Attention Deficit Disorder as they move down the document, it is vitally important to get your key points across as quickly as possible. One of the very best ways to do this with respect to your new credential is to put it at the very top of the page, immediately following your name. For example, say that you earned the aforementioned Associate in Risk Management certificate to go along with your law degree. The best way to imprint your dual credentials on an employer is to note them as follows at the top of your resume: Jane Doe, JD, Associate in Risk Management (ARM)

Since approximately 20–25 percent of Risk Managers have a JD (primarily because many employers send their Risk Managers to law school), coming into the job competition equipped with both credentials is a huge advantage and is very compelling to employers.

A Risk Management credential combined with a JD is well understood by corporate employers. If you apply for such a position, you will not have to do a lot of explaining of its utility in either your resume or cover letter. The mere mention of it will likely be sufficient to get the point across. Risk management offices are fond of attorneys in the Risk Manager role, especially if the attorney also possesses an ARM or something comparable (see Appendix C for the varieties of Risk Management credentialing programs, e.g., healthcare, food safety, workplace, etc.). They know that law students and attorneys deal with risk assessment daily, and also that lawyers are analytical, hard-working individuals.

The savviest among them also understand that American companies have had very positive experiences hiring attorneys for this role.

That may not be the case with some other credentials that are either less well-known or relatively new to employers. These will require more elaboration in your application documents. You can accomplish that by itemizing the specifics of your credentialing program in the Education section of your resume and/or in your cover letter or transmittal email. If you opt for the former approach, be sure to position your Education information so that the employer will actually see it and read it, or make reference early on that you have elaborated on the credential below in your resume. One way to do this is to include such a reference in your Profile (or Summary of Qualifications) at the top of the document, e.g.,

SAMPLE

Profile

JD from a top-tier law school, plus Certified Fraud Examiner (see "Education," below).

Obtaining an additional credential to accompany your law degree has never been easier. Valuable legal and law-related credentialing programs exist in many fields that mesh well with a JD. Appendix C lists selected credentialing programs that have benefited my entry-level legal career counseling clients.

CHAPTER 15

Think Career, Not Job

As a legal career counselor, I am struck by how many young attorneys who have been unsuccessful job hunters for some time become so desperate to find a job—any job—that they are willing to settle for just about anything that comes along. Although I experienced some success in talking them out of bad decisions that might have a lifelong career impact, I was certainly less than 100 percent successful. That translated to some of my clients accepting paralegal positions, jobs as legal secretaries, or other jobs that were decidedly off the attorney career path and about which they would likely have a difficult time explaining in future legal job-hunting endeavors.

I understand that the time eventually comes when financial pressures loom very large and paying the bills becomes an immediate concern. Nevertheless, you make a big mistake when you settle for less than you could have, or for a job that will do little to advance your legal career.

Why You Might Still Be Unemployed

Before you decide to settle for the next job that comes along, regardless of its nature and legal career impact, you owe yourself an in-depth analysis of (1) yourself and (2) your job-search strategy and its implementation, in order to determine what, if anything, you might be doing wrong. I guarantee that you will almost always discover one or more flaws that, once corrected, can transform a sinking job campaign into a flourishing one. It is the extremely rare legal job candidate that goes about the business of job hunting as well as s/he could.

There are a great many reasons why a candidate encounters job-hunting failure. The constant refrains (excuses?) that I hear in my counseling capacity from discouraged job seekers are something along these lines:

"I sent my resume to over a hundred employers and didn't get a single response."
"I responded to hundreds of job ads, and…nothing."

"I have had a number of interviews, but they always say I don't have enough experience."

"I often get invited to interviews, but I never get the job offer."

It is worth examining each of these excuses in depth.

The unsolicited resume barrage. *"I sent my resume to over a hundred employers and didn't get a single response."*

One of my counseling clients came into my office frustrated by the lack of any action resulting from his job search. He had been applying for hundreds of attorney positions for six months with nothing to show for it. At best, he would receive an impersonal, stock communication from an employer simply stating that his resume or application had been received. Otherwise, no communication at all. He had not managed to secure a single job interview.

> Even if you have less experience than the competition, it's up to you to show why you are the best candidate.

Supremely discouraged, he was ready to give up entirely on becoming an attorney and wanted my advice on what else he might do. Instead, I suggested that he allow me to examine and, if necessary (it is almost always necessary), revise his resume and give his legal career a second chance.

His resume was a disaster.

It was illogical, disorganized, crammed full of type (more than 500 words on a single page), and virtually unreadable. Together, we transformed his resume using some of the techniques described in this book and I sent him on his way. Two months later, I received a call from him where he updated me on what had ensued since our counseling sessions. I was floored when he actually complained about receiving too many invitations to legal job interviews!

As you may know, there are companies that will send your resume to hundreds of law firms and corporate human resources offices while proclaiming this to be a terrific legal job-search strategy. Some of these companies charge a small fortune for this so-called service. It isn't worth it; it's almost always a complete waste of time and money. And it may even delude you into believing that you are doing something productive vis-à-vis your job search campaign. You are not.

If employers do not have any jobs available, they are most likely going to throw out your resume as soon as it comes across their desk. And if they do have a job, it is highly unlikely that your resume will be one that matches the job's qualifications. And, do not assume that the resume mailing company is sending only your resume and no others to an employer. They are barraging the same offices with the resumes of *all* of their clients. Sending your resume, unsolicited, to hundreds of employers is about as effective as throwing them against a wall and hoping one of them sticks. It almost never does.

Responding to hundreds of job ads. *"I responded to hundreds of job ads, and… nothing."*

It has been my consistent experience that what this really means is that the candidate applied for almost every legal job ad s/he ran across, regardless of whether it matched his or her interests or qualifications. The vast majority of my clients who stated this particular frustration also did almost no probing into prospective employers beyond reading their job ads. They relied exclusively on the spare language found in the ads, and that was the extent of their research. One could hardly call this lackadaisical, ad hoc approach a job campaign. If this is you, go to Chapter 11.

The "no experience" excuse. *"I have had a number of interviews, but they always say I don't have enough experience."*

This may be the lamest of all rationalizations for failing to net a job offer. Before you were invited to interview, the employer knew that you lacked experience from reading your resume or online application. Nevertheless, something about your background prompted an invitation to you to interview anyway. No employer wants to waste time interviewing a candidate s/he knows s/he is not going to hire. True, you may have been competing against candidates with experience. But the important point is that you still got to compete at the interview stage. It was up to you to employ techniques to demonstrate why you were the best candidate regardless of any experience gap.

Many interviews, no offers. *"I often get invited to interviews, but I never get the job offer."*

This is related to the "No Experience" excuse in that, again, something about your application materials landed you an interview. However, you never get beyond the interview. This almost always means that you are doing something wrong during your interviews. This is where vigorous, "Maoist-style" self-criticism during your interview debriefings can help you overcome your interview deficiencies. When you emerge from an interview, you can benefit immensely from debriefing your interview performance in writing while it is still fresh in your mind. When you do this, you need to be honest and cold-blooded in your self-assessment. Then, you need to think hard about the deficiencies you have identified and how to correct or mitigate them.

What else might explain why you haven't gotten hired? In addition to a less-than stellar resume and cover letter, and poor interviewing, the other most common reasons for legal job-search failure are:

Misdirection. Legal job seekers frequently look for the wrong job in the wrong place at the wrong time (it could be one or two or all of the above). Pursuing attorney positions in Baghdad in early 2003 would definitely qualify as misdirection. So would a lot of job targeting that attorneys do—or fail to do. If you want to practice water law, for example, you will find many more opportunities in the arid Rocky Mountain West, Southwest and California than you will in the waterlogged Pacific Northwest. You need to find out enough about the practice areas in which you have an interest, and in which there is some logical link between your background and skills and the practice area, before leaping into a job search. Medicare fraud defense, for example, is a nationwide practice, but it is exponentially more acute in South Florida than anywhere else, by far. This is information that is readily available and easy to find.

Lack of effort. You might believe that you are doing everything possible to advance your job search when, in reality, you are only making a half-hearted effort. Far too many attorneys convince themselves they are job-hunting by emailing a resume to a headhunter. Given that legal headhunters want to place only the top 1 or 2 percent of the attorney population and never handle entry-level attorneys, you may as well submit your resume into a black hole where it will be accorded the same consideration that a headhunter will give it.

Being a "serial applier." On several occasions, I had career counseling clients who thought that the way to find an attorney position was to apply for only one at a time, let the application and evaluation process play out, and then if no job offer was forthcoming, apply for another job. The serial approach is a killer because it requires you, the candidate, to pass up opportunities that may arise during one of these single application cycles. I suppose if you have unlimited resources, you can survive being a job-hunting tortoise. Unlike the fable, however, the race almost always goes to the quickest.

Think Several Moves Ahead

The traditional legal career model where a law grad went to work for an employer and remained there until retirement is gone. Technology and globalization are among the factors that have seen to that. Nowadays, the legal job market is more volatile than ever. And in all likelihood, an attorney who graduates from law school now is going to hold quite a few jobs during his or her career.

This fundamental fact means three things for newly-minted lawyers:

- You need to do a great deal of planning and research both while you are in law school and after graduation. Actually, you need to adjust your legal career model continually throughout your career in order to stay ahead of trends and unanticipated career "shocks" and to grab opportunities when they arise. Fortune favors the prepared.
- You need to accept that you may not fall into your ideal legal position immediately upon emerging from law school. That may take some time and one or more "transitional" positions.
- You need to evaluate a job offer in terms of how it will impact your long-term career goals. Ask yourself, "Am I going to gain valuable knowledge and skills that will position me for the next job? Do I risk practicing in an area for which there is little demand? Does my practice area have staying power? Could my practice area disappear because of technological advances? Might I find myself "typecast" by future employers?"

The more uncertain and unstable the legal job market, the more sweat equity and due diligence you need to invest in your future. Complacency is not an option.

CHAPTER 16

Prepare Your Contacts Roadmap

Psychologists who study such matters say that the three things people fear most are death, snakes and public speaking. After three decades of legal career advising, I'll add a fourth: *networking*.

For many attorneys, job-hunting is as lonely as serving a stint in solitary confinement. Virtually every attorney who seeks my legal career advice and assistance comes in awash in the erroneous assumption that "nobody knows the troubles I've seen." This is especially true of entry-level legal job-seekers who graduated from law school without a job and who think that they won't find one.

This is the worst possible attitude you can have going into a job search.

One essential way to temper it is to develop an effective network of contacts who can advise and assist you. This is particularly critical for newly-minted lawyers and can be one of the keys to overcoming joblessness.

One of the biggest problems that I have seen in many recent law school graduates is a certain degree of social awkwardness. Without overstating it, it is my observation that many attorneys are, by nature, loners, not exactly social butterflies. They much prefer spending the evening reading a good book or watching TV—or even working—than clubbing or partying. Fear or anxiety about human interaction appears to be high. The vast majority of attorneys, judging by my own empirical tally after counseling several thousand lawyers, would much rather work on a problem alone than as part of a team, and over-whelmingly prefer contemplating a research and writing assignment than appearing in court or sitting across the table in a transactional negotiation. And keep in mind that fewer than 10 percent of attorneys ever go to court.

It does not—and should not—have to be this way. But...

- If you believe that no one can possibly help you, you are wrong.
- If you insist on going it alone, you're likely to be unemployed much longer than if you enlist the aid of others.

- If you believe that it is supremely embarrassing to have to "network," you are wrong because it is quite possible to make good and even great contacts without feeling like a supplicant.

So, set aside any personal trepidation you might harbor about networking. Look at it this way. The better your contacts and the more effective your invoking of them, the more likely it will be that your job hunt will be successful. The four steps that follow are intended as a guide to effective attorney networking.

Step 1: Your Initial Contacts

Anyone and everyone you know or have ever met qualifies as an initial networking contact. What follows is a list of the most obvious potential contacts that you should contemplate contacting before going further afield. This initial group of potential networking intermediaries is also the easiest one with which to communicate.

- Friends
- Relatives
- Friends of friends
- Friends of relatives
- Neighbors
- Friends of neighbors
- Fellow academic alumni/ae
- Teachers and school administrators (law school, graduate school, college, high school, other)
- Current classmates
- Current employer (if s/he knows about your job search)
- Former employers (if they know about your job search, *and* you left under amicable circumstances)
- Colleagues at your current and former jobs
- Workplace alumni/ae at your current and former jobs
- Other professional colleagues
- Job interviewers you impressed
- Political contacts (if any)
- Members of clubs and organizations to which you belong (such as bar associations, community and cultural organizations, service clubs, church groups, etc.)
- Clergy

- Other people whom you regularly see, e.g., postal carrier, barber, hairdresser, other "vendors"

Step Two: Draft a Contacts Roadmap

In addition to the fear and loathing that most attorneys and law students have for networking, the other major deterrent is the sense (often backed up by empirical experience) that contacts usually don't really do much of anything for you. *It does not have to be that way.* By using a networking technique I developed over the years for my own counseling clients, you can both (1) overcome your fear and loathing, and (2) motivate your contacts to go the extra mile for you. You do it with what I call a Contacts Roadmap. It's a document you should develop at the same time—if not before—you sit down to draft your resume(s). The reason for doing this might appear to be counterintuitive, timing-wise. However, crafting your Roadmap beforehand will help you prepare and target more effective resume(s).

> **Developing a network of contacts to advise you is particularly critical for newly-minted lawyers.**

What is the Roadmap? It's nothing less than your personal job-hunting "strategy-and-objectives" document. Think of it as a campaign plan or business plan. However you describe it, the Roadmap will lay out, in some detail three things: *what you want to do, where you want to do it, and why you should be considered a serious candidate.* Example: Let's say that Jane X wants to work in a government contracts practice. Her Contacts Roadmap might look something like this:

Jane X
12345 Main Street, Apt. 765
Arlington, VA 22203
(C) 703-555-5555
janex@xmail.com

This document maps out my legal job-hunting campaign. In it, I discuss my career objective, prospective employers in which I am interested, and my qualifications/rationale for targeting those employers. My intention is to provide you with a "roadmap" in the event that you can assist me with my job search.

Objective

To work in government contracting. Specifically, I am interested in negotiating and documenting government contracts, contract administration, contract disputes practice, and debarment and suspension practice. While I prefer working as a government contract attorney, I am not averse to launching my government contracting career in a law-related position, such as a Contract Specialist, Contract Negotiator, Contract Officer, Contract Administrator, Contract Termination Specialist, Contract Compliance Specialist or Procurement Analyst as a "transitional position" toward my goal.

Prospective employers

I would like to work for either the U.S. government or a corporation. I am not interested in working at a law firm. My preferred employers are indicated below: U.S. Government, preferably:

Department of Defense
- Office of General Counsel
- Office of Inspector General (IG)
- Defense Logistics Agency (DLA)
- Defense Contract Management Agency (DCMA)
- Defense Contract Audit Agency (DCAA)
- Defense Advanced Research Projects Agency (DARPA)
- Office of the Undersecretary of Defense for Acquisition, Technology, and Logistics
- U.S. Army Corps of Engineers—Office of Chief Counsel and Office of Real Estate
- Defense Commissary Agency (DeCA)—Office of General Counsel

Author note: IG, DLA, DCMA, DCAA, DARPA and DeCA all have both their own legal offices as well as numerous law-related contracting positions in other offices.

Department of Homeland Security
- Office of General Counsel
- Office of Inspector General (IG)
- Science and Technology Directorate (SCI)
- Office of the Chief Procurement Officer
- Transportation Security Administration (TSA)
- Federal Emergency Management Agency (FEMA)
- U.S. Customs and Border Protection (CBP)
- U.S. Immigration and Customs Enforcement (ICE).

Author note: IG, TSA, FEMA, CPB and ICE all have their own legal offices as well as numerous law-related contracting positions in other offices.

Department of Transportation
- Office of General Counsel
- Federal Aviation Administration
- Federal Highway Administration
- Federal Railroad Administration
- Federal Transit Administration
- Maritime Administration
- Research and Innovative Technology Administration
- Office of Inspector General (IG).

Author note: The six referenced modal administrations all have a Chief Counsel's Office as well as numerous law-related contracting positions in other offices. IG also has its own law office and some contracting positions.

While I prefer these three federal departments, I am also interested in working in government contracting in any other federal department or major agency, in either one of its law offices or in a law-related contracting position.

Colleges and Universities
- Georgetown University
  Office of General Counsel
  Medical Center Office of Counsel
  Medical Center Office of Technology Transfer
  Contracting and Procurement Office
- George Washington University
  Office of General Counsel
  Contracting Office
- University of Maryland at College Park
  Office of General Counsel
  Office of Contracts and Procurement
- George Mason University
  Office of General Counsel
  Contracting Office
- American University
  Office of Counsel
  Office of Contracts and Grants
- Howard University
  Office of General Counsel
  Procurement Office

> **A Contacts Roadmap will help you articulate what you want to do, where you want to do it, and why you should be considered a serious candidate.**

- Johns Hopkins University
  Office of General Counsel
  Purchasing Office
  Technology Transfer Office

Corporations. I am interested in the contracting offices (note: it is almost impossible for an entry-level attorney to work for a major corporation's general counsel office without several years of experience) of the following major corporations in the Washington, DC area:

- Lockheed Martin
- Northrup Grumman
- General Dynamics
- CSC Corporation
- AES Corporation
- Capital One
- Marriott
- Daneher Corporation
- GEICO
- Pepco
- NVR Inc.
- Discovery Communications
- W.R. Grace
- Verizon
- Giant Food
- Constellation Energy

I am also interested in legal and law-related contracting positions with any member company of the Northern Virginia Technology Council. These slightly smaller companies are likely to be more open to hiring an entry-level attorney than their larger counterparts.

My qualifications and rationale. As a law student, in addition to my two-semester Contracts course, I also took the following courses that gave me an excellent grounding in government contract law and administration:

- Basic government contracts
- Contract suspension and debarment
- Commercial transactions
- Technology licensing
- Negotiations

> During my 2L summer, I worked in the Office of General Counsel at the National Association of General Contractors, where I was exposed to a great many contracting and subcontracting matters. I have applied to the National Contract Management Association (NCMA) to sit for the Certified Federal Contract Manager certification course of study and examination. I anticipate taking the NCMA Federal Knowledge examination in September, 20__.

The value of a Contacts Roadmap to legal job hunting has proven immense.

In my experience with clients, the Roadmap's greatest value seems to be its ability to boost a candidate's self-confidence, help overcome any inhibitions you might have regarding networking, and—even more than a resume—demonstrate to prospective contacts that you bring something tangible and concrete to your job search. Like nothing else, a Contact Roadmap will force you to carefully and methodically think through your job-search goals, and to document them in considerable detail. In so doing, you will find direction and achieve a strategic objective (not to be confused with the typical, throw-away objective so many job seekers put at the top of their resumes, e.g., *"I want to work for a dynamic organization where my talents mesh with the goals of the organization and where I can contribute to achieving those goals."*).

Where traditional resumes are often subject to considerable misunderstanding and misinterpretation, a Contact Roadmap is a pragmatic directional tool; a map to help guide the thinking and acting of your networking contact. The second most important benefit is its value as a motivational tool for the contact. Seeing what you've put together, the contact will more likely be impressed and inspired to actually do something to advance your job-hunting campaign. The third benefit is what it does to enthuse your contact, and that translates to a more energetic and persuasive endorsement of your candidacy when the contact speaks to prospective employers or additional intermediaries.

Without a Roadmap, most networking contacts simply do not pan out and wind up doing nothing for you.

Everything that I say about the Roadmap has been tested in the real world by my legal career counseling clients. It is, far and away, the best networking "icebreaker" extant, and my clients have found that, more often than not, their networking contacts were able to direct them much more effectively than without such a device at their disposal.

Step Three: Intelligent Use of Social Networks

Social networks like Facebook, Twitter, LinkedIn, etc., have become unavoidable components of a job-search campaign.

No substitute for direct, face-to-face networking. For many attorneys, the advent of social networking has been an exciting development because it implies that they no longer must email, pick up the phone and call, or meet with, a potential contact in person. The emergence of email in the 1990s was equally exciting for a similar reason; again, it implied distance—no longer did a candidate have to pick up the phone and actually speak to someone. In both cases, total or even substantial reliance on these impersonal communications media is a bad idea. Face-to-face interaction with your contacts is essential to (1) getting them to agree to be part of your network, and (2) motivating them to perform on your behalf. They need to see you and assess your affect, intelligence and personality. No one wants to recommend someone or advocate on their behalf without a pretty good feel for the "cut of their jib." You do not get this from email or a visit to a social networking site.

Social (and anti-social) networking. This is not to say that you cannot make effective use of social networks. You can, but you have to be extremely careful. Social networking sites can provide you with job leads and possible contacts that you should follow-up with a phone call, at least, and a personal visit if at all possible. They also can serve a modest collateral purpose in demonstrating to a prospective employer that you possess some computer-savvy and are up on contemporary technological developments. Then, when you get a job offer, these media can be useful in performing some of the employer due diligence that is essential before you accept a position. But that's where their utility ends.

Last year I took an informal poll of law firm recruiters and posed two questions:

- *Have you visited a social networking site in the past year in order to see what a job applicant posted?*
- *Has a visit to a social networking site ever been determinative of your decision to hire—or not hire—a job applicant?*

The responses surprised me.

Every one of the surveyed respondents had visited a social networking site for the purpose of assessing job applicants. Ninety percent told me that they do this as a matter of routine. Every respondent said that a visit to a social networking site had been determinative of their hiring decision. However, they also said that they had never decided to hire someone on the basis of what they read or saw on a social networking site. Rather, 100 percent of them said that they had rejected a candidate because of what they discovered that either the candidate said about himself or herself, or what someone else posting to the site said about them.

> **A Contacts Roadmap forces you to think through your job-search goals carefully and methodically, and document them in considerable detail.**

My straw poll indicated that social network information is rarely, if ever, determinative of a decision to hire someone. Like Woody Hayes, the legendary Ohio State football coach who eschewed the forward pass because two of the three possible outcomes were bad, I am not a fan of social networking. You can only control what you say about yourself and, at best, that is likely to leave an employer with a neutral impression of you. You cannot control what others say about you, and that is where the biggest threat to your job-hunting success lies.

In April, 2011 the Columbia University Computer Science Department released a study that revealed interesting results about Columbia undergraduates who used Facebook:

- All of the respondents said they knew how to use Facebook's advanced security features and were sure that the information on their Facebook pages that they wanted to restrict was secure.
- 95 percent of the undergrads had put something on their Facebook page that they did not want anyone else to see, or had not put something on their Facebook page that they thought they had and wanted everyone else to see.

If you insist on including social networking as part of your job campaign strategy, I recommend that you restrict yourself to LinkedIn, which is very professional and less likely to attract scurrilous commentary about you than the other social network options.

Moral for job seekers: don't put up anything you don't want your grandmother to see.

Step Four: Networking Organizations

Membership in organizations is another method of effective networking that also has the advantage of easing into the networking mode without the usual anxieties and insecurities.

One of the principal reasons why membership organizations exist at all is for networking purposes, whether business development or job-hunting. In other words, all of the other members know exactly why you—and they—are participating in the organization. No one has to dance around that fact. Attorney and law-related membership organizations have value beyond their networking advantages. They are highly effective at keeping the members up-to-date on trends and developments in their area of interest and can serve as early warning systems about intelligence that you need to know in order to job-hunt successfully. Such organizations abound; they are everywhere. Appendix B contains the names and Web sites of more than 250 legal and law-related membership organizations, most of them happy to take your dues money in return for the benefits of membership.

CHAPTER 17

Differentiate Yourself from the Competition

Professional football scouts look for speed at every position. But when it comes to wide receivers, there is something even more important that they look for—it's called *separation*, or the ability of the receiver to put some distance between himself and his defender(s).

Jerry Rice, the greatest wide receiver in NFL history, was nowhere close to being the fastest man at his position. But he more than compensated by his uncanny ability to get separation. That's what made him great.

Take a lesson from Jerry Rice, and apply it to your legal job-search strategy. In this context, what I mean is to make it clear to prospective employers that you are different from your competitors in as many important ways as possible. Doing so separates you—distinguishes you—from other entry-level candidates.

The following *separation* techniques are ones that history shows will impress employers:

Deconstructing the Legal Resume

You know what they say: *you only get once chance to make a first impression.*

It's true. First impressions are critically important in any interaction with anyone about anything, whether you are face-to-face, speaking on the phone, emailing, or otherwise communicating in writing. It's even truer with respect to prospective employers and potential networking contacts. Resumes are often the first impression that a prospective employer or networking contact will see of you. Naturally, you want your first impression to be the very best possible impression because it sets the tone for everything that follows and can be determinative in getting you considered for a position regardless of your level of experience.

Contact information. The very first impression your resume makes comes from what the reader sees first when examining your resume. What is it? It's the mundane contact information you include at the very top of your resume. The most important objective here is getting the reader through this information without eliciting a negative vibe. If you have the misfortune of doing that, it is likely that the employer will obsess about what you have done up front to the detriment of the key information in your resume that you want him or her to focus on and remember.

So, to begin, consider these "don'ts" when identifying yourself:

- **Don't be cute.** Nicknames are out. Only your first name and last name belong here (middle initial optional). Cute email addresses are also out. If that is all you have, get a new one that brands you as professional.
- **Don't be ambiguous.** If your name does not clearly identify your gender, add "Mr." or "Ms." before your name, as appropriate. Gender uncertainty makes employers uncomfortable because they do not know how to address you when they communicate with you.
- **Don't be incomplete.** Make it easy for the employer to contact you. Include your mailing address, phone numbers, and email address.
- **Don't go overboard.** One email address is sufficient, provided it is one that you regularly check. I have actually seen resumes that included irrelevant identifying information such as beeper numbers, CB radio handles, and ham radio call signs. Also, leave out your social network addresses. If the employer wants to view your Facebook, LinkedIn or Twitter pages, s/he will locate them without your help.

On the other hand, there is something you can add to your contact information that can give you an edge, and enhance your competitive advantage.

If you have a credential (undergraduate major, advanced degree or certificate) in addition to your law degree that bolsters your candidacy, by all means include it after your name and law degree, e.g., "Jane Doe, JD, LLM (Tax)." This can earn you immediate positive points. If the credential's abbreviation is possibly unfamiliar to a particular employer, spell it out, e.g., "Associate in Risk Management" instead of "ARM." Of course, the opportunity to make a great first resume impression does not end with your identifying and contact information. Once you have finished with this section, you must decide what comes next in the substantive section of your resume: a Career Objective (not recommended) or a Profile or Summary of Qualifications (highly recommended):

The career objective. If you seek a mainstream legal position, you don't need a Career Objective. Everyone knows your career objective is to practice law without having to be told. Most legal employers view a Career Objective with disdain bordering on contempt. This is because, in addition to being irrelevant, it is usually just meaningless drivel on the order of: *"To work for a dynamic, forward-looking organization where I can apply my talents to help it achieve its goals."* This is, to be blunt, offensive and off-putting. Don't waste your time or resume space on something this inane. There is one exception: if you are going in a completely new career direction that would not be obvious from reading your resume. For example, if you want to become a lion tamer, a Career Objective is definitely in order. In the event you are embarked on a major career change from mainstream law, keep your Career Objective short and include at least a hint as to why you are changing direction after spending all that money on law school, e.g., *"To use my legal education and concentration on contracts and transactions toward a career in government contracting."*

The Profile/Qualifications Summary. This section is always useful, and can do much to advance your candidacy. You can use it to…

- Grab the employer's attention immediately and entice him or her to read on with interest. Absent something compelling here, most employers are likely to either dispense with the rest of the document or slog through it with decreasing attention.
- Bring key points you want to get across, but that may otherwise be buried deep down in your resume, up to the beginning of the document. Foreign language fluency or proficiency, for example, is always good for this kind of up-front treatment. This way you can make certain the employer (1) sees your important selling points and (2) is paying attention.
- Emphasize your most compelling selling points. If you attended top schools, don't delay informing the reader about those achievements.
- Imprint your distinctive qualifications on the reader.

A few lines and sentences will suffice. This is not the place for a Proustian soliloquy. Avoid subjective statements such as "outstanding legal researcher" that would be difficult for either you or the reader to verify via objective assessments. Below are several examples of strong Profiles/Qualifications Summaries developed by some of my entry-level legal career transition clients. Each example contributed to a successful job search outcome.

"Extensive academic and clinical course background in all phases of litigation from inception of lawsuit through settlement, including appellate practice (via moot court competitions), conducting mediations, and handling trial proceedings

(two trial practice clinics and 3L admission on behalf of legal aid clinic [eight civil court appearances, including three bench trials])."

"Experienced and successful certified mediator of family court referral cases and foreclosure disputes during last two semesters in law school. Law review. Yale BA; Harvard JD."

"Experienced editor, writer and legal/political advisor at a 28,000-member non-profit corporation prior to and during law school. Extensive background drafting and editing legislation and regulations. Proficient in Spanish."

"Intellectual Property attorney. Admitted to practice before U.S. Patent & Trademark Office; MS in Biotechnology; BS in Biology. Worked for boutique IP law firm during last two years in law school; exposure to the full range of IP matters, including patents, trademarks, copyrights, licensing, trade secrets, and diverse technology agreements. Extensive academic background in IP and international business."

The next critical resume decision you will have to make has to do with how you present the substantive material about yourself, i.e., your work experience and education. The sequence and the manner of presentation are decisions that can make or break a job campaign. How you present the substantive material about yourself in a resume is a critical threshold decision that is not going to be the same for every attorney. You need to decide (1) the placement of your key information, and (2) what you will include in addition to the "Big Two" resume components, education and experience.

What Comes First: Education or Experience?

You cannot arrive at the best decision for yourself about what comes first without considering what an employer might want to see first.

The decision is generally an easy one if you are a third-year law student or recent graduate applying for your first job. For most of you, education needs to come first. Your legal work experience is, at this stage of your career, probably limited to summer positions and part-time legal positions that you held during the school year. Since your legal education is what you have been doing most recently, it is likely to be the most important factor in how you are going to be judged.

But that is not always the case. An exception might be if you have had extensive, strong, or very interesting work experience prior to or coterminous with going to law school, or worked as a non-lawyer in a field or for an employer related to the kind of position you are currently seeking. The law students that I teach average 42 years of age, and have almost all come from highly successful careers in medicine, science, engineering, finance, education, technology, accounting, etc. It makes little sense for most of them to lead their resumes with their educational background.

In determining what to lead with, you have to balance the significance of your work experience against that of your education, and you have to do this with each specific employer to whom you apply. If you had great work experience, but you also performed exceptionally well in law school, this may not be a close question. You would likely want to put your education first because you want the employer to be immediately impressed with your stellar academic credentials. If you were a less-than-outstanding law student, you may want to put your prior work experience at the top of the resume. Similarly, if you have great prior work experience and you attended elite schools but did not shine academically, you still may have more to gain by leading with your education.

> **When weighing your prior work experience, don't overlook the "intangibles", or soft skills, that you developed at work or elsewhere.**

When weighing your prior work experience against the job(s) you are seeking, do not discount the "intangibles" that you developed at work or elsewhere (see Chapter 19), e.g., the soft skills such as teaming, multi-tasking, interpersonal communications skills, organizational skills, etc. While not related to the substance of your potential jobs, these are nevertheless skills that any savvy employer would value.

The decision about what to place first—education or experience—is somewhat more complicated if you have been out of law school for a while and are still unemployed. The reason is that more variables must be considered. For most such candidates, education should still come first. However, the longer you have been out of school without a job, the closer the question becomes. In most cases, an employer will not have much to go on by examining your work/volunteer experience, such as it might be. If you have only worked as a contract lawyer (aka attorney temp) since law school, your experience usually would not give an employer enough information on which to judge you.

If you have been underemployed (say that you were unable to find a job out of law school and have spent some time as a paralegal), education may prevail over work experience. If your work experience has not been on a par with your strong educational background (e.g., Harvard undergrad, Yale Law School, followed by volunteering as a legal services intake attorney), your academic background should also probably come first.

This question can be a very difficult one, especially in the uncertain and increasingly volatile legal employment environment that prevails today. You have to assess very carefully which selection advantages you best, mindful that your answer may vary with each employer to whom you are applying.

Bar Status

Your bar status always needs to be included in your resume. This is important even if you are seeking a position for which bar admission is not required. Taking and passing a state bar examination is another indicator of your capabilities. If you are not yet a bar member, indicate when you (hope you) will be. Mentioning this at the end of your Profile is as good a place as any to position this information. It gets it up near the top and thus answers a question that may linger in the employer's mind as s/he reads through the document.

Community or Volunteer Activities

Such activities are also valuable additions: first, they demonstrate that you have a life outside the law and are not just a tunnel-visioned grinder. The implications of this can be interesting for an employer keen on evaluating your client development potential. Second, these activities and the knowledge and experience that you derived from them may compensate for thin, paid work experience. You will have to judge for yourself—generally on a case-by-case basis with respect to each specific employer—whether to include activities that might "brand" you politically, ideologically, religiously or otherwise. One employer's enthusiasm may be another employer's antipathy.

Honors and Awards

Legitimate ones need to be included. "Legitimate" precludes items such as an entry in *Who's Who,* since many such compilations are open to anyone at all who meets very minimal criteria or merely submits an application and accompanying fee, or the National Defense Service Medal, which is conferred on every member of the armed forces who still has a pulse at the conclusion of boot camp. However, do not leave out work-related honors and awards, since they indicate third-party vetting of your capabilities. When you cite honors and awards, make sure that you accompany them with a brief explanation of their significance unless, like Phi Beta Kappa, they are well-known to virtually everyone.

"Hybridizing" Your Presentation

Another way to separate yourself from your competitors is to take a different approach to your resume structure than the traditional, reverse chronological approach used by the vast majority of legal job candidates; provided, of course, that you have a very good reason for deviating from the traditional. A good reason would be if you have non-legal or quasi-legal work experience preceding or coterminous with attending law school that adds value to your pitch to employers.

For example, let's say that you worked for a few years as a Certified Public Accountant before deciding on law school, and continued working as a CPA through your 1L year. And let's say that you worked both summers for two different legal employers and as a research assistant for a law professor during your 3L year. If you employ the traditional resume approach, the resume example that appears immediately below is what your document might look like at its best (which is still pretty good). Note: I have omitted the Profile wording, and have cut off the resume after getting through the Experience section; also, that the hypothetical candidate very wisely divided Professional Experience into two different professional categories to draw employer attention to her dual background, thus partially distancing herself from the pure reverse chronological approach.

SAMPLE #1

Linda B.T. Numbers, JD, CPA
222 Jumping Frog Court, #123
Calaveras, CA 95425
(H) 555-555-5555
(C) 555-444-4444
LBTNumero@frogsnottoads.com

PROFILE: (profile omitted)

EDUCATION:
JD, High Sierra Night School of Law, Mountainside, CA, 2011
BA (Finance & Accounting), Pacific Rim University, Ocean Landing, CA, 2004

PROFESSIONAL EXPERIENCE
Legal Experience
- Research Assistant to Professor Singh Singh, High Sierra Night School of Law, Mountainside, CA, 2010–2011. Researched and prepared initial drafts for Professor Singh's book, "Cases and Materials on South Asian Corrections Law" (East Publishing, 2011).

- Summer Associate, San Ramon, CA, 2010. Prepared pleadings and motions for boutique criminal defense firm, including two murder cases.
- Summer Associate, Thrift & Penury, Carlsbad, CA, 2009. Participated in drafting of two appellate briefs for the California Supreme Court and the federal Ninth Circuit Court of Appeals.
- Participated in numerous aspects of a securities class action lawsuit involving 30,000 class members and three major financial institution defendants. Interviewed class members, prepared extensive discovery documents, and discussed case strategy with partners and associates.

Business and Accounting Experience
- Eyeshade and Green, CPAs, Dry Gulch, NV, 2004–2009. Manager, 2007–2009,
  - Senior Accountant, 2005–2007, Staff Accountant, 2004–2005
- Advised business clients, including two law firms and a corporate in-house counsel office on various matters, including business development strategies, streamlining operations and litigation management.
- Managed annual audits of client companies.
- Audited legal fees on behalf of federal government agency clients.
- Received two promotions to higher positions during tenure at firm.
- Participated in annual audits.
- Made numerous presentations to prospective clients and business membership organizations.

SAMPLE #2

Here is what her resume would look like if she liberated herself from the strictures of the reverse chronological approach. The wording of some of the bullets is slightly changed for better impact.

Linda B.T. Numbers, JD, CPA
222 Jumping Frog Court, #123
Calaveras, CA 95425
(H) 555-555-5555
(C) 444-444-4444
LBTNumero@frogsnottoads.com

PROFILE (profile omitted)

EDUCATION
JD, High Sierra Night School of Law, Mountainside, CA, 2011
BA (Finance & Accounting), Pacific Rim University, Ocean Landing, CA, 2004

EMPLOYMENT HISTORY

- Research Assistant to Professor Singh Singh, High Sierra Night School of Law, Mountainside, CA, 2010–2011
- Summer Associate, Mobbed & Up, San Ramon, CA, 2010.
- Summer Associate, Thrift & Penury, Carlsbad, CA, 2009.
- Eyeshade and Green, CPAs, Dry Gulch, NV, 2004–2009.
  Manager, 2007–2009
  Senior Accountant, 2005–2007
  Staff Accountant, 2004–2005

PROFESSIONAL EXPERIENCE

Litigation

- Participated in numerous aspects of a securities class action lawsuit involving 30,000 class members and three major financial institution defendants. Interviewed class members, prepared extensive discovery documents, and discussed case strategy with partners and associates.
- Prepared pleadings and motions for boutique criminal defense firm, including two murder cases.
- Participated in drafting of two appellate briefs for the California Supreme Court and the federal Ninth Circuit Court of Appeals.

Litigation/Outside Counsel Management

- Advised law firms and a corporate in-house counsel office on effective litigation management, including selecting outside counsel, litigation budgeting, partnering with outside counsel on case strategies and related matters.
- Audited legal fees on behalf of federal government agency clients.

Client Development

- Made numerous presentations to prospective clients and business membership organizations.
- Headed auditing and management consulting teams in client audits and consulting assignments.

Business operations

- Managed annual audits of client companies.
- Advised clients of auditing results and recommended corrective actions.
- Received two promotions to higher positions during tenure at CPA firm.

Comparative law

- Researched and prepared initial drafts for Professor Singh's book, "Cases and Materials on South Asian Corrections Law" (East Publishing, 2011).

This "hybridized" resume—one that combines the reverse chronological approach (**employment history**) with a knowledge/skills approach (**professional experience**)—represents our hypothetical job-seeker much more effectively than the traditional resume. It permits her to categorize her experience to mesh with what specific employers are seeking, and to move both her category headings and their bullets around for best impact, depending on the position. Note that she put her **employment history** near the top in order to allay any fears that an employer might have that she was covering up any temporal gaps. The hybrid approach enhances her chances of competing for positions and, in her case, mitigates her lack of experience. It also serves an important collateral purpose by impressing potential employers with her organizational skills as manifested in how she structured her resume.

Achievements, Accomplishments, Outcomes, Results

Whenever you come to the point in your resume or cover letter/transmittal email where you need to describe what you did, try to do so in terms of your results. It makes for both a livelier and more interesting document, and a much more compelling reason for any employer to keep you in the game. It also forces you to think in achievement-oriented terms, which will help you both reconstruct your history and boost your self-confidence, as well as put you in the proper mindset for communicating with prospective references, contacts and employers.

Work experiences that sound like position descriptions are boring to write and, worse, boring to read and quickly forgotten. Results are far better because they need to address specifics and it is detail that sticks in one's mind. *When crafting your resumes, remember that employers are not interested in process, just results.*

The point here, like the others in this chapter, is to do something different than what other candidates for the position do; something that is to your advantage because you need an advantage to be seriously considered. Despite the fact that many employers themselves just go through the motions, they become hypocrites when considering others for jobs, and want to see results regardless of their own possible lack of performance.

Storytelling

Everyone enjoys a good story.

While "enjoy" may not be exactly the reaction of most employers to the unwelcome task of having to read through a stack of job application materials, they will at least appreciate a candidate who makes an otherwise stultifying task somewhat interesting and entertaining. It is not easy to satisfy that urge, but one way to do it is to append a "Highlights Addendum" to your resume where you can devote a full page to relating how you tackled a specific problem and devised a solution, whether you did that on a job, in school, or elsewhere. It does not necessarily have to be something legal or law-related. What you are trying to impress on the employer is that you are a problem-solver. See Chapter 19 for a sample "Highlights Addendum". The Addendum is the best place prior to a job interview in which to tell your story. If you decide on this tactic, make sure that you direct the employer to the Addendum in the body of your resume. The best way to accomplish this is by referencing it in a parenthetical at the end of one of your resume bullet statements. For example:

"As a 3L specially admitted to handle civil cases in the New York courts for the law school's Legal Aid Clinic, I created a new, more streamlined constructive abandonment (divorce) complaint that a New York Supreme Court Judge announced from the bench 'should be a model for all similar complaints in my court' (see Significant Highlights, attached)." Note: this is not a fictional example; it actually happened.

Every Job Search Document is a Writing Sample

By now I hope I have impressed you with the notion that you must take the utmost care in putting together every single legal job-search document that you intend to employ in your legal job campaign. The effort that you put into this can have a big pay-off. If you neglect this effort, the downside can be career-altering. You will spend much of your legal career writing documents of one sort or another: pleadings, briefs, memoranda of law, contracts, leases, licenses, settlement agreements, regulations, regulatory comments, legislation, etc. This is why legal employers put a very high premium on writing ability. You need to be sensitive to this when you are crafting your job-search documents. In addition to the very best writing you can present, you also need to spend time, energy and attention on making certain that your job-search documents are as reader-friendly as possible. Put yourself in the employer's shoes. What would you want to see (and not see)? Make the employer's resume reading experience as tolerable as you can. Again, the pay-off can be huge.

> Every document you intend to employ in your job campaign should be done with care because every job-search document is a writing sample.

The Job Interview

Legal job interviews are central to attorney hiring decisions. That is one reason law firms spend so much time and money each year on on-campus recruiting at law schools. In years when the job market for new law grads is a positive one, the top law schools even charge law firms for the privilege of coming on campus to interview their students. If you make it to the interview, it means that you did something at an earlier stage to impress a prospective employer, or the employer is seeing you because of an endorsement by one of your contacts or as a courtesy to an intermediary that s/he does not want to disrespect. In addition to the boost this should give your confidence level going into the interview, it means that you have put yourself in a great position to seal the deal and secure a job offer despite your lack of experience.

Here are some tips about doing just that:

Before the interview. Find out as much as you can about what to expect in order to prepare adequately to confront it.

- Will you be interviewed by one person? A group? By more than one person sequentially? Will a meal be part of the interview?
- Where will the interview take place? What kind of travel and logistic problems might you encounter on your way to the interview? Do you need to make a trial run to the interview site?
- What kind of preparation do you need to do? Where can you go for the information you need? With whom can you role-play? What personal conversational quirks do you need to work on (such as interrupting, failure to make eye contact, verbal crutches such as *"ah,""umm,""you know?""Right?""You know what I'm saying?""Are you with me?"* or speaking in a monotone, or slouching, or poor or negative body language)?
- What will you wear to the interview?

During the interview. There are a great many things that you need to be cognizant of during a job interview. The following are the most important:

- Exuding confidence, energy and enthusiasm without going overboard.
- Answering the interviewer's questions with specific examples.
- Having a mental list of great questions to ask when it becomes your turn to become the interrogator.
- Closing the interview by reiterating your interest in the position (unless, of course, the interview has turned you off to the job), determining the next step in the hiring process, and thanking the interviewer(s).

After the interview. In the sense of an employer assessing your worth, the interview is not over when you walk out of the door. There is follow-up involved, and that means that you need to send a thank you note or email to the interviewer in which you reaffirm your interest. You also need to "de-brief" yourself in writing, being as critical as you can of your performance, in the event that you do not receive a job offer or accept one from this particular employer. Such a debriefing will be of immense value to you during succeeding interviews. Each one of these ways of gaining separation from your competitors is critical for any legal job candidate, and even more essential for a recent law school grad.

CHAPTER 18

Extenuate and Mitigate
Your Resume Weaknesses

Without exception, employers tend to zero in on what they perceive as weakness in a resume.

This can happen at two critical junctures in the hiring process: when the employer begins evaluating resumes, and, later, during the interviews (assuming the weakness/es in a candidate's resume did not result in a quick rejection).

Whatever possible weaknesses in your own resume, it is *essential* that you extenuate them—that is, minimize them—if you want to be invited for an interview. What's involved? You need to employ certain techniques that (without engaging in a subterfuge, of course) tend to mitigate, or de-emphasize, the weakness or make it more difficult to pinpoint. You can address some weaknesses directly in the body of the resume, others in your cover letter… and most in the job interview.

If your resume does make it through the gate, and you are invited to an interview, you must prepare even more thoroughly for these "weakness" issues than for the "home run" questions that you know you can answer easily. Unfortunately, most legal job seekers do just the opposite; they hone their responses to the questions that they know will make them feel good and look good, and they ignore the ones that will make them squirm because they know how difficult and discomfiting these are.

You simply must avoid the tendency to stay within your comfort zone.

This chapter briefly identifies the most common resume weaknesses, and recommends strategies for dealing with them at both of these critical hiring process decision points.

What Does Your Resume Say About You?

As I explained, weaknesses in one's resume are often what rivet the attention of prospective employers. For each weakness cited below, I am providing sample mitigating or extenuating explanations. Some of these weaknesses may appear, at first glance, to be inapplicable to you. However, an increasing number of recent law school graduates have gone into law as a second career, and if you fall into that category, your resume may exhibit these weaknesses. Caveat: You should not use these measures if they don't apply to you.

The eight most common resume weaknesses are:

Resume weakness #1. **Your academic performance was less-than-stellar.** Explain that you worked your way through school in order to support yourself and/or your family and were unable to devote as much time to study as your more fortunate, better-heeled colleagues.

Resume weakness #2. **There are gaps in your employment record.** Explain that you took time off to do something else important (caring for a sick relative; raising children; taking a sabbatical to travel around the world; working in a political campaign; relocating for family reasons).

Resume weakness #3. **You're currently unemployed.** If you were laid off from your job and are currently unemployed, explain that your practice area dried up due to the economy. If you were fired, make sure that what you tell the interviewer will be consistent with what s/he might hear from your prior employer. You may want to discuss this with your prior employer and agree on what will be said. If you have been unemployed for a long period of time, your resume will look much better if you fill in the gap with something, such as a supplemental credential or volunteer activity (see Chapter 7, *Doing Nothing is Not an Option*).

Resume weakness #4. **You have a checkered work history, or an unremarkable career progression.** Get this out of the way fast in your cover letter or during your interview, and counter it with the substantive expertise and skill sets that you developed along the way.

Resume weakness #5. **Your job titles are undistinguished.** Talk to your prior employers about how, with their approval, you might label yourself, Paralegal → Law Clerk or Legal Researcher or Legal Analyst; Alternative Dispute Resolution Specialist → Mediator or ADR Manager.

Resume weakness #6. **You have too much "seasoning".** Don't waste your time applying to places where age could likely be an issue, and don't omit dates of education on your resume. It's a sure sign that you are hiding your age. Instead, put education at the end of the document so that all of your positives will be seen first. Make sure you include your strenuous outside activities on your resume: sports, other involvements, etc. Point out how your seasoning would benefit an employer, e.g., mentoring younger attorneys; extensive substantive knowledge.

Resume weakness #7. **You seem to lack a life outside of work**. Join something; volunteer; get some noteworthy activities on your resume.

Resume weakness #8. **You have a history of job-hopping**. The explanations for your leaving jobs might include: the firms went belly-up or practice areas suffered a decline in business. Consider leaving very short-term jobs off your resume. State your dates of employment in years only, not months and years. What follows below are two examples of resumes with different approaches to the handling of dates of employment. In the example that follows,"Before" shows that the candidate held her job for only one month, then was unemployed for almost a full year;"After"presents an alternative treatment of dates that eliminates both of these weaknesses:

- Before
  Associate, Barracuda & Serpent, Redding, CA, December 2006–Present
  Associate, Serendipity & Chance, Eureka, CA, December 2004–January 2005

- After
  Associate, Barracuda & Serpent, Redding, CA, 2006–Present
  Associate, Serendipity & Chance, Eureka, CA, 2004–2005

What Can You Expect from Employers

Employer reactions to resume weaknesses typically take the following form:

- Outright rejection of your candidacy upon reading the resume.
- Obsession with the perceived resume weakness, to the exclusion of the positive selling points and gems about you that you have addressed elsewhere in your resume.
- Seeking an explanation from you in your cover letter.
- Seeking an explanation from you during your job interview. In order to overcome any resume weaknesses, you have to: identify them for yourself and attempt to extenuate or mitigate them.

CHAPTER 19

Emphasize Your Intangibles

Too many candidates focus exclusively or disproportionately on their *tangibles*, i.e., academic achievements, substantive knowledge of the law, technical legal experience, etc. Few spend much time identifying their *intangible* skills or strategizing how to exploit them in a job-search campaign. This is a huge mistake, particularly for entry-level attorneys. And if you lack some or all of the tangible markers, there may be other strengths you can bring to the table to compensate. Intangibles are much more difficult to pinpoint than tangible strengths. They are much more subjective, not as objective or as clearly and easily defined as tangible strengths. The most important intangibles are listed below. They are listed in alphabetical order rather than according to any hierarchy of employer needs because each employer is different and will have his/her own opinions about which intangibles are the most important:

- Accountability
- Analytical Ability
- Anticipation
- Attention to Detail
- Being a Quick Study
- Business Bottom-Line/Budget Consciousness
- Client Development/Marketing Skills
- Energy Level
- Enthusiasm
- "Fit" (your alignment with the organization and the interviewer)
- Flexibility
- Follow-Through
- Foresight
- High-Level Social Skills
- Initiative

- Intelligence
- Interpersonal Skills
- Leadership or Leadership Potential
- Leading by Example
- Likeability
- Listening Skills
- Meeting Deadlines
- Mentoring Ability (of Attorneys or of Staff)
- "Normalcy"
- Optimism
- Organizational Skills
- Persuasive Ability
- Problem-Anticipation Ability
- Problem-Solving Ability
- Productivity
- Self-confidence
- "Team-player" attitude
- Temperament
- Thorough Preparation
- "Whatever-It-Takes" Attitude
- Writing Ability
- Work Ethic

Hiring decisions, like almost every other important decision in life, are rarely if ever arrived at on the basis of just one isolated factor. In fact, smart legal employers base their hiring decisions on a combination of factors that are important to them and to success in the position. You may have all of the conceivable Securities Law experience in the world, but if you have the personality of a Star Trek Vulcan, you probably will not get the job offer. Intangible skills and talents can often compensate for lack of experience. I'll repeat that:

Intangible skills and talents can often compensate for lack of experience.

Example #1: I once needed to hire an attorney for my staff, and I sorted through many applications before rejecting all but two.

One candidate was law review and ranked second in his class at a top law school. The other candidate attended a second-tier law school and was an average student, but his resume and transmittal email evidenced an appealing earnestness and diverse work experience while in law school that was intriguing. I scheduled back-to-back interviews with both candidates.

Academic Superstar came into my office, shook hands rather weakly, slouched down in the chair, hardly ever looked me in the eye, and appeared lackluster and disinterested. By the time he left, I was almost as deflated as he had come across. The *Average Student* marched crisply into my office, shook hands firmly, was engaging, listened politely, asked me a series of good questions that he had obviously prepared in advance after thoroughly researching both me and my company, and closed the interview by expressing his interest in and enthusiasm for the job.

It was no contest.

Next day I offered *Average Student* the job and never regretted it. He made up for his lack of academic achievement with a healthy dose of common sense, very hard work, and eagerness to learn.

Example #2: One of my career counseling clients was a young man who finished in the bottom quartile of his law school graduating class. He hadn't bothered to go through the on-campus interview season in the fall of his 3L year, and graduated without any job prospects at all.

He came to see me while he prepared for the bar examination, and I was immediately struck by his dynamism, native intelligence, energy, and enthusiasm. His personality was infectious; it was impossible not to like him.

In devising a legal job-search strategy, I urged him to go down parallel paths; one, a traditional, conservative approach to small law firms and government agencies where I thought he would have a stronger chance of impressing a more flexible employer not hung up on academic achievement, and a second path I called the "Pipedream Path". For this second path, I suggested he contact large law firms in his home city. After all, he had nothing to lose.

We put together a "template" cover letter that succeeded in getting him an informational interview—expressly not a job interview—with a partner at a large firm that sought two years of transactional experience. To my mind, the job was clearly beyond my client's reach. But following his meeting with the partner, my client called me brimming with excitement. Despite his mediocre academic record and his lack of the requisite experience, the firm offered him the job at the end of the interview, contingent on the approval of the hiring partner and a check of his references. My client remained with the firm for three years, was successful at his job, and then was contacted by a headhunter and moved to another major firm at higher compensation.

These examples taught me two important lessons: one, *never say never.* I've seen enough job-search triumphs to make me very reluctant to advise anyone to forget about their dreams, no matter how unrealistic or unachievable they might have appeared to me upon initial consideration. And, lesson #2, I am reminded of the supreme importance of a candidate's "intangibles" to overcome gaps in experience.

The Four Kinds of Intelligence

While on the subject of intangibles, it's necessary to spend a little time on one intangible in particular: intelligence. We need to dissect "intelligence" because this is not as easy a concept as it might appear to be at first glance. In fact, it is rather complicated, and very important to any aspiring legal job seeker. After many years of observing attorneys in their work places and interacting with them in my role as legal career counselor, I concluded that there are actually four different kinds of intelligence, at least insofar as attorneys are concerned.

My rough, unscientific sorting of kinds of intelligence came up with the following:

Academic intelligence. This is the kind of intelligence that most assume is what is meant by the term "intelligence." Period. An individual with academic intelligence is "book-bright," blessed with the ability to quickly absorb information, process it swiftly and accurately, and recite it back on demand. An academically intelligent person has superior ability to understand the theoretical and to sort through and understand complexity. Objectively, this kind of intelligence is manifested by high grades in school and high standardized test scores. Some of the individuals who possessed amazing academic intelligence were presidents Herbert Hoover, Jimmy Carter, and Bill Clinton, and Robert Oppenheimer, the theoretical physicist who guided the atomic bomb-making work of the Manhattan Project during World War II. (Note: Presidents are good exemplars of the different kinds of intelligence because we know so much about them and can easily make the necessary connections. Hence they appear disproportionately in this analysis.)

Creative intelligence. This might also be called "relational intelligence," the ability to connect the dots, to see the long view, to understand the implications of disconnected facts, activities and events, and to learn from history. People with creative intelligence tend to be information sponges and "strong sorters," i.e., able to separate the "wheat from the chaff." They are *ideophoric*, meaning that they are interested in a wide diversity of things and are constantly searching for new ideas and ways to do things. Creatively intelligent individuals demonstrate this by being result-oriented problem solvers. They like problems, anticipate them, and are likely to see looming issues before they jell. Exemplars are presidents George Washington, Thomas Jefferson, Dwight Eisenhower, and George H.W. Bush, and inventor Thomas Edison.

Situational intelligence. This is also known as common sense, "street smarts," judgment and knowing what to do in the moment. These folks are logical, realistic, quick studies, and naturally tend to do what is in their own best interests. Exemplars are presidents FDR, Harry Truman, JFK, and Ronald Reagan, and Wealth of Nations economist Adam Smith.

Emotional intelligence. This fourth kind of intelligence means having "people skills," oral communications ability, listening ability, "feeling someone's pain." Manifestations are likeability, social comfort, enthusiasm for interaction with others, and sales prowess (that demonstrates client development capability or potential). Exemplars are presidents Teddy Roosevelt, Ronald Reagan, and Bill Clinton.

Intelligence is worth dissecting in some detail because legal employers make it so central to their hiring considerations. My point here is that, while academic intelligence may be paramount in employer assessments of candidates, you need to be cognizant of the other kinds of intelligence so that you can make the best case for yourself. Ideally, you are one of those extremely rare individuals who possesses some degree of all four kinds of intelligence. The point is that, even if you did not shine academically in law school, you are likely to have shone with respect to one or more of the other three kinds of intelligence, and this is something that you need to think about very carefully and thoroughly when you embark on a job campaign.

> **Your resume must be logically constructed and reader-friendly. It needs to impress an employer with your organizational skills.**

One additional point about intelligence: there is no precise separation between one kind of intelligence and another. It is possible for there to be some overlap. For example, creative intelligence and situational intelligence are not necessarily always discrete concepts.

Promoting Your Intangible Skills

First, let's look briefly at how not to tout your intangibles to an employer. I am beginning with the negatives because so very many attorneys fall into these traps, which are often ones that kill opportunities:

Avoid overreaching. Don't make highly subjective, self-serving pronouncements about your intangible qualities. I encounter these all too often in resumes and cover letters/transmittal emails from attorneys. Here is a classic example from the Career Objective section at the top of one attorney's resume: *"I am an energetic, go-getter constantly seeking new challenges in a dynamic law office where I can apply my ability to come up the learning curve quickly in order to contribute to growth."* Statements like this are worthless, annoying, irritating, and highly off-putting to employers. Once seen by a prospective employer, they are almost always the "kiss-of-death" to your chances of employment. In fact, Career Objectives are usually completely unnecessary and may be dangerous. Unless you are changing careers and not just jobs, you don't need to waste precious resume space by including one.

Exercise some restraint. Select the intangibles likely to matter most to each specific employer, and go just with those. Hopefully, your analysis of what those are will mesh with those that are your strongest ones. Once you understand what not to do, you can concentrate on what you should do in order to get your intangibles across to an employer:

Cite specific examples. It is not enough to offer a conclusive statement and leave it at that. Without some detail that supports your assertion, it will be easy to discount it completely. Making such a statement without elaboration tends to annoy and anger employers.

Use a resume "highlights addendum" to elaborate. If you feel you cannot get your point across in the confines of a resume or transmittal document, draft an addendum that liberates you from the one-to-two pages of a typical resume. An addendum allows you to narrate exactly how your intangible(s) enabled you to solve a problem, achieve a positive result, or develop as a capable attorney. I have yet to hear from a legal employer that such an addendum violated a resume length restriction.

The most effective addendum format roughly follows the scientific method:

Question

↓

Hypothesis

↓

Experiment or Observations

↓

Conclusions (and Publication)

The adaptation of this for attorney resume addenda looks something like this:

Problem

↓

Analysis

↓

Proposed Solution

↓

Implementation

↓

Results

Your examples do not necessarily have to be associated with law. They could be prior career achievements, things that you did in law school, or associated with community or volunteer activities.

Link your intangibles to the employer's needs. Demonstrate how your intangibles would be valuable in the new position. To do that, you need to thoroughly research prospective employers so that their needs become well-known to you, and enable you to sort through your intangibles and select suitable examples of them in action.

Keep "hammering." Entry-level attorneys above all others need to rely on their intangibles in order to distinguish themselves from competitors and get past any employer predilection for experience. That means that you must be vigilant for any opportunity to get the intangibles point across. You need to do this at the networking stage (see Chapter 16), the application stage, and the interview stage.

A TYPICAL RESUME HIGHLIGHTS ADDENDUM

The following resume highlights addendum was developed by a third-year law student in the fall of his 3L year.

Significant Highlights

During the summer following my 2L year, I worked as a Summer Associate for Orka & Mako, a small personal injury defense boutique law firm in Santa Ana, CA. One of my diverse assignments at the firm was to draft pleadings and motions in current cases:

Issue. One of the firm's litigation clients was a heavy machinery maintenance and repair company that was sued for alleged negligent repair of an agricultural combine that resulted in plaintiff's injury.

Analysis. After attending all of the depositions in the case, I was asked to draft a Motion for Summary Judgment. I spent several weeks reviewing all of the discovery documents and interviewing the relevant individual employees of our client. I then drafted the Motion for Summary Judgment, my argument being that the combine part that injured the plaintiff had never been touched by the client. The final work product constituting the Motion was 95 percent my work.

Result. Summary Judgment was granted and the case against our client was dismissed.

Evaluation. In her ruling, the judge commented: "This is what all summary judgment motions should look like." I received a special award from the firm at the end of the summer that praised my central role in the case, and was told, informally, that I would be the only summer associate who would receive a permanent job offer upon graduation next spring.

Honing Your Intangibles

If you buy into what I am saying about the value of intangibles in a legal job search, and you realize that you (1) either do not possess some important ones, or (2) some that you do have are weak, you can do something about it. Here are two examples of how you can acquire or strengthen your intangibles:

Intangible #1: Being a Quick Study. Put yourself into situations at work or in volunteer activities where you are forced to come up a learning curve quickly. The more experience you have tackling new and unfamiliar subject matter, the better you will be at it and the more you will be able to say about it to a prospective employer.

Intangible #2: Organizational Skills. There are a variety of ways to get this very important message across to a prospective employer:

- Craft a reader-friendly and logically constructed resume. This is the first opportunity you have to impress an employer with your organizational skills. "Reader-friendly" means plenty of white space, bullets, and less-than-an-overwhelming amount of type. You do not want the employer's first impression of your resume to be that slogging through it is going to be a chore.
- Put together an impressive reference list. I don't mean one with a lot of dazzling celebrity names on it. Rather, a dynamite reference list contains five elements for each reference:

The name of the reference

His/her job title and employer

His/her relationship to you

The best time and method of communicating with the reference

Something you did with, for or under the supervision of, the reference

You can actually get additional mileage out of such a reference list beyond "points" for your organizational skills. This kind of reference list also demonstrates your ability to anticipate and your sensitivity to needing to accommodate both the employer and the reference.

- Develop a writing sample cover sheet. This is your opportunity to place the writing sample in context for the employer. Without a cover sheet, the employer may wonder what your writing sample is all about rather than paying attention to your writing and advocacy style.
- Ask great questions at the interview. This locks in the message about your strong organizational skills and foresight. Employers warm to candidates who ask good questions and award plus points for your forethought that went into preparing them. When you leave the interview, it is your great questions that are imprinted on the employer and what s/he remembers about you when it comes time for the hiring decision.

The Most Important Intangible for Job Interviews

When you strip away all of the other factors that go into a hiring decision—experience, skills both tangible and intangible—the most important thing you can accomplish at a job interview is to get the employer to like you. No one hires someone that they do not like.

When I interviewed a job seeker for my company, I visualized what it would be like to spend 8+ hours a day in close contact with that person, five days a week, for an indeterminate time period. If my visualization did not unambiguously return positive vibes, I did not offer the job. Likeability is infectious. You naturally want to be around people whom you like. Likeability is related to other intangibles, among them listening skills, energy, enthusiasm, a whatever-it-takes attitude, optimism, self-confidence and interpersonal skills. If you can get these across to the interviewer, you are well on the way to being liked.

Intangibles are a great compensation for lack of experience. Legal employers today are much more sensitive to the great value that such skills can contribute to their practice.

CHAPTER 20

Accentuate the Positive

What do you think of this for an opening sentence in a job resume: *"Although I do not have any experience in Securities Law…"*

In my capacity as a law career counselor, I have seen this sort of opening sentence hundreds of times in attorney cover letters and transmittal emails. And I still can't believe someone would put that in writing. What could s/he be thinking? I mean, if there was ever a way to guarantee that you will be rejected for a position, this is it. Why should any employer read further than an opening statement about your lack of qualifications? My point is this: it's not enough to merely avoid launching your job pitch with something negative. You need to avoid mentioning *anything* negative about yourself that would be detrimental to your chances of competing for the position. Period. No exceptions!

The purpose of your resume is to talk about your *positives*; the attractive things about you that you can offer the employer. Application documents are not a place to spill your guts about your deficiencies. Save it for your therapist.

Think of your resume as a marketing document, a platform to tout your pluses. The only time that you might need to address a negative is if a job ad or government vacancy announcement expressly demands that you address a background or experience that you do not possess. Even then, it is possible to turn your response into something positive and beneficial to you. For example, a job ad says something like this: *"You must respond with specifics to each of the evaluation factors listed below"*, and one of the factors is, *"…At least two years of experience with Securities Law."*

You don't want to respond with something like this: *"I do not have any Securities Law experience."* The following would serve you better:

"In addition to my three law school courses in Securities Law, I worked on 8–K and 10–K filings with the Securities and Exchange Commission on behalf of

clients while a Summer Associate at Barracuda, Shark & Ray. Additionally, I participated in the Regulatory Comments clinical program at Plymouth Rock Law School, where I learned a great deal about complex commercial regulatory matters that transfers very well to securities regulation."

Note that nothing was said about the candidate's lack of two years of Securities Law experience.

While she may not have gotten the job, she increased the likelihood of surviving a first cut by countering with relevant education, summer employment, and transferable technical knowledge. In this example, the candidate could have helped herself even more if she had elaborated on precisely how those skills and experience make her suitable for consideration as a securities lawyer.

Savvy legal employers understand the value of "parallel experience", and how that can translate to their needs. If someone with experience in or understanding of one complex regulatory practice area applies for a position in another, equally complex regulatory practice area—e.g., telecommunications regulation to securities regulation—that will often boost a candidate's competitiveness even in the absence of substantive knowledge of the practice area. In other words, technical skills and background count for something significant. For most practice areas, coming up the learning curve about the substantive law is not that difficult. Of course, much depends on the personality, exposure, and possibly the idiosyncrasies of the particular employer. But if you play the percentages, you will find that most employers understand the value of parallel experience or knowledge, i.e., of bridging whatever gap there might be by analogy.

> **The purpose of your resume is to talk about the attractive things you can offer...not a place to spill your guts about your deficiencies. Save that for your therapist.**

Know How to Position Your Positives

The worst thing you can do is bury the most compelling information about you and your qualifications deep within your resume, cover letter, or transmittal email. Employers are often overwhelmed to the point of attention deficit by so many resumes and job applications. That's why you need to plan how you will position your positives. Because by the time they get to your resume—assuming they get to it at all—they may no longer be paying attention.

The most important information about you needs to be first, followed by the next most compelling information, and so forth.

You want to grab an employer's attention immediately. But what you believe is your most important information needs to be sublimated to what you see as the most important information from the prospective employer's perspective.

Remember, this is less about you than it is about how you can best meet the employer's needs. This principle may mean that you adjust your hierarchy of pluses differently for different employers.

Entry-level attorneys need to do these things and do them well, and without hyperbole, in order to compete effectively and neutralize the experience gap if they are also competing with experienced attorneys. This takes forethought and strategic planning, not to mention targeting to specific employers.

As I indicated earlier, one way to look at this is to view every job ad as an indication of a problem that the employer needs to solve. Once you have scoped out the problem, think of yourself and your communications to the employer as the solution.

One final word:

I have actually had clients who argued with me about this on the grounds that steering clear of any mention of your lack of qualifications is "not honest." I beg to differ. Your cover letter/transmittal email is a marketing piece, something that promotes you. If you tout your positives and omit your negatives, this has nothing to do with honesty or ethics. Rest assured that employers will quickly figure out what you lack in terms of knowledge or experience. What you are doing here is more psychological than anything else. You are laying the groundwork for serious consideration of you as a candidate. Broadcasting what you do not possess means that you will probably not have that opportunity.

CHAPTER 21

Write Your Way to a Job

Writing is an excellent way to advance any legal career at any career stage. And these days, the opportunities to write for publication are vast. Print and online publications directed at a legal audience number in the thousands, and, as a consequence, interesting and well-written content almost always has a strong shot at being published. The purposes of writing an article are twofold: To bolster your legal career credentials, and to open the door to making useful contacts who can then help your career aspirations be realized.

How to Begin

Choose a topic that gets you in front of (in person or by phone) people whom you would like to call upon later as networking contacts. Ideally, you will want to identify topics that are compatible with your career goals. But if, along the way, you find topics that excite you—but do not fulfill those immediate career goals—save them for a later time. Naturally, your media outlet does not necessary have to be one that is read only by lawyers. Thousands of print and online publications publish pieces concerning the law or legal developments. Even publications far afield from law often contain legal analyses that impact on their fields. For example:

- *ArtNews* often contains articles on Art Law.
- *Sports Illustrated* increasingly covers legal matters that affect athletics.
- *Technology Review* covers innovations in medicine, science, engineering, materials, and much more, and is unable in our highly regulated society to avoid publishing legal think pieces that affect these new technologies.

Again, the main purpose of your article writing is not to see your name in print (although there's a lot to be said for having written a bylined article); the purpose is to open up an opportunity to return to the people you interviewed (and who you hopefully impressed with your questions, insights, and professional approach), and invoke them as possible job-search contacts.

How One Lawyer Wrote Her Way into a New Career

"Jennifer"was a recent graduate of a New England law school.

While job-hunting, she volunteered for a local legal aid organization, primarily doing intakes and assisting the legal aid attorneys with case research and management. Her dream job was to do"something involved with international law,"but opportunities were difficult to find. She came to us to help her (1) identify and sort through realistic international law possibilities and (2) position herself to compete effectively for such jobs.

In our assessment of Jennifer, it was strikingly apparent that she possessed excellent interpersonal and social skills. She was lively, alert, and eager to contribute her talents to an organization. As career counselors, our assessment led us to recommend that, among other jobs, she pursue a position with a state or municipal economic development agency, more specifically in the "business attraction"component of economic development. She had no idea what this was all about, but quickly warmed to the idea when we told her what it involved, including a brief history of the concept.

The individuals necessary to do the complex deals and manage the collateral matters that constitute business attraction come from many different disciplines and must also possess a variety of"intangible"skills and talents, including very strong communications abilities, marketing prowess, and social skills. They must be able to deal with corporate C-level officers and senior government officials with ease and confidence. With the focus having changed from domestic to foreign business attraction, familiarity with foreign languages and cultures is also at a premium. All this being said, states and municipalities that want to be successful in attracting business must do several things, many of which require the services, expertise, skills, backgrounds and talents of attorneys:

Marrying Your Writing Projects to Your Job Search

There are more than 1,500 economic development agencies at the state and local level. In addition, there are hundreds of utilities that are also involved in attracting businesses to their regions.

We crafted a two-tier strategy for Jennifer, boosting her credentials by having her enroll in an economic development certificate program, and challenging her to write about cutting-edge issues in economic development. Both strategies were designed to enhance her economic development bona fides.

Jennifer opted for a Penn State University online Certificate in

Community and Economic Development. Simultaneously, she decided to research possibilities for article ideas by visiting relevant Web sites (the International Economic Development Council, the National Association of Development Organizations, the National Association of Counties, the National Governors Association, the National League of Cities, and the U.S. Conference of Mayors).

Jennifer found a wide selection of possible article topics, and crafted two articles *with the specific intention of making contact with prospective employers.* The first article was about New England region economic development agencies' foreign business attraction initiatives, focusing primarily on the legal issues surrounding business attraction and its follow-up. What made her first article especially enticing was her analysis of "clawbacks" in agency agreements with foreign investors, something that was in a nascent stage at the time she was job-hunting. Clawbacks are withdrawals of relocation or new plant construction enticements in the event a target business does not live up to its side of the bargain.

One trade journal immediately accepted the first article and, once in publication, took the second article, too.

The nexus of Jennifer's interest and an emerging practice area benefited from good timing. Her article hit the legal and economic development communities at a very good time. Researching her article required her to communicate with economic development agency personnel in all six New England states, and interviewing them about their clawback philosophies, specific clawback provisions, and how those provisions might be activated in the event of investor non-compliance with the agreement.

Following publication, Jennifer sent copies to each of the individuals she interviewed, along with a cover note reminding them of their prior connection.

She also included the article in both the Profile and Publications sections of her resume, and mentioned her economic development certificate under both the Profile and Education sections of her resume. And with that accomplished, Jennifer actively began applying for economic development jobs.

Write About Evolving Law

New practice areas are constantly emerging.

The first decade of the 21st century has seen the emergence of such practice areas as Homeland Security, e-Commerce, e-Discovery, and Climate Change, to name just a few. Practice areas can also suddenly awaken from periods of dormancy. Copyright Law and Privacy Law are both experiencing new life, thanks to the Internet and other technological leaps forward.

New legislation and accompanying regulations also have a profound impact on practice area health. Sarbanes-Oxley, the Patriot Act, Bioterrorism Act, Patient Protection and Affordable Care Act, and the Wall Street Reform and Consumer Protection Act gave impetus to numerous practice areas. The regulations that flowed from the Financial Modernization Act of 1999 (Graham-Leach-Bliley Act) generated several thousand public and private sector attorney and law-related positions. Treaties such as the Patent Cooperation Treaty, Madrid Protocol, the Central American Free Trade Agreement (CAFTA), and the PRO-IP Act spurred the hiring of intellectual property and international trade attorneys.

All of these exemplify cutting-edge writing opportunities that can make an attorney attractive to the content-eager media and, in turn, can serve as a foot-in-the-door to employment opportunities.

Article and blogging ideas are everywhere and do not necessarily have to meet a purely legal litmus test. Scanning the pages of the daily newspaper or idea-filled magazines such as *The Economist, Scientific American, Technology Review, People, Sports Illustrated*, or even an airline magazine will invariably turn up interesting article ideas.

Moreover, you always have a fall-back.

You can publish your own blog and direct readers to it through social media Web sites and other means. If what you write is sufficiently interesting, readers will find you.

CHAPTER 22

Understand the Cosmetics of Legal Job Hunting

A young man who once applied for a position with my company arrived at the interview wearing jeans and a glossy jacket with his college logo on the front and the name of the institution on the back. On paper, he was a dream candidate: top law school, top grades, great summer jobs. In person, he looked like a slob. I gave him a 10-minute, go-through-the-motions interview, escorted him quickly out of my office, and threw his resume into the trash.

I wondered, "*What could he have been thinking*"?

I was once on a panel of legal career experts from a variety of different callings. Two of the panel members—a woman and a man—had come from an upscale national clothing store chain. They were there to instruct the attorney audience on "dressing for success." Unfortunately, they resorted to a bit of "shock and awe," actually highlighting attorneys in the audience who they felt were guilty of fashion faux pas.

"*Look at the tie this guy is wearing. Are you kidding me*!?"

"*Honey, I can't believe you go to work in shoes like that. And that hairdo!*"

It was embarrassing, discomfiting, and humiliating all at once. To the audience and to the other panel members. In fact, the moderator apologized to the audience, and then asked the two dress-for-success experts to leave.

As a member of the panel, I was as appalled as anyone.

But the more I thought about it, the more I realized that their assessments were spot on, albeit crudely delivered. And it got me to thinking about the external trappings that legal job candidates have to factor into their job search campaigns (and subsequently, their work places) if they want to be successful. Consequently, I devised my own set of cosmetic standards that I suggested to my legal career counseling clients. However, before I settled on them, I consulted the only experts that count—legal employers.

A Little Conservatism Goes a Long Way

Most legal employers are risk-averse in their hiring, and when it comes to sizing up job candidates they look for indicators that express or imply risk. For the most part, they home in on external factors—grooming, attire, resume structure, and any overt signs of deviance from a conservative approach to life and work.

It's safe to say that legal employers don't want to see candidates outfitted like Lady Gaga or the lead singer in a Goth band, and when it comes to resumes they don't want to see exotic typefaces, or resumes that are either outsized or undersized with colors other than white or some shade of off-white. And regardless of your personal taste—in clothing, piercings, tattoos, hairstyles, face-painting, or other cosmetic assertions of your unique and fascinating personality—you need to sublimate all of these when you apply for a legal job. In short, you need to document, dress and groom as conservatively as you can, for two reasons: the overwhelming majority of legal employers expect you to, and it is difficult to go wrong if you do, whereas if you don't you might as well send a "don't-hire-me" message.

Some Gender-Specific Cosmetic Tips

I always felt uncomfortable speaking frankly to my counseling clients about their dress and grooming. Nevertheless, I concluded that I would not be doing them a favor if I felt they needed to hear this kind of advice.

Men

- Hair should be neat and in place.
- Facial hair should be trimmed and non-hirsute areas should be clean-shaven and not fashionably stubbly.
- Clothes should be clean and well-tailored.
- A dark suit is appropriate.
- A white or blue shirt works well.
- A conservative tie that is not garish is suitable.
- Dark socks should be long enough to hide any skin when you sit.
- Shoes should be polished and not frayed or have soles with holes in them.
- If you are overweight, do not wear a shirt with a too-tight collar.

Women

- Hair should be neat and in place.
- Clothes should be clean and well-tailored.
- A dark suit is appropriate.

- Pants suits are acceptable.
- Shoes should be "sensible."
- Stiletto heels are out.
- If you travel in running shoes, make sure you change into work shoes before you arrive at the interview.
- Be modest in applying make-up.
- A handbag or purse should not resemble a suitcase in size.

Gender-Neutral Tips

- Keep the "bling" to a minimum.
- Do not overload on accessories. A nice briefcase is sufficient.
- If you think you look too young, a pair of drugstore glasses can "age you up."
- Do not wear a Mickey Mouse watch or something equally juvenile.
- Watching a candidate switch glasses several times is both annoying and distracting. If you need more than one pair of glasses to get through an interview, consider getting line-free progressive lens bifocals or trifocals. Traditional bifocals and trifocals can make you look older than you wish to come across.

EPILOGUE

In closing, I want you to be conscious of—and hope you retain—three key points:

1. Entry-level attorneys can compete effectively for jobs, even against attorneys with several years of experience, if they follow some or all of the strategies described in this book to enhance their competitive status. Each one of the suggested strategies has a track record of success, which I attribute to (1) their positive impact on legal job hunters' self esteem, self-confidence and overall ego and affect, all of which are often severely challenged by the rigors and inevitable disappointments of legal job hunting, and (2) because they impress and imprint your foresight and sophistication on employers and make you memorable when it comes to decision time.

2. The more strategies you adopt (and adapt to your particular situation and preferences), the more effective your legal job search is likely to be, and the more upside there is likely to be to your legal career down the road.

3. We live in an increasingly complicated and information overloaded world that is deeply and inextricably interconnected. To maneuver through this interwoven and rapidly changing matrix, you need to be able to be continually cognizant of the multitude of external events that could affect your career and be able to make sense of what is happening and how it might positively or negatively impact you. In other words, you need to become reasonably adept at connecting the barrage of dots that come at us continuously from all sides, and that we must make sense of if we are to maximize our career potential.

Here are just some of the "dots" that occurred in only a two-week period last year:

- The 9.0 magnitude Japan earthquake followed by a tsunami followed by the world's worst nuclear reactor accident since Chernobyl.
- The civil war in Libya into which the United States and Europe injected themselves.
- Civic unrest and demands for democracy and economic opportunity spread throughout much of the Middle East.
- Congress' continuing inability to agree on raising the debt ceiling, budget cuts, a budget for the remainder of Fiscal Year (FY) 2011, or an FY 2012 budget.
- The largest insider trading case in history went to trial.
- The European Union freed banks from some of its most rigorous regulations.
- Both Greece and Ireland, balked at key EU bailout terms, while Portugal appeared to be following these two countries into economic free-fall.
- Midwestern governors went after the collective bargaining rights of some of their public employee unions
- The House of Representatives held hearings on Islamic terrorism in the U.S.
- An expert panel commissioned by the World Health Organization (WHO) to investigate its handling of the H1Ni swine flu pandemic of 2009 slammed mistakes made by WHO and warned that tens of millions could die if there is a severe flu outbreak in the future.
- GAO issued a report on duplication in federal programs and agencies.
- China announced shockingly high quarterly inflation despite efforts to rein it in.
- The price of a barrel of oil hit $108 per barrel, a three-year high representing a more than 25 percent increase in only one month.
- Wholesale food prices in the U.S. increased month-to-month at a faster rate than at any time in the last 37 years.
- The Indian middle class was reported to now number more than 400 million people.
- The Securities and Exchange Commission engaged a headhunter to find legal job candidates, an unprecedented move by a government agency and utterly inexplicable in an agency that receives hundreds of unsolicited attorney resumes every week.
- Actor Charlie Sheen melted down and sued his studio for $100 million.

Each one of these rapid-fire occurrences could have a legal employment impact. Several represent opportunity; others may be a warning not to commit yourself to a particular career path. For example:

- This may not be the best time to seek employment with either the nuclear reactor industry or the federal Nuclear Regulatory Commission, given the heightened global wariness of relying on nuclear energy. So far the Obama Administration is claiming that it intends to move ahead with its stated policy of promoting nuclear power as part of Energy Independence, but the proof will be in the pudding. Right now the pudding is looking rather unformed, as evidenced by an abrupt slowdown in Nuclear Regulatory Commission legal hiring.
- Middle Eastern nations that overthrow their dictators and oligarchs might be ripe for international organization, government and Non-Governmental Organization (NGO) Rule of Law projects in the region. This is especially true of Tunisia, Egypt, and Libya; the jury is still out as to Syria and Yemen.
- Securities and commodities regulation, enforcement and compliance could be a very solid career choice for both regulators (e.g., the Securities and Exchange Commission, Commodity Futures Trading Commission, Financial Industry Regulatory Agency, and other Self-Regulatory Organizations) and regulated financial services companies and industries.
- Unions under siege by ideologically-motivated governors appear reinvigorated and may, at least temporarily, reverse their 40-year decline, thus opening up more labor law and labor-management relations jobs.
- Alternative renewable energy may get considerably more attention and resources directed at it, along with increased domestic exploration and development of fossil fuel resources, all of which will demand more energy lawyers, landmen and other legal talents.
- Inflation appears to be much closer than the Federal Reserve Board would have us believe. The industries most affected by rapidly rising costs, such as airlines, may not be the best places to look for a legal job.
- Companies focusing on India are looking at one of the world's largest and fastest-growing consumer markets with new discretionary income to spend. A check of the India Desk at the United States and Foreign Commercial Service reveals that U.S.-India trade has increased 7-fold in 20 years with no ceiling in sight. Moreover, the number of U.S. exporters to India is growing even more rapidly, creating job opportunities for attorneys as well as law-related positions for international trade specialists and contracting officers, among others.

- Hollywood studios and their celebrities are becoming more contentious. Entertainment lawyers should thrive.

While this is, to some degree, speculation on my part, doing this kind of analysis of external events will always pay off where your legal career is involved. And the more you do it, the better you will become at connecting the dots, and the more rewarding will be your legal career. You do not have to be a genius to identify the connections between disparate events and their possible legal career impacts. Lawyers are superb at absorbing and processing enormous quantities of information, sorting the good stuff from the bad (issue identification, sound familiar?) and applying the quality items to the construction of a compelling argument. We spend three years learning to do this in law school. In addition to applying this training and experience to your day-to-day law practice, you can also apply it to how you pursue and manage your entire legal career. That is what *From Lemons to Lemonade in the New Legal Job Market* is all about.

Now that you have the recipes, go out and make the best legal lemonade that you can.

APPENDIX

APPENDIX A

U.S. Government Honors Programs for Legal Employment

U.S. government honors legal employment programs are not always consistently offered from year-to-year. Consequently, this list may change from one year to the next. Check with your law school career services office for updated information.

U.S. Department of Homeland Security General Counsel's Honor Program

U.S. Department of Housing and Urban Development Legal Honors Program

U.S. Department of Justice Attorney General's Honors Program

U.S. Department of Labor Office of the Solicitor Honors Program

U.S. Department of Transportation Office of the Secretary Honors Attorney Program

Central Intelligence Agency Office of the General Counsel Honors Attorney Program

Comptroller of the Currency Chief Counsel's Employment Program for Law Graduates

Environmental Protection Agency Office of General Counsel Honors Fellowship Program

Equal Employment Opportunity Commission Attorney Honor Program

Federal Bureau of Investigation Honors Internship Program

Federal Communications Commission Attorney Honors Program

Federal Deposit Insurance Corporation Legal Division Honors Attorney Program

Federal Trade Commission Entry Level Attorney Program

Internal Revenue Service Chief Counsel Honors Program

National Labor Relations Board Attorney Honors Program

Nuclear Regulatory Commission Honor Law Graduate Program

Securities and Exchange Commission Advanced Commitment Program

U.S. Army Corps of Engineers Chief Counsel's Civilian Honors Program

U.S. Postal Service Honor Attorney Program

Legal and Law-Related Networking Organizations

The following list of over 250 legal and law-related membership organizations is a compilation of useful networking, business development and educational opportunities. Most of these organizations charge relatively modest annual membership dues. Note that some organizations require that a new member be nominated or sponsored for membership by one or more current members:

Academy for Health Services Research and Health Policy (www.academyhealth.org)

Academy of Legal Studies in Business (http://alsb.roundtablelive.org/)

American Academy of Adoption Attorneys (www.adoptionattorneys.org)

American Academy of Assisted Reproductive Technology Attorneys (www.adoptionattorneys.org/aaarta.htm)

American Academy of Criminal Defense Attorneys (www.ameracadcrimdefattys.org)

American Academy of Estate Planning Attorneys (www.aaepa.com)

American Academy of Matrimonial Lawyers (www.aaml.org)

American Agricultural Law Association (www.aglaw-assn.org)

American Arbitration Association (www.adr.org)

American Association for Justice (www.atlanet.org)

American Association of Attorney-Certified Public Accountants (www.attorney-cpa.com)

American Association of Jewish Lawyers and Jurists (www.jewishlawyers.org)

American Association of Legal Nurse Consultants (www.aalnc.org)

American Association of Motorcycle Injury Lawyers (www.lawtigers.com)

American Association of Nurse Attorneys (www.taana.org)

American Association of Visually Impaired Attorneys (www.visuallyimpairedattorneys.org)

American Bankruptcy Institute (www.abiworld.org)

American Bar Association (Sections and Committees) (www.abanet.org)

American Catholic Lawyers Association (www.americancatholiclawyers.org)

American Civil Liberties Union (www.aclu.org)

American College of Bankruptcy (www.amercol.org)

American College of Construction Lawyers (www.accl.org)

American College of Family Trial Lawyers (www.acftl.com)

American College of Legal Medicine (www.aclm.org)

American College of Real Estate Lawyers (www.acrel.org)

American College of Tax Counsel (www.actonline.org)

American College of Trial Lawyers (www.actl.com)

American College of Trust & Estate Counsel (www.actec.org)

American Constitution Society for Law and Policy (www.acslaw.org)

American Foreign Law Association (www.afla-law.org)

American Health Lawyers Association (www.healthlawyers.org)

American Immigration Lawyers Association (www.aila.org)

American Inns of Court (www.innsofcourt.org)

American Intellectual Property Law Association (www.aipla.org)

American Judicature Society (www.ajs.org)

American Land Title Association (www.alta.org)

American Law and Economics Association (www.amlecon.org)

American Law Institute (www.ali.org)

American Masters of Laws Association (www.amola.org)

American Prepaid Legal Services Institute (www.aplsi.org)

American Property Tax Counsel (www.aptcnet.com)

American Society for Bioethics and Humanities (www.asbh.org)

American Society for Healthcare Risk Management (www.ashrm.org) American Society for Pharmacy Law (www.aspl.org)

American Society of Association Executives (www.asaenet.com)

American Society of Comparative Law (www.comparativelaw.org)

American Society of Corporate Secretaries (www.ascs.org)

American Society of International Law (www.asil.org)

American Society of Law, Medicine and Ethics (www.aslme.org)

American Taxation Association (http://aaahq.org/ata/index.htm)

American Veterinary Medical Law Association (www.avmla.org)

Animal Legal Defense Fund (www.aldf.org)

Asia Pacific Legal Institute (http://apli.org)

Association for Children for Enforcement of Support (www.ismi.net/aces)

Association for Conflict Resolution (www.acrnet.org)

Association of Attorney-Mediators (www.attorney-mediators.org)

Association of Certified Anti-Money Laundering Specialists (www.acams.org)

Association of Certified Fraud Examiners (www.acfe.com)

Association of Certified Turnaround Professionals (www.actp.org)

Association of Corporate Counsel (www.acc.com)

Association of Family and Conciliation Courts (www.afccnet.org)

Association of Federal Defense Attorneys (www.afda.org)

Association of Insurance & Risk Managers (www.airmic.com)

Association of Legal Administrators (www.alanet.org)

Association of Life Insurance Counsel (www.alic.cc)

Association of Professional Responsibility Lawyers (www.aprl.net)

Association of Real Estate License Law Officials (www.arello.org)

Association of Record Managers & Administrators (www.arma.org)

Association of Student Judicial Affairs (www.asjaonline.org)

Association of Trial Lawyers of America (www.atla.org)

Association of University Technology Managers (www.autm.org)

Association of Women in International Trade (www.witt.org)

Black Entertainment & Sports Lawyers Association (www.besla.org)

Center for Telehealth & E-Health Law (www.ctel.org)

Christian Legal Society (www.clsnet.com)

Christian Trial Lawyers Association (www.christiantriallawyers.org)

Commercial Law League of America (www.clla.org)

Copyright Society of America (www.csusa.org)

Council of Parent Attorneys and Advocates (www.copaa.org)

Council of School Attorneys (www.nsba.org/SecondaryMenu/COSA.aspx)

Council on Law in Higher Education (www.clhe.org)

Council on Litigation Management (www.litmgmt.org)

Counselors of Real Estate (www.cre.org)

Criminal Justice Legal Foundation (www.cjlf.org)

Customs and International Trade Bar Association (www.citba.org)

Cyberlaw Association (www.cyberlawassociation.com)

Cyberspace Bar Association (www.cyberbar.net)

Decalogue Society of Lawyers (http://decaloguesociety.org)

Defense Research Institute (www.dri.org)

Education Law Association (http://educationlaw.org)

Electronic Frontier Foundation (www.eff.org)

Energy Bar Association (www.eba-net.org)

Enterprise Content Management Association (www.aiim.org)

Environmental Defense Fund (www.edf.org)

Environmental Law Institute (www2.eli.org)

Equal Justice Works (www.equaljusticeworks.org)

Ethics and Compliance Officers Association (www.theecoa.org)

Federal Bar Association (www.fedbar.org)

Federal Circuit Bar Association (www.fedcirbar.org)

Federal Communications Bar Association (www.fcba.org)

Federation of Defense & Corporate Counsel (www.thefederation.org)

Federation of Regulatory Counsel (www.forc.org)

Federation of Insurance & Corporate Counsel (www.thefederation.org)

Food and Drug Law Institute (www.fdli.org)

Georgia Association of Counsel for Children (http://gaccchildlaw.org/)

Global Association of Risk Professionals (www.garp.com)

Half-Norwegian American Bar Association (http://www.lawzone.com/half-nor/)

Health Care Compliance Association (www.hcca-info.org)

Hellenic Bar Association (www.hellenicbarassociation.com)

Hispanic National Bar Association (www.hnba.com)

Home School Legal Defense Association (www.hslda.org)

Human Rights First (www.humanrightsfirst.org)

Indian Law Resource Center (www.indianlaw.org)

Institute for Professionals in Taxation (www.ipt.org)

Inter-American Bar Association (www.iaba.org)

Inter-Pacific Bar Association (www.ipba.org)

International Academy of Estate & Trust Law (www.international-academy.org)

International Academy of Matrimonial Lawyers (www.iaml.org)

International Association of Risk & Compliance Professionals (www.risk-compliance-association.com)

International Association of Defense Counsel (www.iadclaw.org)

International Association of Entertainment Lawyers (www.iael.org)

International Association of Facilitators (http://iaf-world.org)

International Association of Hedge Funds Professionals (www.hedge-funds-association.com)

International Association of Jewish Lawyers and Jurists (www.intjewishlawyers.org)

International Association of Privacy Professionals (www.privacyassociation.org)

International Association of Sports Law (http://iasl.org)

International Association of Young Lawyers (www.aija.org)

International Bar Association (www.ibanet.org)

International Catholic Lawyers Society (www.catholiclawyers.net)

International Center for Not-for-Profit Law (www.icnl.org)

International Collegiate Licensing Association (www.nacda.com/icla/nacda-icla.html)

International Compliance Professionals Association (www.icpainc.org)

International Criminal Defence Attorneys Association (www.aiad-icdaa.org)

International Criminal Law Network (www.icln.net)

International Institute for Conflict Resolution & Prevention (www.cpradr.org)

International Law Association (www.ila-hq.org/)

International Legal Technology Association (www.iltanet.org)

International Litigation Management Association (www.litigationmanagement.org)

International Masters of Gaming Law (www.gaminglawmasters.com)

International Media Lawyers Association (www.internationalmedialawyers.org)

International Municipal Lawyers Association (www.imla.org)

International Society of Certified Employee Benefit Specialists (www.iscebs.org)

International Tax Planning Association (www.itpa.org)

International Technology Law Association (www.itechlaw.org)

International Trademark Association (www.inta.org)

Internet Bar Association (http://lawyers.org)

Jewish Lawyers Guild (www.jewishlawyersguild.org)

Judge Advocates Association (www.jaa.org)

Justinian Society (www.justinian.org)

Law and Society Association (www.lawandsociety.org)

Lawyers' Committee for Civil Rights Under Law (www.lawyerscommittee.org)

Lawyer Pilots Bar Association (www.lpba.org)

Legal Marketing Association (www.legalmarketing.org)

Lesbian and Gay Law Association (www.le-gal.org)

Licensing Executives Society (www.usa-canada.les.org)

Lithuanian-American Bar Association (http://javadvokatai.org)

Maritime Law Association of the United States (www.mlaus.org)

National Academy of Elder Law Attorneys (www.naela.org)

National Asian Pacific American Bar Association (www.napaba.org)

National Association for Athletics Compliance (www.nacda.com)

National Association for Community Mediation (www.nafcm.org)

National Association for Rights Protection & Advocacy (www.narpa.org)

National Association of Blind Lawyers (www.blindlawyer.org)

National Association of Bond Lawyers (www.nabl.org)

National Association of College and University Attorneys (www.nacua.org)

National Association of Consumer Bankruptcy Attorneys (http://nacba.com)

National Association of Counsel for Children (www.NACCchildlaw.org)

National Association of Criminal Defense Lawyers (www.criminaljustice.org)

National Association of Drug Court Professionals (www.nadcp.org)

National Association of Enrolled Agents (www.naeahq.org)

National Association of Environmental Professionals (www.naep.org)

National Association of Estate Planners and Councils (www.naepc.org)

National Association of Guardians ad Litem (www.nagalro.com)

National Association of Insurance and Financial Advisors (www.naifa.org)

National Association of Legal Fee Analysis (www.thenalfa.org)

National Association of Legal Search Consultants (www.nalsc.org)

National Association of Patent Practitioners (www.napp.org)

National Association of Railroad Trial Counsel (www.nartc.org)

National Association of Retail Collection Attorneys (www.narca.org)

National Association of Tax Practitioners (www.natptax.com)

National Association of Women Lawyers (www.abanet.org/nawl/)

National Bar Association (www.nationalbar.org)

National Contract Management Association (www.ncmahq.org)

National Council of University Research Administrators (www.ncura.edu)

National Court Appointed Special Advocate Association (www.nationalcasa.org)

National Crime Victim Bar Association (www.victimbar.org)

National District Attorneys Association (www.ndaa.org)

National Employment Lawyers Association (www.nela.org)

National Guardianship Association (www.guardianship.org)

National Human Resources Association (www.humanresources.org)

National Immigration Law Center (www.nilc.org)

National Lawyers Association (www.nla.org)

National Lawyers Guild (www.nlg.org)

National Legal Aid and Defender Association (www.nlada.org)

National Lesbian and Gay Law Association (www.nlgla.org)

National Native American Bar Association (www.nativeamericanbar.org)

National Obscenity Law Center (www.moralityinmedia.org)

National Organization of Bar Counsel (www.nobc.org)

National Organization of Social Security Claimants' Representatives (www.nosscr.org)

National Organization of Veterans Advocates (www.vetadvocates.com)

National Structured Settlements Trade Association (www.nssta.com)

National Tax Association (http://ntanet.org)

National Transportation Safety Board Bar Association (www.ntsbbar.org)

National Whistleblower Center (www.whistleblowers.org)

Native American Rights Fund (www.narf.org)

Natural Resources Defense Council (www.nrdc.org)

Nonprofit Risk Management Center (www.nonprofitrisk.org)

Open Compliance and Ethics Group (www.oceg.org)

Phi Alpha Delta (www.padcommunity.org)

Professional Association for Compliance and Ethics (www.pacecompliance.com)

Professional Mediation Association (www.promediation.com)

Professional Risk Managers International Association (www.prmia.org)

Public Agency Risk Managers Association (www.parma.com)

Public Risk Management Association (www.primacentral.org)

Risk and Insurance Management Society, Inc. (www.rims.org)

Risk Management Association (www.rmahq.org)

Sarbanes Oxley Compliance Professionals Association (www.sarbanes-oxley-association.com)

Society for Human Resource Management (www.shrm.org)

Society of Corporate Compliance and Ethics (www.corporatecompliance.org)

Society of Corporate Secretaries & Governance Professionals (www.governanceprofessionals.org)

Society of Maritime Arbitrators (www.smany.org)

Sports Lawyers Association (www.sportslaw.org)

State and Local Bar Associations (Sections and Committees)

State Risk and Insurance Management Association (www.strima.org)

Tau Epsilon Rho Law Society (www.ter-law.org)

The Rutherford Institute (www.rutherford.org)

Trial Lawyers for Public Justice (www.tlpj.org)

Transportation Lawyers Association (www.translaw.org)

Turnaround Management Association (www.turnaround.org)

United States Ombudsman Association (www.usombudsman.org)

University Risk Management & Insurance Association (www.urmia.org)

Victim Offender Mediation Association (www.voma.org)

Women in Government Relations (www.wgr.org)

Workplace Injury Law & Advocacy Group (www.wilg.org)

Legal and Law-Related Certificate & Credential-Building Programs

Two things are important to note when considering the following list: credentialing programs are in constant flux. It is likely that there will be changes to certain programs and their web addresses between the time this list was prepared and publication of this book. Secondly, certain programs require that you meet minimum threshold qualification requirements in order to enroll. These are always explained on the program's Web site:

Alternative Dispute Resolution

American Arbitration Association Programs (www.adr.org)

Association for Conflict Resolution (www.acrnet.org). Approved Family Mediation Training Programs

Boise State University - Certificate in Dispute Resolution (www.boisestate.edu)

Center for Legal Studies (www.legalstudies.com). Alternative Dispute Resolution Certificate (online option)

Hamline University School of Law (www.hamline.edu/law). (1) Certificate in Dispute Resolution; (2) Certificate in Global Arbitration Law and Practice

Hawaii Pacific University (www.hpu.edu). (1) Certificate in Mediation and Conflict (online); (2) Commercial Mediation Certification (online); (3) Commercial Arbitration Certification (online)

Institute for Conflict Resolution (www.icmadr. com). Family Mediation Certification (online)

Marquette University (www.marquette.edu). Graduate Certificate in Dispute Resolution

Marylhurst University (www.marylhurst.edu). Certificate in Conflict Resolution & Mediation (online)

Mediation Matters (www.mediationmatters.com/ training.html). (1) Basic Mediation Training; (2) Business and Employment Mediation Training; (3) Divorce Mediation Training; (4) Marital Property Mediation Training; (5) Child Access Mediation Training

Mountain States Employers' Council (www.msec.org). Mediating Workplace Disputes

New York University (www.nyu.edu). Certificate in Conflict & Dispute Resolution

Northeastern University (www.cps.neu.edu/ programs/certificates/). Conflict Resolution Studies Certificate

Northern Virginia Mediation Service (www.nvms.us). Virginia Mediator Certification

Southern Methodist University (www.smu.edu). Dispute Resolution Graduate Certificate Program

World Trade Organization (www.wto.org). (1) Dispute Settlement System Training Module; (2) General Agreement on Trade in Services

Art & Museums

Boston University (www.bu.edu). Metropolitan College - Graduate Certificate in Arts Administration

DePaul University College of Law (www.law.depaul.edu). Certificate in Intellectual Property: Arts & Museum Law

Harvard College (www.harvard.edu). Certificate in Museum Studies

Banking & Finance

American Institute of Banking (www.aba.com). (1) AIB Banking and Finance Diploma; (2) AIB Personal Trust Diploma

Association of Certified Anti-Money Laundering Specialists (http://www.acams.org/). Certified Anti-Money Laundering Specialist (online)

Boston University (www.bu.edu). Metropolitan College - Graduate Diploma Program in Banking and Financial Services

Credit Union National Association (http://training.cuna.org). Regulatory Training & Certification Program

Florida International University (http://business.fiu.edu). Certificate in Banking

Hedge Funds Association (www.hedge-funds-association.com). Certified Hedge Fund Compliance Expert (CHFCE)(online)

Institute of Certified Bankers (www.aba.com/ICBCertifications). (1) Certified Regulatory Compliance Manager (CRCM); (2) Certified Corporate Trust Specialist (CCTS)

Keller Graduate School of Management of DeVry University (www.directdegree.com). Graduate Certificate in Financial Analysis

Lorman Education Services (www.lorman.com). Certificate of Banking Compliance

Northeastern University (www.cps.neu.edu/programs/certificates/). Financial Institutions and Markets Certificate

University of the Pacific (www.pacific.edu). Banking Leadership Certificate Program

Bankruptcy Law

American Board of Certification (www.abcworld.org). (1) Business Bankruptcy Certificate; (2) Consumer Bankruptcy Certificate; (3) Creditors' Rights Law Certificate

Bioethics

Indiana University (www.iupui.edu). Purdue University Indianapolis - Bioethics Certificate

Loyola University Chicago (http://bioethics.lumc.edu/online_masters.html). Certificate in Bioethics and Health Policy (online)

Medical College of Wisconsin (www.mcw.edu). Certificate in Clinical Bioethics Program (online)

Montefiore Medical Center (www.montefiore.org). Montefiore-Einstein Certificate Program in Bioethics and Medical Humanities

Union Graduate College (www.bioethics.union.edu). Mount Sinai School of Medicine - Certificate in Bioethics: (1) Specialization in Clinical Ethics; (2) Specialization in Research Ethics; (3) Specialization in Health Policy & Law

University of Nevada, Reno (www.unr.edu). Graduate Certificate in Bioethics, Bioterrorism Preparedness

Penn State University (www.worldcampus.psu.edu/certificates.shtml). Certificate in Bioterrorism Preparedness (online)

Georgetown University (http://grad.georgetown.edu/pages/certif_biohazard.cfm). (1) Biohazardous Threat Agents and Emerging Infectious Diseases Certificate Program (online); (2) Biodefense and Public Policy Certificate

Child Welfare Law

National Association of Counsel for Children (www.naccchildlaw.org). Certified Child Welfare Law Specialist

Center for Guardianship Certification (www.guardianshipcert.org). (1) Registered Guardian Certification; (2) Master Guardian Certification

Climate Change

University of California (http://unex.uci.edu). Irvine Extension - Decision Making for Climate Change (online) [in conjunction with the University of Washington Educational Outreach, Northwestern University School of Continuing Studies and the University of British Columbia Continuing Studies]

Compliance

ABS Consulting (www.absconsulting.com). (1) Environmental and Quality Certification Programs; (2) Clean Air Compliance (CAC) Specialist; (3) Clean Water Compliance (CWC) Specialist; (4) EMS Compliance (EMSC) Specialist; (5) Hazardous Waste Compliance (HWC) Specialist; (6) QMS Compliance (QMSC) Specialist; (7) Regulatory Compliance Specialist (RCS)

Association of Health Care Compliance Professionals (www.hcca-info.org). Certificate in Healthcare Compliance

Compliance LLC (www.compliance-llc.com). (1) Certified Basel ii Professional (online); (2) Certified Sarbanes Oxley Expert (online); (3) Certified Risk and Compliance Management Professional (online)

Compliance Resources (www.complianceresources.com). (1) Certified Healthcare Compliance Officer (CHCO) (online); (2) Certified Healthcare Compliance Consultant (CHCC)(online)

Credit Union National Association (http://training.cuna.org). Regulatory Training & Certification Program

Financial Industry Regulatory Authority (www.finra.com). FINRA Compliance Boot Camp

Florida Gulf Coast University (www.fgcu.edu). Graduate Compliance Certificate Program (online)

George Washington University (www.gwu.edu). Graduate Certificate in Healthcare Corporate Compliance

Hamline University School of Law
(http://law.hamline.edu). Health Care
Compliance Certification Program
Health Care Compliance Association
(http://hcca-info.org). (1) Certified in
Healthcare Compliance Professional (CHC);
(2) Healthcare Research Compliance
Certification (CHRC); (3) Certified in
Healthcare Compliance Fellowship (CHC-F)
Hedge Funds Association (www.hedge-funds-
association.com). Certified Hedge Fund
Compliance Expert (CHFCE)(online)
Institute of Certified Bankers (www.aba.com/
ICBCertifications). Certified Regulatory
Compliance Manager (CRCM)
International Import-Export Institute
(http://expandglobal.com). Certified U.S. Export
Compliance Officer
LOMA (www.loma.org). Associate, Insurance
Regulatory Compliance® (AIRC)(online)
Lorman Education Services (www.lorman.com).
(1) Certificate of Banking Compliance;
(2) Construction Compliance Certification
National Regulatory Services
(www.nrs-inc.com). Investment Adviser
Compliance Certificate Program
National Safety Council (www.nsc.org).
Certificate in OSHA Compliance
Purdue University (www.purdue.edu). Regulatory
& Quality Compliance Graduate Certificate
Program
St. Thomas University (FL) School of Law
(www.stu.edu/lawschool). International Tax
Law Program: Anti-Money Laundering &
Compliance Certificate
Seton Hall University School of Law
(www.law.shu.edu). Health Care Compliance
Certification Program
Sheshunoff (www.sheshunoff.com). Regulatory
Compliance Certification Program
Society of Corporate Compliance & Ethics
(www.corporatecompliance.org). (1) Certified
Compliance & Ethics Professional;
(2) Certified Compliance and Ethics
Professional-Fellow
Quinnipiac University (www.quinnipiac.edu).
Healthcare Compliance Certificate
University of Washington Extension
(www.extension.washington.edu). Certificate
Program in Healthcare Regulatory Compliance

Construction Law
Lorman Education Services (www.lorman.com).
Construction Compliance Certification

University of California at Davis
(http://extension.ucdavis.edu). Certificate
Program in Construction Management

Consulting
Nexient Learning (www.nexientlearning.com).
Associate Certificate in Consulting
Kaplan University (www.kaplan.edu). Legal
Nurse Consulting Certificate
American Association of Legal Nurse Consultants
(www.aalnc.org). Legal Nurse Consultant
Certificate

Contracts & Procurement
Villanova University (www.villanova.edu).
Master Certificate in Government Contract
Management (online)
University of Virginia (www.uva.edu). Graduate
Certificate Program in Procurement and
Contracts Management
National Contract Management Association
(www.ncmahq.org). (1) Certified Commercial
Contracts Manager; (2) Certified Professional
Contracts Manager; (3) Certified Federal
Contracts Manager

Corporate Governance
Compliance LLC (www.compliance-llc.com).
Certified Sarbanes Oxley Expert (online)
University of North Carolina Greensboro
(www.uncg.edu). Corporate Governance &
Ethics Certificate
Harvard Business School Executive Education
(www.exed.hbs.edu). Corporate Governance
Series
Tulane University (www.corpgovonline.com).
Excellence in Corporate Governance Certificate
New York University School of Continuing and
Professional Studies (http://www.scps.nyu.edu).
Certificate in Ethics and Corporate Governance

Corporate Restructuring
Association of Insolvency & Restructuring
Advisors (www.airacira.org). Certified
Insolvency & Restructuring Advisor (CIRA)
Association of Certified Turnaround Professionals
(www.actp.org). Certified Turnaround
Professional
Post University Online (www.post.edu/online).
Graduate Certificate in Corporate Innovation
(online)

Counseling

University of California—Santa Cruz (www.ucsc.edu). Human Services Certificate in Counseling

Capella University (www.capella.edu). Graduate Certificate in Professional Counseling

Creditors' Rights

American Board of Certification (www.abcworld. org). Creditors' Rights Law Certificate

Criminal Justice

National Board of Trial Advocacy (www.nbtanet.org). Criminal Trial Certificate (online)

Association of Certified Fraud Examiners (www.acfe.com). Certified Fraud Examiner

University of Massachusetts(http://umass.edu). Criminal Justice Studies Certificate

Post University Online (www.post.edu/online). Criminal Justice Certificate in Homeland Security (online)

Boston University—Metropolitan College (www.bu.edu). Criminal Justice Certificate Program

Utica College (www.utica.edu). Financial Crimes Investigator Certificate (online)

Northeastern University (www.spcs.neu.edu). Graduate Certificate in Community Justice Studies

Association of Certified Anti-Money Laundering Specialists (www.acams.org). Anti-Money Laundering Specialist Certificate

University of Virginia in conjunction with the Federal Bureau of Investigation (www.uva.edu). Certificate Program in Criminal Justice Education

California State University at Fullerton (www.csufextension.org). Certificate in Crime and Intelligence Analysis

Disability Law

National Board of Trial Advocacy (www.nbtanet.org). Social Security Disability Certificate (online)

University of Illinois—Chicago (www.uic.edu). Disability Ethics Certificate Program

Mountain States Employers' Council (www.msec.org). Americans with Disabilities Act: Managing Disabilities in the Workplace

National Board of Social Security Disability Advocacy (www.nblsc.us). Social Security Disability Specialist

E-Commerce

University of Virginia (www.uva.edu). Graduate Certificate Program in E-Commerce

Eastern Michigan University (www.emich.edu). Graduate Certificate in E-Business

Keller Graduate School of Management of DeVry University (www.directdegree.com). Graduate Certificate in Electronic Commerce Management (online)

E-Discovery/IT/Records Management

University of Washington Extension (www.extension.washington.edu/ext/ certificates/edm/edm_gen.asp). Certificate in Electronic Discovery Management

California State University at Fullerton (www.csufextension.org). Certificate in Electronic Discovery

AIIM - The Enterprise Content Management Association (www.aiim.org). Electronic Records Management Certificate Program (online)

Keller Graduate School of Management of DeVry University (www.directdegree.com). (1) Graduate Certificate in Information Security (online); (2) Graduate Certificate in Information Systems Management (online)

Association of Record Managers & Administrators (www.arma.org). Certified Records Manager

Stevens Institute of Technology Web Campus (http://webcampus.stevens.edu/Legal-Issues-IT.aspx). Legal Issues in IT Graduate Certificate (online)

Economic Development

Penn State University (www.worldcampus. psu.edu/certificates.shtml). Certificate in Community and Economic Development (online)

National Development Council (http:// nationaldevelopmentcouncil.org/index.php/ site/training_schedule/category/certification/). Economic Development Finance Professional Certification Program™

Education Law

Student Affairs Administrators in Higher Education (www.naspa.org). NASPA Certificate Program in Student Affairs Law and Policy

National Alliance for Insurance Education and Research (www.scic.com/CRM/CRMmain. htm). Certified School Risk Manager (CSRM) [California and Texas only]

Elder Law and Affairs
National Elder Law Foundation (www.nelf.org). Certified Elder Law Attorney

Marylhurst University (www.marylhurst.edu). Graduate Certificate in Gerontology (online)

University of Toledo (www.utoledo.edu). Elder Law Graduate Certificate Online (online)

Emergency Management
American Military University (www.amu.apus. edu). Graduate Certificate in Emergency and Disaster Management

Penn State University (www.worldcampus.psu. edu/certificates.shtml). Graduate Certificate in Disaster Preparedness (online)

Emergency Management Institute (http://training.fema.gov/EMI/). 50 Certificate Programs

Employee Benefits

Georgetown University Law Center (www.law.georgetown.edu). Employee Benefits Law Certificate

John Marshall Law School (www.jmls.edu). Graduate Certificate in Employee Benefits Law

Temple University, James E. Beasley School of Law (www.law.temple.edu). Employee Benefits Certificate Program

Villanova University School of Law (www.law. villanova.edu). Employee Benefits Certificate

eCornell (www.ecornell.com). Benefits and Compensation Online Certificate

Mountain States Employers' Council (www.msec.org). Compensation and Benefits Certificate Program

Department of Veterans Affairs (www.va.gov). Accredited Veterans Benefits Representative

Institute for Applied Management and Law (www.iaml.com). Certificate in Employee Benefits Law (sm) Seminar

Energy & Natural Resources
University of Vermont Law School (www.vermontlaw.edu). Summer Energy Programs

University of Denver, Sturm College of Law (www.law.du.edu). Certificate of Studies (CS) in Natural Resources Law and Policy

University of Houston Bauer College of Business (www.bauer.uh.edu). (1) Energy Risk Management Certificate; (2) Energy Investment Analysis Certificate; (3) Energy Finance Certificate

University of California-Davis Extension (http://extension.ucdavis.edu/certificates/).

(1) Energy Resource Management Certificate (online); (2) Certificate Program in Renewable Energy (partially online)

American Association of Professional Landmen (www.aapl.org). (1) Certified Professional Landman; (2) Registered Professional Landman Designation (www.nea.fr/html/law/isnl/index. html). (3) Registered Landman Designation

Centenary College - Graduate Certificate in Oil & Gas Management (www.centenary.edu)

International School of Nuclear Law - Introductory Course on Nuclear Law

Entertainment, Sports & Media
UCLA Anderson School of Management (www.anderson.ucla.edu). Summer Intensive Certificate Program in Entertainment/Media Management

American Military University (www.amu.apus. edu). (1) Graduate Certificate in Athletic Administration; (2) Graduate Certificate in Sports Management

Southern New Hampshire University (www.snhu. edu). (1) International Sport Management Graduate Certificate (online); (2) Sport Management Graduate Certificate (online)

United States Sports Academy (www.ussa.edu). Sports Management Certificates: (1) Sports Administration (online); (2) Sports Agents (online); (3) Sports Law and Risk Management (online); (4) Sports Business (online)

National Football League Players Association (www.nflplayers.com). (1) Agent Certification; (2) Player Financial Advisor Registration

National Basketball Players Association (www.nbpa.org). NBPA Player Agent Certification

Columbia Southern University (www.columbiasouthern.edu). Certificate in Sport Management (online)

Environmental Law & Regulation
Harvard University (www.extension.harvard.edu). Certificate in Environmental Management (online)

University of Denver University College (www.universitycollege.du.edu). Environmental Policy Certificate

University of Colorado (www.colorado.edu). Graduate Certificate in Environment, Policy, and Society

Pace Law School (www.law.pace.edu). Certificate in Environmental Law

Tufts Institute of the Environment
(www.tufts.edu/tie). Certificate in
Environmental Management
University of Georgia (www.uga.edu).
Environmental Ethics Certificate Program
University of Washington Extension
(www.extension.washington.edu). Certificate
Program in Environmental Law and Regulation
The Academy of Board Certified Environmental
Professionals (www.abcep.org). Certified
Environmental Professional Designation
National Registry of Environmental Professionals
(www.nrep.org). (1) Registered Environmental
Manager Certificate; (2) Associate
Environmental Professional Certificate
ABS Consulting (www.absconsulting.com).
Environmental and Quality Certification
Programs: (1) Clean Air Compliance (CAC)
Specialist; (2) Clean Water Compliance (CWC)
Specialist; (3) EMS Compliance (EMSC)
Specialist; (4) Hazardous Waste Compliance
(HWC) Specialist; (5) QMS Compliance
(QMSC) Specialist; (6) Regulatory Compliance
Specialist (RCS)
Johns Hopkins University Bloomberg School of
Public Health (http://commprojects.jhsph.edu/
academics/Certificate.cfm). Humane Sciences
and Toxicology Policy Certificate
United Nations Educational, Scientific and
Cultural Organization (www.unesco.org). Water
& Environmental Law and Institutions
University of California-Davis Extension
(http://extension.ucdavis.edu/certificates/).
Certificate in Land Use and Environmental
Planning

Estate Planning, Planned Giving & Trusts
National Association of Estate Planners &
Councils (www.naepc.org). (1) Estate Planning
Law Specialist; (2) Accredited Estate Planner
Georgetown University Law Center (www.law.
georgetown.edu). Estate Planning Certificate
St. Thomas University (FL) School of Law
(www.stu.edu/lawschool). Certificate in the
International Tax Law Program:
Capital University Law School
(www.law.capital.edu). Certificate in Estate
Planning
Temple University, James E. Beasley School of
Law (www.law.temple.edu). Estate Planning
Certificate Program
Villanova University School of Law (www.law.
villanova.edu). Estate Planning Certificate

College of William & Mary (www.wm.edu).
Certificate in Planned Giving
American Institute of Banking (www.aba.com).
AIB Personal Trust Diploma
Institute of Certified Bankers (www.aba.com/
ICBCertifications). (1) Certified Corporate
Trust Specialist (CCTS); (2) Certified Trust and
Financial Advisor (CTFA)
University of Washington—Tacoma - Fundraising
Management Certificate (www.tacoma.
washington.edu/pdc/schedule/fundraising_cert.
html)

Ethics
University of North Carolina (www.uncg.edu).
Greensboro - Corporate Governance & Ethics
Certificate
University of New Mexico (www.unm.edu).
(1) Business Ethics Certificate Program;
(2) Health Care Ethics Certificate Program
University of Illinois—Chicago - Disability Ethics
Certificate Program (www.uic.edu)
Southern Methodist University - Accounting
Ethics Certificate Program (www.smu.edu)
University of Florida - Pharmacy Law and Ethics
Certificate Program (www.ufl.edu)
University of Georgia - Environmental Ethics
Certificate Program (www.uga.edu)
Public Responsibility in Medicine and Research
(PRIM&R)—(1) Certified Institutional Review
Board Professional (CIP®); (2) Certified
Professional Institutional Animal Care & Use
Committee Administrator (CPIA)
(www.primr.org)
Society of Corporate Compliance & Ethics -
Certified Compliance & Ethics Professional
(www.corporatecompliance.org)

Family Law
National Board of Trial Advocacy
(www.nbtanet.org). Family Law Certificate
(online)
Association for Conflict Resolution
(www.acrnet.org). Approved Family Mediation
Training Programs

Food, Drugs & Devices
University of Maryland (www.umd.edu).
Graduate Certificate of Professional Studies in
Food Safety Risk Analysis
Michigan State University (www.msu.edu).
International Food Law Internet Certificate
Program

Purdue University (www.purdue.edu). Regulatory & Quality Compliance Graduate Certificate Program

Temple University Quality Assurance & Regulatory Affairs Graduate Program (www.temple.edu). (1) Drug Development Certificate; (2) Clinical Trial Management; (3) Medical Device Certificate

University of Florida (www.ufl.edu). Pharmacy Law and Ethics Certificate Program

Northeastern University (www.spcs.neu.edu). (1) Biopharmaceutical Domestic Regulatory Affairs (online option); (2) Biopharmaceutical International Regulatory Affairs (online option); (3) Medical Devices Regulatory Affairs (online option))

Fraud Investigation

Association of Certified Fraud Examiners (www.acfe.com). Certified Fraud Examiner

Utica College (www.utica.edu). Financial Crimes Investigator Certificate (online)

Association of Certified Anti-Money Laundering Specialists (www.acams.org). Anti-Money Laundering Specialist Certificate

California State University at Fullerton (www.csufextension.org). Certificate in Healthcare Fraud and Abuse in the Application of Medical Coding (online)

Globalization

Thunderbird School of Global Management (www.thunderbird.edu). Globalization: Merging Strategy with Action

Grants Management

Management Concepts (www.managementconcepts.com). Grants Management Certificate Program

Guardianship

Center for Guardianship Certification (www.guardianshipcert.org). (1) Registered Guardian Certification; (2) Master Guardian Certification

Health Law & Administration

George Washington University Law School (www.law.gwu.edu). (1) Graduate Certificate in Public Health; (2) Graduate Certificate in Healthcare Corporate Compliance

DePaul University College of Law (www.law.depaul.edu). Certificate in Health Law

Seton Hall University School of Law (www.law.shu.edu). Health Care Compliance Certification Program

University of Maryland (www.umd.edu). Graduate Certificate of Professional Studies in Food Safety Risk Analysis

University of Florida (www.ufl.edu). Graduate Certificate in Health Care Risk Management

Kaplan University (www.kaplan.edu). Legal Nurse Consulting Certificate

University of New Mexico (www.unm.edu). Health Care Ethics Certificate Program

Mountain States Employers' Council (www.msec.org). HIPAA: Privacy Rules and Portability

Florida International University Legal Studies Institute (www.fiu.edu). Medical/Legal Consultant Certificate

American College of Healthcare Executives (www.ache.org). Fellows Program

American Association of Legal Nurse Consultants (www.aalnc.org). Legal Nurse Consultant Certificate

The Association of Health Care Compliance Professionals (www.hcca-info.org). Certificate in Healthcare Compliance

American Hospital Association Certification Center (www.aha.org). Certified Professional in Healthcare Risk Management (online)

Healthcare Quality Certification Board (www.cphq.org). Certified Professional in Healthcare Quality (online)

Center for Insurance Education & Professional Development (www.insuranceeducation.org) Long-Term Care Professional (LTCP) Designation

Cleveland State University (www.csuohio.edu/ce). Patient Advocacy Certificate Program (online)

National Safety Council (www.nsc.org). Certificate in OSHA Compliance

University of Washington Extension (www.extension.washington.edu). Certificate Program in Healthcare Regulatory Compliance

Quinnipiac University (www.quinnipiac.edu). Healthcare Compliance Certificate

Johns Hopkins University (http://commprojects.jhsph.edu/academics/Certificate.cfm). Certificate in Health Policy

American Society for Healthcare Risk Management (www.ashrm.org). Barton Certificate Program in Healthcare Risk Management

Northeastern University (www.spcs.neu.edu).
(1) Biopharmaceutical Domestic Regulatory
Affairs (online option); (2) Biopharmaceutical
International Regulatory Affairs (online option);
(3) Medical Devices Regulatory Affairs (online
option)

University of California-Davis Extension
(http://extension.ucdavis.edu/certificates/).
(1) Health Informatics Certificate Program
(online); (2) Intensive Certificate Program in
Workplace Health and Safety

California State University at Fullerton
(www.csufextension.org). Certificate in
Healthcare Fraud and Abuse in the Application
of Medical Coding (online)

Compliance Resources
(www.complianceresources.com). (1) Certified
Healthcare Compliance Officer (CHCO)
(online); (2) Certified Healthcare Compliance
Consultant (CHCC)(online)

Health Care Compliance Association
(http://hcca-info.org). (1) Certified in
Healthcare Compliance Professional (CHC);
(2) Healthcare Research Compliance
Certification (CHRC); (3) Certified in
Healthcare Compliance Fellowship (CHC-F)

Hamline University School of Law
(http://law.hamline.edu). Health Care
Compliance Certification Program

City University of New York
(www.workered.org). The Murphy Institute -
The Graduate Certificate in Health Care Policy
and Administration

Historic Preservation

University of Hawaii (www.hawaii.edu). Graduate
Certificate in Historic Preservation

University of North Carolina-Greensboro
(www.uncg.org). Post-Baccalaureate Certificate
in Historic Preservation

Human Resources

Society for Human Resource Management
(www.shrm.org). (1) Professional in Human
Resources; (2) Senior Professional in Human
Resources

Southern New Hampshire University
(www.snhu.edu). Certificate in Human
Resources Management (online)

Human Capital Institute (www.hci.org). Human
Capital Strategist Designation

Villanova University (www.villanove.edu). Master
Certificate in Human Resource Management
(online)

Cornell University (www.cornell.edu).
(1) Human Resources Management Certificate
(online); (2) HR: Benefits and Compensation
Certificate (online)

Strayer University
(http://strayer.edu-info.com). Executive
Graduate Certificate in Business Administration
- Human Resource Management

Human Rights

Center for International Humanitarian
Cooperation (www.cihc.org). (1) International
Diploma in Humanitarian Assistance;
(2) Humanitarian Negotiators Training Course;
(3) Forced Migration Program

Columbia University Continuing Education
(http://ce.columbia.edu). Human Rights
Certificate Program

University of Iowa Center for Human Rights
(http://international.uiowa.edu). Certificate in
Human Rights

University of Cincinnati (www.uc.edu).
International Human Rights Certificate

Insurance & Risk Management

Kaplan University (www.kaplan.edu). Risk
Management Certificate (online)

American Institute for CPCU & Insurance
Institute of America (www.aicpcu.org).
(1) Associate in Risk Management (ARM);
(2) Associate in Risk Management for Public
Entities (ARM-P)

Compliance LLC (www.compliance-llc.com).
Certified Risk and Compliance Management
Professional (online)

National Alliance for Insurance Education and
Research (www.scic.com/CRM/CRMmain.htm).
(1) Certified Risk Manager (CRM); (2) Certified
School Risk Manager (CSRM)[California and
Texas only]

Stanford University (www.stanford.edu).
Certificate Program: Strategic Decision and
Risk Management

Institute of Risk Management (www.theirm.org).
Certificate in Risk Management

University of Maryland (www.umd.edu).
Graduate Certificate of Professional Studies in
Food Safety Risk Analysis

University of Florida (www.ufl.edu). Graduate
Certificate in Health Care Risk Management

Mountain States Employers' Council
(www.msec.org). Workplace Risk Management
Certificate Program

University of Houston Bauer College of Business (www.bauer.uh.edu). Energy Risk Management Certificate

American Hospital Association Certification Center (www.aha.org). Certified Professional in Healthcare Risk Management (online)

American Society for Healthcare Risk Management (www.ashrm.org). Barton Certificate Program in Healthcare Risk Management

Professional Risk Managers International Association (www.prima.org). Professional Risk Manager (PRM™) Certification Program

LOMA (www.loma.org). Associate, Insurance Regulatory Compliance® (online)

Boston University Distance Education (http://www.bu.edu/online/online_programs/certificate_programs/). Online Graduate Certificate in Risk Management and Organizational Continuity (online)

Institute of Consumer Financial Information (www.icfe.us). Certified Identity Theft Risk Management Specialist

Intellectual Property

DePaul University College of Law (www.law.depaul.edu). (1) Certificate in Intellectual Property: Arts & Museum Law; (2) Certificate in Intellectual Property: General; (3) Certificate in Intellectual Property: Patents

Licensing Executives Society (www.usa-canada.les.org). Intellectual Asset Management Certificates

Franklin Pierce Law Center (www.piercelaw.edu). Intellectual Property Diploma

U.S. Department of Agriculture Graduate School (www.grad.usda.gov). Technology Transfer Program

University of California, Berkeley Extension (www.unex.berkeley.edu). Certificate in Technology Transfer and Commercialization

World Intellectual Property Organization (www.wipo.int). (1) Primer on Intellectual Property (online); (2) General Course on Intellectual Property (online); (3) Introduction to the Patent Cooperation Treaty (online); (4) Copyright and Related Rights (online); (5) Biotechnology and Intellectual Property (online); (6) Patents (online); (7) Trademarks, Industrial Designs and Geographic Indications (online); (8) Arbitration and Mediation Procedure Under the WIPO Rules (online); (9) Patent Information Search

(online); (10) Basics of Patent Drafting (online)

University of San Diego (www.sandiego.edu). Intellectual Property Professional Certificate

Northeastern University (www.spcs.neu.edu). Graduate Certificate in Intellectual Property

New York University School of Continuing and Professional Studies (http://www.scps.nyu.edu). Certificate in Intellectual Property Law

Foundation for Advanced Education in the Sciences (http://faes.org/grad/certificate_programs/technology_transfer). Technology Transfer Certificate Program

Intelligence, Homeland Security & National Security

Texas A&M University (www.tamu.edu). (1) Graduate Certificate in Homeland Security; (2) Certified Training Professional

Post University Online (www.post.edu/online). Criminal Justice Certificate in Homeland Security

Michigan State University (www.msu.edu). Online Certificate in Homeland Security Studies

Point Park University (www.pointpark.edu). Certificate in Intelligence and National Security

University of New Haven (www.newhaven.edu). National Security Certificate

American Military University (www.amu.apus.edu). (1) Graduate Certificate in Homeland Security; (2) Graduate Certificate in Intelligence Studies; (3) Graduate Certificate in National Security Studies

George Washington University (www.gwu.edu). International Security Policy Certificate

Long Island University (www.southampton.liu.edu). Advanced Certificate in Homeland Security Management (online)

Penn State University (www.worldcampus.psu.edu/certificates.shtml). (1) Certificate in Bioterrorism Preparedness (online); (2) Graduate Certificate in Disaster Preparedness (online)

Eastern Kentucky University (www.eku.edu). Certificate in Homeland Security (online)

International Affairs & Business

St. Thomas University (FL) School of Law (www.stu.edu/lawschool). Certificates in the International Tax Law Program: (1) International Financial Centers; (2) United States Taxation; (3) E-Commerce; (4) Anti-Money Laundering & Compliance; (5) Trusts and Estate Planning

Illinois Institute of Technology, Chicago-Kent College of Law (www.kentlaw.edu). Certificate in International Law & Practice

Hamline University School of Law (www.hamline.edu/law). Certificate in Global Arbitration Law and Practice

Pace Law School (www.law.pace.edu). Certificate in International Law

Ellis College of New York Institute of Technology (http://ellis.nyit.edu). Graduate Certificate-International Business (online)

University of Maryland University College (www.umuc.edu). Certificate in International Trade (online)

World Trade Organization (www.wto.org). (1) Dispute Settlement System Training Module; (2) General Agreement on Trade in Services

University of the Pacific (http://web.pacific.edu). International Trade Certificate Program

Berkeley City College (http://berkeley.peralta.edu). International Trade Certificate of Completion

Long Island University (www.liu.edu). United Nations Advanced Certificate On-Line

International Import-Export Institute (http://expandglobal.com). (1) Certified International Trade Law Specialist; (2) Certified U.S. Export Compliance Officer; (3) Certified International Trade Manager; (4) Certified International Trade Professional; (5) Certified International Trade Marketing Specialist; (6) Certified International Trade Documentation Specialist; (7) Certified International Trade Logistics Specialist; (8) Certified International Trade Finance Specialist; (9) Certified Exporter; (10) Certified International Trade Educator

International Maritime Law Institute (www.imli.org). (1) Certificate: General Introduction to Public International Law; (2) Certificate: The Law of International Institutions; (3) Certificate: Introduction to Shipping Law; (4) Certificate: International Marine Environmental Law; (5) Certificate: Maritime Legislation Drafting; (6) Certificate: EC Maritime and Shipping Law; (7) International Law of the Sea Certificates: (a) Introduction to the International Law of the Sea; (b) The High Seas Legal Status and Freedoms; (c) Common Heritage of Mankind; (d) Coastal Zone Regimes; (e) Fisheries;

(f) LLS & GDS; (g) Marine Scientific Research; (h) International Dispute Settlement; (8) Shipping Law Certificates: (a) Nationality, Registration and Ownership of Ships; (b) Proprietary Interests in Ships; (c) Enforcement of Maritime Claims; (d) Carriage of Goods by Sea; (e) Carriage of Passengers and their Luggage; (f) Maritime Labour Law; (g) Law of Maritime Safety; (h) Law of Marine Collisions; (i) Law of Salvage and Wreck; (j) Law of General Average; (k) Law of Towage; (l) Law of Marine Pilotage; (m) Global Limitation of Liability; (n) Law of Marine Insurance

George Washington University (www.gwu.edu). 1) International Security Policy Certificate; (2) International Science and Technology Policy Certificate; (3) International Trade Policy Certificate

Southern New Hampshire University (www.snhu.edu). (1) Certificate in International Business (online); (2) Certificate in International Finance (online)

Thunderbird School of Global Management (www.thunderbird.edu). (1) Executive Certificate in International Management (online); (2) Doing Business in China Certificate (online)

World Intellectual Property Organization (www.wipo.int). (1) Introduction to the Patent Cooperation Treaty (online); (2) Trademarks, Industrial Designs and Geographic Indications (online); (3) Arbitration and Mediation Procedure Under the WIPO Rules (online)

Hofstra University (http://www.hofstra.edu/Academics/grad/grad_postbacc.html). International Business Certificate

Investigations

Utica College (www.utica.edu). Financial Crimes Investigator Certificate

Association of Certified Fraud Examiners (www.acfe.com). Certified Fraud Examiner Designation

Center for Legal Studies (www.legalstudies.com). Graduate Certificate in Legal Investigation

Southern New Hampshire University (www.snhu.edu). Certificate in Forensic Accounting and Fraud Examination

Association of Certified Anti-Money Laundering Specialists (www.acams.org). Anti-Money Laundering Specialist Certificate

Investment Banking

New York University (www.nyu.edu). Certificate in Investment Banking

Journalism

University of Massachusetts (http://umass.edu). Online Certificate of Journalism

Labor & Employment

eCornell (www.ecornell.com). Foundations of Employee Relations Certificate

Rutgers University (www.rutgers.edu). Public Sector Labor Relations Certificate Program

Mountain States Employers' Council (www.msec.org). (1) Employment Law Certificate Program; (2) Unions: Labor Relations Certificate Program; (3) Employee Handbooks: Revising or Developing; (4) Mediating Workplace Disputes; (5) Workplace Risk Management Certificate Program

University of California-Davis Extension (http://extension.ucdavis.edu/certificates/). (1) Certificate in Labor-Management Relations; (2) Specialized Studies Program in Employee Relations

Columbia Southern University (www.columbiasouthern.edu). Employment Law Specialist - Certification Program

Expert Rating (www.expertrating.com). Employment Law Certification (online)

CAI (www.capital.org). Employment Law Certification Series

City University of New York (www.workered. org). The Murphy Institute - The Graduate Certificate in Labor Studies

Law and Business

University of Pennsylvania (http://executiveeducation.wharton.upenn. edu). Wharton School - Wharton Business and Law Certificate

Hofstra University (http://www.hofstra.edu/ Academics/grad/grad_postbacc.html). International Business Certificate

Law Office Management

Florida International University Legal Studies Institute (www.fiu.edu). Law Office Management Certificate

Association of Legal Administrators (www.alanet.org). Certified Legal Manager Program

Legal Marketing

University of Miami (www.educationmiami.edu). The UM Marketing Program for Lawyers

Legislation

Georgetown University Government Affairs Institute (http://gai.georgetown.edu). Certificate Program in Legislative Studies

Licensing

International Licensing Industry Merchandisers Association (www.licensing.org). Certificate in Licensing

Licensing Executives Society (www.usa-canada. les.org). Intellectual Asset Management Certificates

U.S. Department of Agriculture Graduate School (www.grad.usda.gov). Technology Transfer Program

University of California, Berkeley Extension (www.unex.berkeley.edu). Certificate in Technology Transfer and Commercialization

Life Sciences

American Health Lawyers Association (www.healthlawyers.org). Life Sciences Law Institute

Indiana University Kelley School of Business (http://kelley.iu.edu). Kelley Executive Certificate in the Business of Life Sciences (ECBLS)

University of Buffalo (www.buffalo.edu). Life Sciences Certificate Program

Local Government

University of Missouri (www.umsl.edu/divisions/ graduate/ppa/local-gov/certificate.html). St. Louis - Graduate Certificate Program in Local Government Management

Negotiation

University of Notre Dame Mendoza School of Business (www.nd.edu). (1) Executive Certificate in Negotiation (online); (2) Advanced Negotiations Certificate (online)

Center for International Humanitarian Cooperation (www.cihc.org). Humanitarian Negotiators Training Course

Nonprofit Management

Capella University (www.capella.edu). Graduate Certificate in Management of Non-Profit Agencies

American Society of Association Executives
(www.asaecenter.org). Certified Association
Executive

Duke University
(http://www.learnmore.duke.edu). Nonprofit
Management Certificate

Arizona State University (www.asu.edu).
Graduate Certificate Program in Nonprofit
Leadership and Management

Northeastern University (www.spcs.neu.edu).
Nonprofit Management Certificate (online
option)

Privacy

International Association of Privacy Professionals
(www.iapp.org). (1) Certified Information
Privacy Professional (CIPP); (2) Certified
Information Privacy Professional/Government
(CIPP/G)

Institute of Consumer Financial Information
(www.icfe.us). Certified Identity Theft Risk
Management Specialist

HIPAA Academy (www.trainforhipaa.com/
certification.html). (1) Certified HIPAA
Administrator; (2) Certified HIPAA
Professional; (3) Certified HIPAA Security
Specialist

American Health Information Management
Association (www.AHIMA.org). AHIMA
Certified in Healthcare Privacy

Joint Commission on Accreditation of Healthcare
Organizations (www.jcaho.org). Privacy
Certification Program for Business Associates

HIPAA Training.Net
(www.training-hipaa.net). (1) Certified HIPAA
Privacy Expert; (2) Certified HIPAA Privacy
Associate

Professional Liability

American Board of Professional Liability
Attorneys (www.abpla.org). (1) Medical
Professional Liability Certificate; (2) Legal
Professional Liability Certificate

Public Administration

Central Michigan University (www.cmich.edu).
Graduate Certificate in Public Administration

Brookings Institution (www.brookings.edu/
execed/certificateprograms.aspx). Certificate in
Public Leadership

Public Policy

North Carolina State University (http://pa.chass.
ncsu.edu/prosStud/gradCert/publicPolicy.php).
Public Policy Certificate Program

University of Houston Hobby Center for Public
Policy (www.uh.edu/hcpp/certification/cpm.
htm). Certified Public Manager Program

University of Southern California
http://www.usc.edu/schools/sppd/programs/
certificate/public_policy.html). Certificate in
Public Policy

City University of New York (www.workered.org).
The Murphy Institute - Graduate Certificate in
Public Administration and Public Policy

American University (www.american.edu).
Graduate Certificate in Public Policy Analysis

Real Estate

University of Wisconsin (www.wisc.edu). Real
Estate Certificate Program

Chartered Realty Investor Society
(www.crisociety.org). CRI Charter Designation:
(1) Chartered Realty Investor One Certification;
(2) Chartered Realty Investor Two Certification

University of California-Davis Extension
(http://extension.ucdavis.edu/certificates/).
Certificate in Land Use and Environmental
Planning

International Right of Way Association - Right
of Way Certification: (1) Asset (Property)
Management; (2) Environmental Negotiation/
Acquisition (www.irwaonline.org)

Regulatory Affairs

Northeastern University (www.spcs.neu.edu). (1)
Biopharmaceutical Domestic Regulatory Affairs;
(2) Biopharmaceutical International Regulatory
Affairs; (3) Medical Devices Regulatory Affairs

San Diego State University (www.ces.sdsu.edu/
regulatoryaffairs.html). Advanced Certificate in
Regulatory Affairs

Lehigh University (www.distance.lehigh.edu).
Certificate in Regulatory Affairs in a Technical
Environment

Securities

Financial Industry Regulatory Agency
(www.finra.com), (1) Compliance Boot Camp;
(2) FINRA Institute at Wharton Certificate
Program

National Regulatory Services
(www.nrs-inc.com). Investment Adviser
Compliance Certificate Program

Tax

University of San Diego School of Law (www.sandiego.edu). The Diploma in Taxation

St. Thomas University (FL) School of Law (www.stu.edu/lawschool). Certificates in the International Tax Law Program:
(1) International Financial Centers; (2) United States Taxation; (3) E-Commerce; (4) Anti-Money Laundering & Compliance; (5) Trusts and Estate Planning

New York University School of Law (www.law.nyu.edu). Advanced Professional Certificate in Taxation

Cleveland State University, Cleveland-Marshall School of Law (www.law.csuohio.edu). Tax Certificate Program

Southern New Hampshire University (www.snhu.edu). Certificate in Taxation

Bentley College (www.bentley.edu). Advanced Professional Certificate in Taxation

National Business Institute (www.nbi-sems.com). Taxation Law Certificate

Technology Transfer

U.S. Department of Agriculture Graduate School (www.grad.usda.gov). Technology Transfer Program

University of California, Berkeley Extension (www.unex.berkeley.edu). Certificate in Technology Transfer and Commercialization

University of Southern California—Marshall School of Business (www.marshall.usc.edu/tccm). Certificate in Technology Commercialization

Trial Advocacy

National Board of Trial Advocacy (www.nbtanet.org). (1) Civil Trial Certificate (online); (2) Criminal Trial Certificate (online); (3) Family Law Certificate (online); (4) Social Security Disability Certificate (online)

National College for DUI Defense (www.ncdd.com). DUI Defense Law Certificate

Training

Texas A&M University (www.tamu.edu). Certified Training Professional

International Import-Export Institute (http://expandglobal.com). Certified International Trade Educator

Victims' Rights

Center for Legal Studies (www.legalstudies.com). Graduate Certificate in Victim Advocacy

Water Law

United Nations Educational, Scientific and Cultural Organization (www.unesco.org). Water & Environmental Law and Institutions

Oregon State University (http://ecampus. oregonstate.edu). Water Conflict Management Graduate Certificate (online)

Wealth Management

University of California, Irvine (www.uci.edu). Personal Financial Planning Certificate

New York Institute of Finance (www.nyif.com). Professional Certificate in Wealth Management

What Can You Do With a Law Degree? 800+ Options

The following 800+ law-related job titles, arranged into 30 broad career fields, derive from career transitions made by (1) the author's clients, and (2) other attorneys who moved from law to a law-related career and shared their experiences with the author.

Alternative Dispute Resolution
Adjudications Officer (Immigration)
Administrative Judge
Administrative Law Judge
ADR Intake Specialist
Alternative Dispute Resolution Coordinator
Arbitration Administrator
Arbitrator
Asylum Officer
Civil Mediation Program Manager
Community Relations Representative
Conciliator
Consumer Complaints Manager
Contractor Industrial Relations Specialist
Convenor
Court ADR Resources Director
Director of Student Mediation and Dispute
    Resolution
Dispute Resolution Consultant
Dispute Resolution Professional
Domestic Relations Mediation Program Manager
Domestic Relations Mediator
Domestic Resolution Specialist
Early Dispute Resolution Manager
Equal Employment Manager (Complaints and
    Resolution)
Fair Housing Specialist
Facilitator
Family Mediator
Family Support Magistrate
Foreclosure Mediator
Health Care Ombudsman
Hearing Officer
Loan Modification Mediator
Mediation Analyst
Mediation Coordinator
Mediation Trainer
Mediator
Neutral Advisor
Ombudsman
Ombudsman for Private Property Rights
Settlement Judge
Small Claims Mediation Program Manager

Small Claims Mediator
Structured Settlements Professional

Civil Rights
Accessibility/Compliance Specialist
Advocacy Coordinator
Affirmative Action Specialist
ADA Coordinator
ADA Compliance Manager
Civil Rights Analyst
Civil Rights Coordinator
Civil Rights/Affirmative Action Investigator
Community Relations Specialist
Conciliation Specialist
Cultural Diversity Director
Equal Opportunity Compliance Specialist
EEO Manager/Officer
Human Rights Administrator
Judiciary AA/EEO Investigator
Legal Compliance Officer

College and University Administration
Law School
Academic Compliance Affairs
Academic Support Program Coordinator
Advocacy Programs Director/ Assistant
Career Placement Officer
Career Services Counselor/Officer
Cooperative Legal Education Coordinator
Clinical Program Supervisor
Development/Fundraising
Director of Admissions
Director of Alumni Affairs
Director of Institutional Advancement
Director of Marketing
Director of Student Affairs
Faculty Computer Consultant
Law Librarian
Law Librarian—Electronic Services
Law Information Technology Director
Legal Education Director
Publication Support Specialist
Researcher

Campus Administration

Affirmative Action/EEO Officer
Agricultural Mediation Service Negotiator
Assistant to the President/Chancellor
Athletic Conference Compliance
Business Affairs Director/Officer
Chief of Staff to President
Clinical Risk Specialist
Contract Staff Analyst
Contract Specialist
Compliance Officer
Corporate Liaison Officer
Director of Corporate Compliance
Director of State Compliance
Director of Student Mediation and Dispute
    Resolution
Disability Services Coordinator
Discrimination Investigator
Diversity Management Director
Employee Relations Specialist
Environmental Programs Professional
Equity Coordinator
Estate Recovery Case Coordinator
Ethics Officer
Federal/State Relations Professional
Governance Officer
Grants and Contract Compliance Specialist
Grants and Contracts Manager
Healthcare Licensing Manager
Human Resources Director
Immigration Specialist
Immigration Compliance Officer
International Student Affairs Coordinator
Judicial Affairs Officer
Labor Relations Specialist
Laboratory Business Manager
Land Use Director
Legislative Affairs Professional
Mediator
Ombudsman
Paralegal Program/School Administrator
Planned/Deferred Giving Officer/Director
Policy Development Specialist
Pre-Law Advisor
Public Policy Associate
Real Estate Acquisitions and Leasing Specialist
Real Estate Director/Officer
Real Estate Ventures Director
Risk Manager
Security Compliance Officer
Sexual Harassment Counselor
Sponsored Research Officer
Student Affairs Professional
Student Conflict Resolution Coordinator

Student Legal Affairs Officer
Subcontracts Manager
Technology Licensing Associate
Trademark Licensing Officer
Trust Officer
Trusts and Estates Officer
University Press Legal Editor

College and University Teaching
Law School
Academic Support Instructor
Assistant/Associate/Full Professor
Clinical Program Director
Clinical Program Director/Instructor
Foreign Law School Professor/Lecturer
Legal Research and Writing Instructor

Undergraduate/Graduate
Business Law Professor
Criminal Justice Program Instructor
Dispute Resolution Teacher
Environmental Policy Teacher
Ethics Instructor
Labor Relations Instructor
Law and Anthropology Professor
Law and Economics Professor
Law and History Professor
Law and Psychology Professor
Law and Society Professor
Legal Administration Professor
Legal Studies Program Coordinator
Legal Studies Program Teacher
Paralegal Program Instructor
Real Estate Instructor
Security Assistance Management Instructor
Tax Instructor

Contracts, Procurement, and Grants
Competition Advocate
Contract Negotiator
Contract Administrator/Manager
Contract Specialist/Officer
Contract Staff Analyst
Contract Termination Specialist
Contract and Rights Manager
Federal Contract Compliance EEO Specialist
Grants Administration Specialist
Grants Supervisor
Industrial Property Manager
Master Negotiator
Procurement Officer/Analyst
Purchasing Officer/Director
Self-Determination Specialist
Small Business Advocate

Subcontracts Manager
Technology Transfer Professional
Transactions Coordinator

Corporate, Law Firm and Government Legal Training
Legal Trainer
Persuasion Consultant

Court Administration
ADR Project Coordinator
ADR Resources Director
Alternative Sanctions Coordinator
Assistant Circuit Executive for Legal Affairs
Assistant District Executive for Legal Affairs
Attorney Admissions Deputy
Bankruptcy Administrator
Bankruptcy Appeals Clerk
Bankruptcy Case Administration Manager
Bankruptcy Examiner
Bankruptcy Group Manager
Bar Admissions Administrator
Case Calendaring Clerk
Circuit/District Court Executive
Clerk of Court
Court Administrator
Court Analyst
Court Improvement Programs Manager
Court Mental Health Services Manager
Court Operations Specialist
Court Services Director
Court Technology Advisor
Deputy Clerk
Disciplinary Administrator
Estate/Probate Administrator
Friend of the Court
Government Relations Specialist
Guardian Ad Litem
Guardianship Clerk
Jury Commissioner
Land Commissioner
Legal Documents Officer/Supervisor
Legal Research Director
Legal Researcher
Parole Officer
Pretrial Services Officer
Probation Director
Probation Officer
Public Guardian
Registrar
Reporter of Decisions
Settlement Director
Supervisor of Public Trust Accounts
Support Payments Officer

Training Professional
Victim Services/Restitution Coordinator
Violations Bureau Manager

Criminal Justice and Law Enforcement
Alcohol, Tobacco and Firearms Inspector
Asset Forfeiture Specialist
Bank Fraud Investigator
Border Patrol Agent
Child Abuse Investigator
Child Support Enforcement Case Analyst
Civil Penalties Officer
Civilian Complaint Review Board Officer
Compliance Support Inspector
Computer Crime and Security Specialist
Computer Fraud Investigator
Consumer Safety Inspector
Crime Analyst
Crime Prevention Coordinator
Criminal Investigator
Criminal Justice Administrator/Analyst
Criminal Research Specialist
Customs Inspector
Deputy Inspector General for Investigations
DEA Special Agent
Domestic Investigator
Drug Investigator
Economic Crimes Investigator
Employment Investigator
Enforcement Analyst
Enforcement Professional
FBI Special Agent
Federal Trade Investigator
Financial Enforcement Specialist
Fines, Penalties and Forfeiture Specialist
Foreign Service Narcotics Control Officer
Forensic Investigator
Fraud/White Collar Crime Investigator
Fugitive Witness Investigations Specialist
Game Law Enforcement Officer
General Investigator/Inspector
Hidden Assets Investigator
Immigration Inspector
Inspector General
Inspector General Complaints Analysis Specialist
Intellectual Property Loss Investigator
Internal Affairs Director
Investigations Review Specialist
Law Enforcement Coordination Manager
Law Enforcement Specialist
Missing Persons Investigator
Municipal Code Enforcement Officer
Postal Inspector
Private Investigator

Revenue Officer/Agent
Securities Fraud Examiner
Seized Property Specialist
Software Piracy and Licensing Abuse
   Investigator
Special Agent (Wildlife)
Treasury Enforcement Agent
Victims Compensation Officer
Victim Services Manager
Welfare Investigator
White Collar Prison Counselor

Energy and Natural Resources
Carbon Transactions Manager
Compliance Enforcement Analyst
Compliance Enforcement Analyst-Mitigation/
   Reporting
Compliance Program Auditor
Director of Nuclear Licensing
Energy Advocate
Energy Conservation Program Specialist
Energy Efficiency Program Manager
Energy Regulatory Affairs Professional
Energy Trading Compliance Officer
Landman (Oil and Gas)
Land Agent
Manager of Compliance
Mineral Appeals Analyst
Natural Resources Specialist
Nuclear Regulatory Affairs Director
Oil and Gas Leasing Policy Analyst
Public Utilities Specialist
Rate Analyst
Regulatory Projects Manager
Regulatory Representative
Renewable Energy Program Specialist
Right-of-Way Manager
Transmission Right-of-Way Specialist
Utility Contract Administration Analyst

Environmental Careers
Advisor, Regulatory Management
Carbon Transactions Manager
Coastal Zone Resources Manager
Conservation Field Representative
Director of Environmental Affairs
Director, Legislative Analysis Environmental
   Policy Professional
Environmental/Public Health Advocate
Environmental Claims Examiner
Environmental Compliance Manager
Environmental Consultant
Environmental Ombudsman
Environmental Planning Manager

Environmental Policy Analyst
Environmental Protection Specialist
Environmental Public Participation Specialist
Global Government Affairs Director
Hazardous Waste Management Consultant
Land Protection Specialist
Marine Resource Management Specialist
Remediation Specialist
Resource Policy Analyst
Safety and Occupational Health Specialist
Technological Program Hazards Specialist
Trade Association Environmental Staffer

Ethics/Professional Responsibility
Attorney Ethics Coordinator
Attorney Ethics Investigator
Bar Disciplinary Manager
Client Protection Fund Director/Officer
Code of Ethics Compliance Manager
Corporate Ethics Director/Officer
Ethics Advisor
Ethics Auditor
Ethics Commission Director/Officer
Ethics Program Specialist
Ethics Researcher
Ethics Trainer
Governmental Ethics Manager
Health Professions Investigator
Hospital Ethicist
Judicial Disabilities Commission Investigator
Lawyer Assistance Program Director
License Examining Specialist
Manager of Compliance and Ethics
Professional Licensing Officer
Professional Regulation Compliance Analyst
Situational Awareness and Ethics Officer
Unauthorized Practice of Law Advisor
Unauthorized Practice of Law Investigator

Financial Services
Bank International Trade Specialist
Bank Investment Compliance Officer
Bank Probate Administrator/Officer
Banking Enforcement Advisor
Bankruptcy Analyst
Benefits Professional
Capital Market Consultant
Carbon Transactions Manager
Chapter 13 Trustee
Claims/Settlement/Termination Specialist
Commercial Lending Manager
Community Reinvestment Act Director
Compliance Manager
Compliance Officer (Bank Regulation)

Compliance Officer (Commercial Banking)
Compliance Officer (Commodities)
Compliance Officer (Securities)
Compliance Representative
Compliance Trust Officer
Conflicts of Interest Oversight Officer
Consumer Affairs Examiner
Corporate Finance Executive
Credit Examiner
Employee Benefits Trust Administrator
Equities Compliance Officer
Escrow Agent
Estate/Fiduciary Administrator
Estate and Financial Planner
Financial Enforcement Specialist
Financial Institution Examiner
Financial Planner/Planning Analyst
Financial Services Sales Agent
Futures Trading Investigator
Investment Banking Officer
Legal Advertising/Sales Literature Manager
Legal Fee Auditor/Legal Cost Specialist
Legal Product Manager-Corporate
Legal Product Manager-Private Label Funds
Legal Product Manager-Securities/Brokerage
Loan Administrator/Specialist
Loan Workout Officer
Mergers and Acquisitions Specialist
Mutual Fund Administrator
Pension Benefits Examiner
Pension Law Specialist
Probate Accountant
Public Finance Consultant
Regulatory Control Officer
Securities Compliance Examiner
Securities Firm Executive
Securities Transactions Analyst
Trust Advisor
Trust Benefits Specialist
Trust Business Development Professional
Trust Examiner
Trust Officer/Administrator
Trust Property Manager
Trust Risk Analyst
U.S. Trustee/Assistant U.S. Trustee
Workers' Compensation Auditor

Healthcare
Contract Negotiator
Director, Pharmaceutical Sales and Marketing
   Compliance
Health Plan Member Services Coordinator
Healthcare Compliance Officer
Healthcare Fraud Investigator

Health Care Ombudsman
Hospital Planned Giving Professional
Hospital Contracts/Procurement Officer
Hospital Risk Manager
JCAHO Policy Writer
Legal Services Specialist
Nursing Home Investigator
Patient Rights Advocate
Quarantine Investigator
Sanctions Associate

Human Resources
Employee Benefit Plan Specialist
Employee Disability Programs Manager
Employee Relations Manager/Specialist
Employment and Training Specialist
Government Benefits Director
Human Resources Compliance Officer
Human Resources Director
Lawyer Temporary Agency Manager
Legal Career Counselor
Legal Search Consultant
Manpower Development Specialist
Personnel Management Specialist
Professional Standards Administrator
Reemployment Rights Compliance Specialist
Retirement Systems Administrator
Salary Administration Specialist
Social Security Disability Claimant
   Representative
Veterans Program Specialist
Veterans Reemployment Rights Specialist

Human Services
Aging Services Program Specialist
Child Support Collection Specialist
Children's Advocate
Director of Human Relations
Elder Rights Specialist/Advocate
Geriatric Care Manager/Advocate
Long-Term Care Ombudsman
Mental Healthcare Ombudsman
Women's Rights Advocate/Domestic
Abuse Specialist

Insurance and Risk Management
Bankruptcy Claims Examiner
Casualty Claims Specialist
Civil Service Retirement Claims Examiner
Claims Legal and Regulatory Compliance
Claims Representative/Manager
Commercial Claims Specialist
Dependent and Estates Claims Examiner
Document Compliance Specialist

Environmental Claims Specialist
Errors and Omissions Claims Manager
General Agent
General Claims Examiner
Health Benefits Program Analyst
Health Care Policy Analyst
Health Insurance Specialist
Health Plan Member Services Coordinator
Insurance Agent (Life, Health, and Disability)
Insurance Agent (Property and Casualty)
Insurance Claims Representative
Insurance Consultant
Insurance Fraud Investigator
Insurance Licensing Administrator
Insurance Licensing Consultant
Insurance Market Conduct Examiner
Insurance Officer
Insurance Policy Analyst
Insurance Services Practice Group Head
Insurance Specialist
Issuing Specialist
Liability Claims Analyst
Litigation Examiner
Litigation Manager
Loss and Damage Claims Examiner
Medical Malpractice Claims Analyst
Pension Investigator
Personal Trust Product Manager
Professional Liability Claims Analyst
Professional Liability Insurance Marketer
Professional Liability Underwriter
Recovery Manager
Risk Analyst
Risk Manager
Social Insurance Administrator
Social Insurance Claims Examiner
Transportation Claims Examiner
Unemployment Insurance Administrator
Veterans Claims Examiner
Workers' Compensation Claims Examiner
Workers' Compensation Program Specialist

Intellectual Property
Applications Examiner
Chief Intellectual Property Officer
Chief Strategy Officer
Conveyance Examiner
Copyright Examiner
Corporate Copyright Specialist
Corporate Director of Licensing
Foreign Filing Specialist
Health Care Licensing Manager
Intellectual Asset Manager
Intellectual Property Commercialization
  Specialist

Intellectual Property Director/Manager
Intellectual Property Resources Director
Intellectual Property Rights Enforcement
Intellectual Property Strategist
Licensing Manager/Specialist
Patent Administrator
Patent Analyst
Patent Examiner
Patentability Review Examiner
Patent/Technology Licensing Officer
Rights Manager
Technology Transfer Outreach Professional
Technology Manager - IP
Technology Transfer Director
Trademark Examiner
Trademark Legal Manager

Intelligence/Security
Aviation Security Specialist/Officer
CIA Clandestine Service Agent
Foreign Assets Control Intelligence Analyst
Foreign Service Diplomatic Security Officer
Industrial Property Clearance Specialist
Industrial Security Specialist/Officer
Information Security Consultant
Information Security Specialist/Officer
Intelligence Officer
Intelligence Research Specialist
Internal Security Specialist/Officer
Munitions Export Control Specialist
Personnel Security Specialist/Officer
Physical Security Specialist/Officer
Premises Security Consultant
Security Administration Specialist/Officer
Security Assistance Analyst
Security Classification Specialist/Officer
Security Inspector

International Affairs, Trade, and Investment
Commercial Loan Specialist
Commercial Operations Specialist
Country Risk Analyst
Customs Entry and Liquidation Specialist
Economic Development Director
Economic Development Project Officer
Export Administrator/Manager
Export Control Specialist
Export Credit Manager
Export Factor
Export Insurance Issuing Specialist
Financial Institution Reform Advisor
Foreign Affairs Specialist
Foreign Service Officer
Foreign Trade Zone Manager

Immigration/Benefits Coordinator
Import Compliance Specialist
Import/Export Manager
International Affairs Specialist
International Agency Liaison Officer
International Human Rights Advisor
International Relations Officer
International Trade Specialist
International Trade Consultant
Library Foreign Law Specialist
Manager of Export/Import Compliance
Manager of Global Trading Documentation
Munitions Export Control Specialist
Passport and Visa Examiner
Political Risk Insurance Officer
Tariff and Regulatory Supervisor
Trade Documentation Officer
U.S. Commercial Service Officer

Labor Relations
Industrial Relations Specialist
HR Manager—Labor Relations
Labor Investigator
Labor Management Relations Examiner
Labor Negotiator/Mediator
Labor Relations Clearinghouse Staff
Labor Relations Consultant
Labor Relations Manager/Specialist/Analyst
Labor Relations Planning and Analysis Manager
Labor Relations Specialist
NLRB Field Examiner
Wage and Hour Law Administrator
Wage and Hour Law Compliance Specialist

Legal Administration
Bar Association Professional
CLE Administrator
CLE Training Manager/Specialist
Director of Complex Case Support
Director of Knowledge Management
Law Firm Administrator/Executive Director
Law Firm Management Consultant
Law Firm Marketing Director
Law Firm Trainer
Law Firm Recruiter
Legal Services Program Executive Director
Practice Area Coordinator
Pro Bono Coordinator
Professional Relations Coordinator

Legal Documents/Information/Research
Analyst in Social Legislation
Archivist (Legal)
Economic Research Analyst

Freedom of Information/Privacy Officer
Information Management Specialist
Law Librarian
Law Library Computer Network Manager
Legal Database Manager
Legal Historian
Legal Information Analyst
Legal Instruments Examiner
Legal Researcher
Legal Writer
Public Disclosure Officer
Senior Paralegal
Social Science Research Analyst
Technical Legal Information Specialist

Legislative and Regulatory Affairs
Congressional Affairs Specialist
Congressional Inquiries Program Manager
Congressional Liaison Specialist
Food Program Specialist
Governmental Affairs/Relations Positions
Intergovernmental Affairs Specialist
Legislative Affairs Specialist/Legislative
Analyst/Legislative Director
Legislative Assistant
Legislative Coordinator
Legislative Correspondent
Legislative Drafter
Legislative Program Manager
Legislative Representative
Legislative Staff Director
Lobbyist
Manager of Regulatory Affairs
Policy Advocate
Policy Analyst
Legislative Committee Staff Member
Program Integrity Specialist
Regulations/Rulings Specialist
Regulatory Analyst
Regulatory Compliance Director
Regulatory Impact Analyst
Regulatory Program Specialist
Regulatory Implementation Manager
Telecommunications Regulatory Analyst

Litigation Management/Support
Alternative Sentencing Consultant
Case Assessment Consultant
Director of Complex Case Support
Jury Selection Advisor
Law Firm Director of Litigation Services
Litigation Analyst
Litigation Management Professional
Litigation Management Trainer

Litigation Support Consultant/Specialist
Litigation Support Project Manager
Trial Consultant

Management and Administration
Acquisitions/Divestiture Professional
Association Executive
Automobile Dealer Performance Manager
City/County Clerk/Administrator
Corporate Secretary
Elections Administration Officer
Emergency Management Specialist
Federal Aid Administrator
Foundation Executive/Program Manager
Grants Management Specialist
Industry Specialist
Law Office Management Specialist
Management Analyst
Nonprofit Advocacy Organization Manager
Program Analyst/Officer
Sports Franchise General Manager
Unclaimed Property Administrator

Marketing and Development
Bar Review Regional Director
Business Broker
Gift and Estate Planning Professional
Economic Development Officer
Franchise Development Manager
Law Firm Director of Client Relations
Law Firm Business Development Editor
Law Firm Client Development Director
Legal Cost Management Sales Consultant
Legal Publishing Sales Representative
Public Participation Specialist

Media and Entertainment
Acquisitions Editor
Law Correspondent/Reporter
Law Firm Business Development Editor
Legal Editor
Legal Newspaper/Journal Publisher
Legal Publisher Account Representative
Literary Agent
New Product Development Professional
Public Affairs Specialist
Sports/Talent Agent
Technical Publications Writer/Editor
   (Legal)

Real Estate/Housing
Community Development Block Grant
   Coordinator
Development Specialist
Director of Real Estate
Fair Housing Community Educator
Fair Housing Test Coordinator
Housing Advocate
Housing Authority Director/Professional
Housing Programs Administrator
Housing Services Planner
Land Agent
Land Acquisition Manager
Land Law Examiner
Land Manager
Land Preservation Director
Land Protection Director/Specialist
Lease Negotiator
Real Estate Auction Project Manager
Realty Specialist/Officer
Register of Deeds
Right-of-Way Agent
Tenant's Broker
Title Examiner
Zoning Administrator

Taxation
Estate Tax Examiner
International Tax Analyst
Property and Transaction Tax Manager
Tax Agent
Tax Compliance Manager
Tax Law Specialist
Tax Manager/Tax Planning Manager
Tax Research Manager/Professional
Technical Services Manager
Trust Tax Manager

Transportation
Admeasurer
Boating Law Administrator
Highway Safety Specialist
Marine Inspector
Marine Transportation Policy Analyst
Traffic Management Specialist
Transportation Specialist
Transportation Safety Consultant
Trucking Compliance Specialist
Vessel Traffic Specialist

Selected International Organizations Hiring American Attorneys for JD-Preferred Positions

Each of the listed organizations also has at least one general legal office in addition to its law-related offices:

Organization of American States (Washington, DC) www.oas.org. Inter-American Commission on Human Rights, Inter-American Drug Abuse Control Commission

Inter-American Development Bank (Washington, DC) www.iadb.org. Independent Investigation Mechanism, Office of the Ombudsperson

Pan American Health Organization (Washington, DC) www.paho.org. Ombudsperson Office

Bioethics Unit

Asian Development Bank (Manila, Philippines) www.adb.org. Office of the Compliance Review Panel

International Bank for Reconstruction & Development (World Bank) (Washington, DC) www.worldbank.org.
- Department of Institutional Integrity
- Governance Group
- Office of the Ombudsman
- Mediation Services
- Office of Ethics and Business Conduct
- International Finance Corporation

Office of the Compliance Advisor and Ombudsman

Investor and Corporate Practice Unit

Foreign Investment Advisory Service. Multilateral Investment Guaranty Agency

Legal Affairs and Claims Department

International Monetary Fund (Washington, DC) www.imf.org. Ethics Office

United Nations Headquarters (New York, NY) www.un.org
- UN Development Programme
- UN Office of the Ombudsman
- UN Department of Political Affairs
- UN Office of Internal Oversight Services
- UN Office for Disarmament Affairs
- UN Division for the Advancement of Women
- Women's Rights Section. UN Department of Peacekeeping Operations, UN Office for the Coordination of Humanitarian Affairs

UN Office on Drugs and Crime (Vienna, Austria) www.unodc.org
- Global Programme against Money Laundering
- Global Programme against Corruption
- Global Programme against Organized Crime
- Global Programme against Trafficking in Human Beings
- Terrorism Prevention Branch
- The Commission on Crime Prevention and Criminal Justice. 150 Field Offices Worldwide

UN Office of the High Commissioner for Human Rights (Geneva, Switzerland) www.ohchr.org
- Treaties and Commission Branch
- Special Procedures Branch
- Research and Right to Development Branch. 38 Field Offices Worldwide

UN Environment Programme (Nairobi, Kenya) www.unep.org. Division of Environmental Policy Implementation, Division of Regional Cooperation

UN Commission on International Trade Law (Vienna, Austria) www.uncitral.org

UN Conference on Trade and Development (Geneva, Switzerland) www.unctad.org. Trade Negotiations and Commercial Diplomacy Branch

UN Refugee Agency (Geneva, Switzerland) www.unhcr.org. Protection Operations and Legal Advice Section

World Trade Organization (Geneva, Switzerland) www.wto.org. Secretariat
• Accessions Division
• Council and Trade Negotiations Committee Division
• Intellectual Property Division
• Market Access Division
• Rules Division
• Trade and Environment Division
• Trade and Finance and Trade Facilitation Division
• Trade Policies Review Division

General Council
Dispute Settlement Body

Trade Policy Review Body

International Labour Organization (Geneva, Switzerland) www.ilo.org

Social Dialogue, Labor Law & Labor Administration Department

ILO Ethics Office

Office of the Mediator
Organization for Economic Cooperation and Development (Paris, France) www.oecd.org

International Energy Agency. Corporate Affairs Division, Centre for Tax Policy and Administration, Policy Co-ordination Division (Development Co-operation Directorate)

World Intellectual Property Organization (Geneva, Switzerland) www.wipo.org

PCT (Patent Cooperation Treaty) and Patents Mediation and Arbitration Center and Global Intellectual Property Issues
• PCT Legal Publication Section
• Domain Name Dispute Resolution Section
• Global IP Issues Division
• Institutional Relations Section

Copyright and Related Rights Sector
Copyright Collective Management and Related Issues Division

International Registrations Department

Law and International Classifications Division
Office of Strategic Use of Intellectual Property for Development
• Intellectual Property and New Technologies Division
• Intellectual Property and Economic Development Division
• Division for Public Policy and Development

Internet Corporation for Assigned Names and Numbers (ICANN)(Marina del Rey, CA) www. icann.org

European Bank for Reconstruction and Development (London, UK) www.ebrd.com

Office of the Chief Compliance Officer

The Organization for the Prohibition of Chemical Weapons (The Hague, The Netherlands) www. opcw.org.

International Cooperation and Assistance Division
Wassenaar Arrangement on Export Controls and Dual-Use Goods and Technologies (Vienna, Austria) www.wassenaar.org

Organization for Cooperation and Security in Europe (Vienna, Austria) www.ocse.org. Secretariat

Anti-Trafficking Assistance Unit
Conflict Prevention Centre

Office for Democratic Institutions and Human Rights
Democratization Department

Human Rights Department

Elections Department

Contact Point on Roma and Sinti Issues

Program on Tolerance and Non-Discrimination

Universal Postal Union (Berne, Switzerland) www.upu.int. Economic and Regulatory Affairs Directorate

World Health Organization (Geneva, Switzerland) www.who.int. Ombudsman

International Development Law Organization (Rome, Italy) www.idlo.int. Global Programs

Field Offices in Cairo, Sydney, Kabul, Bishkek, Banda Aceh and Colombo

The International Organization of Securities Commissions (Madrid, Spain) www.iosco.org

Inter-American Institute of Human Rights (San Jose, Costa Rica) www.iidh.ed.cr
- Department of Civil Society Entities
- Department of Public Institutions
- The Center for Electoral Promotion and Assistance

International Institute for the Unification of Private Law (UNIDROIT) (Rome, Italy) www.unidroit.org

International Chamber of Commerce (Paris, France) www.iccwbo.org
- Dispute Boards Centre
- Institute of World Business Law
- Commercial Crime Services

Financial and Investment Fraud Bureau

Counterfeiting Intelligence Bureau

Cybercrime Unit

Convention on Biological Diversity (Montreal, Canada) www.cbd.int. Biosafety Division

Inter-American Center of Tax Administrations (Panama City, Panama) www.ciat.org.
- Executive Secretariat

International Commission of Jurists (Geneva, Switzerland) www.icj.org
- Global Security & Rule of Law Programme
- Judges & Lawyers Programme
- International Economic Relations Programme
- International Law & Protection Programme
- Middle East & North Africa Programme
- Latin America Programme
- Europe/North America & CIS Programme
- Asia-Pacific Programme
- Africa Programme
- Centre for the Independence of Judges and Lawyers

International Confederation of Free Trade Unions (Brussels, Belgium) www.icftu.org

Group on Employment and Labour Standards

Priority Group on Trade Union Rights
International Council on Human Rights Policy (Geneva, Switzerland) www.ichrp.org

Arctic Council Secretariat (TromsØ, Norway) www.arctic-counsel.org

North American Commission for Environmental Cooperation (Montreal, Canada) www.cec.org. Submissions on Enforcement Matters Unit, Law and Policy Program

Commission for Labor Cooperation (Washington, DC) www.naalc.org

Specialized Legal Job-Hunting Resources

Some of the resources listed below contain only attorney jobs; others contain only "JD Preferred" (law-related) jobs; and still others contain both attorney and law-related jobs. Some databases may charge a subscription fee. Others are open only to members of the organization that produces the resource. Most of those organizations charge a membership fee.

Alternative Dispute Resolution

Association for Conflict Resolution (www.acrnet.org)

Association for Student Judicial Affairs (www.asjaonline.org)

Dispute Resolution Employment Opportunities (http://law.pepperdine.edu/straus/careers/jobs.jsp)

Campus Dispute Resolution Jobs (www.campus-adr.org)

Fresno Pacific University Center for Peacemaking & Conflict Studies ADR Jobs (http://peace.fresno.edu/rjjobs.php)

National Association for Community Mediation Jobs (www.nafcm.org)

Banking & Finance

World Bank (www.worldbank.org)

Bank for International Settlements (www.bis.org)

Asian Development Bank (www.adb.org)

Inter-American Development Bank (www.iadb.org)

International Monetary Fund (www.imf.org)

Banking Jobs (www.bankjobs.com)

Securities & Banking Compliance (www.complinet.com)

Children's Law

National Association of Counsel for Children (www.naccchildlaw.org)

Civil Rights

Affirmative Action Register (http://aar-eeo.com)

ACLU Jobs (www.aclu.org/about/jobs/Jobs_post.html)

College & University

Chronicle of Higher Education (www.chronicle.com)

Higher Education Jobs (www.higheredjobs.com)

Council for Advancement & Support of Education (www.case.org)

National Association of College & University Business Officers (www.nacubo.org)

Association of University Technology Managers (www.autm.net)

Association for Student Judicial Affairs (www.asjaonline.org)

College Adjunct Teaching Positions (www.adjunctnation.com)

Student Affairs Administrator Jobs (http://jobslink.naspa.org)

Campus Dispute Resolution Jobs (www.campus-adr.org)

International Collegiate Licensing Association (http://nacda.cstv.com/icla/nacda-icla.html)

Legal Writing Institute (www.lwionline.org)

Compliance

Society of Corporate Compliance & Ethics (www.corporatecompliance.org)

Securities & Banking (www.complinet.com)

Sports Job Opportunities (www.collegesportscareers.com)

National Association of Collegiate Directors of Athletics (http://nacda.cstv.com)

National Collegiate Athletic Association (http://ncaa.thetask.com/market/jobs)

Compliance Jobs (www.jobsinthemoney.com)

Financial Industry Regulatory Authority (www.finra.org)

Health Care Compliance Association (http://hcca-info.org)

Corporations

Association of Corporate Counsel (www.acc.com)

Society of Corporate Secretaries & Governance Professionals (www.governanceprofessionals.org)

Corporate Recovery and Turnaround
Turnaround Management Association (www.turnaround.org)
Association of Insolvency and Restructuring Advisors (www.airacira.org)

Contracts & Procurement
National Contract Management Association (www.ncmahq.org)
U.S. Office of Personnel Management (www.usajobs.gov)

Courts
U.S. Courts (www.uscourts.gov/employment.html)
Alaska Courts (www.state.ak.us/courts/recruit.htm)
California Courts (www.courtinfo.ca.gov/careers/)
Florida Courts (www.flcourts.org/)
Massachusetts Courts (www.mass.gov/courts/jobs)
New York State Courts (www.courts.state.ny.us/careers/)
Pennsylvania Courts (www.jobs.aopc.org/)
Washington State Courts (www.courts.wa.gov/employ)
National Center for State Courts (www.ncsconline.org)

Criminal Law
International Criminal Court (www.icc-cpi.int)
International Criminal Tribunal for Rwanda (http://69.94.11.53/default.htm)
Yugoslav Criminal Tribunal (www.un.org/icty/)
Special Court for Sierra Leone (www.sc-sl.org/jobs.html)
Special Tribunal for Lebanon (approved by UN—establishment pending)
Special Tribunal for Cambodia (approved by UN—establishment pending)
Drug Enforcement Administration (www.justice.gov/dea)

eCommerce
Internet Corporation for Assigned Names and Numbers (www.icann.org). Education Law
National Association of College and University Attorneys (www.nacua.org)
National School Boards Association (www.nsba.org)
Academic Keys for Law (http://law.academickeys.com/)

Energy
Energy Industry Jobs (www.energyjobsnetwork.com). Environmental Law
Earthjustice (www.earthjustice.org)
Land Trust Alliance (www.landtrustalliance.org)
United Nations Environment Programme (www.unep.org)
World Meteorological Organization (www.wmo.ch)

Ethics
Bioethics Jobs (www.bioethics.net)
American Society for Bioethics & Humanities (www.asbh.org)
U.S. Government Inspectors General (www.ignet.gov)

Foundations
Philanthropy News Digest (http://foundationcenter.org)
Chronicle of Philanthropy (www.philanthropy.com)

Government
USAJOBS (www.usajobs.gov)
Capitol Hill Jobs (www.rcjobs.com)
Capitol Hill Jobs (http://thehill.com/employment/)
California State Jobs (www.spb.ca.gov)

Health Law
American Health Lawyers Association (www.ahla.org)
American Society for Healthcare Risk Management (www.ashrm.org)
Healthcare Administration (www.healthcareernet.com)
World Health Organization (www.who.int)
Pan American Health Organization (www.paho.org)
International Red Cross (www.icrc.org)
American Red Cross (www.redcross.org)
Blue Cross Blue Shield Associations (www.resmatic.com/bcbsa/)
Health Care Compliance Association (http://hcca-info.org)

Human Resources
Society for Human Resource Management (www.shrm.org)

Immigration
Immigration Jobs (http://careers.aila.org/hr/)

Information Management/Privacy
Institute of Certified Records Managers
  (www.icrm.org)
International Association of Privacy Professionals
  (www.privacyassociation.org)
International Legal Technology Association
  (www.peertopeer.org)

In-House
Association of Corporate Counsel
  (www.acca.com)

Insurance
Great Insurance Jobs
  (www.greatinsurancejobs.com)

Intellectual Property
World Intellectual Property Organization
  (www.wipo.org)
American Intellectual Property Law Association
  (www.aipla.org)
International Trademark Association
  (www.inta.org)
Internet Corporation for Assigned Names and
  Numbers (www.icann.org)
International Collegiate Licensing Association
  (http://nacda.cstv.com/icla/nacda-icla.html)

International Law
Organization for Economic Cooperation &
  Development (www.oecd.org)
World Trade Organization (www.wto.org)
World Intellectual Property Organization
  (www.wipo.org)
Organization of American States (www.oas.org)
Inter-American Development Bank
  (www.iadb.org)
International Court of Justice (www.icj-cij.org)
International Tribunal for the Law of the Sea
  (www.itlos.org)
International Maritime Organization
  (www.imo.org)
International Monetary Fund (www.imf.org)
Human Rights Watch (www.hrw.org/jobs/)
International Center for Transitional Justice
  (www.ictj.org)
Amnesty International
  (http://web.amnesty.org/jobs)
Human Rights First (www.humanrightsfirst.org)

International Organizations
Organization for Economic Cooperation &
  Development (www.oecd.org)
World Trade Organization (www.wto.org)

World Intellectual Property Organization
  (www.wipo.org)
Human Rights Watch (www.hrw.org/jobs/)
International Center for Transitional Justice
  (www.ictj.org)
Amnesty International
  (http://web.amnesty.org/jobs)
Human Rights First (www.humanrightsfirst.org)
International Criminal Court (www.icc-cpi.int)
International Criminal Tribunal for Rwanda
  (http://69.94.11.53/default.htm)
Yugoslav Criminal Tribunal (www.un.org/icty/)
International Court of Justice (www.icj-cij.org)
United Nations Office for Project Services
  (www.unops.org)
International Tribunal for the Law of the Sea
  (www.itlos.org)
International Maritime Organization
  (www.imo.org)
United Nations Environment Programme
  (www.unep.org)
World Meteorological Organization
  (www.wmo.ch)
Bank for International Settlements (www.bis.org)
Asian Development Bank (www.adb.org)
Inter-American Development Bank
  (www.iadb.org)
International Monetary Fund (www.imf.org)
Organization of American States (www.oas.org)

International Trade
Organization of Women in International Trade
  www.owit.org/en/membership/Index.aspx.
  Labor & Employment
Labor Union Jobs (www.unionjobs.com)

Land Trusts
Land Trust Alliance (www.landtrustalliance.org)

Law Firm "JD Preferred" Jobs
Association of Legal Administrators
  (www.alanet.org)

Legal Journalism
Newspaper Career Bank (www.naa.org)

Legal Services
Legal Services Corporation
  (www.lsc.gov/about/careers.php)
Sargent Shriver National Center on Poverty
  Law (www.povertylaw.org/about-us/job-
  opportunities)
National Legal Aid and Defender Association
  (www.nlada.org/Jobs)

Legislation

National Conference of State Legislatures
(www.ncsl.org)
Capitol Hill Jobs (www.rcjobs.com)
Capitol Hill Jobs (http://thehill.com/employment/)

Licensing/Technology Transfer

Association of University Technology Managers
(www.autm.net)
International Collegiate Licensing Association
(http://nacda.cstv.com/icla/nacda-icla.html)
Technology Transfer Tactics
(http://www.technologytransfertactics.com/
content/job-listings/)

Maritime Law

International Tribunal for the Law of the Sea
(www.itlos.org)
International Maritime Organization
(www.imo.org)

Municipal Law

International Municipal Lawyers Association
(www.imla.org)

Nonprofits

Nonprofit Jobs (www.OpportunityKnocks.org)
Chronicle of Philanthropy
(www.philanthropy.com)
Land Trust Jobs (www.landtrustalliance.org)
Policy Jobs (www.policyjobs.net)
Philanthropy News Digest (http://
foundationcenter.org)
Idealist.org: Action Without Borders
(www.idealist.org)
Nonprofit Career Network
(www.nonprofitcareer.com)
Nonprofit Times (www.nptjobs.com)

Overseas Positions

Organization for Economic Cooperation &
Development (www.oecd.org)
World Trade Organization (www.wto.org)
World Intellectual Property Organization
(www.wipo.org)
National Center for State Courts
(www.ncsconline.org)
Reliefweb Opportunities (www.reliefweb.int)
Human Rights Watch (www.hrw.org/jobs/)
International Center for Transitional Justice
(www.ictj.org)
Amnesty International
(http://web.amnesty.org/jobs)

Human Rights First (www.humanrightsfirst.org)
International Criminal Court (www.icc-cpi.int)
International Criminal Tribunal for Rwanda
(http://69.94.11.53/default.htm)
Yugoslav Criminal Tribunal (www.un.org/icty/)
International Court of Justice (www.icj-cij.org)
United Nations Office for Project Services
(www.unops.org)
International Tribunal for the Law of the Sea
(www.itlos.org)
International Maritime Organization
(www.imo.org)
United Nations Environment Programme
(www.unep.org)
World Meteorological Organization
(www.wmo.ch)
Internet Corporation for Assigned Names and
Numbers (www.icann.org)
Organization of American States (www.oas.org)

Public Interest/Advocacy

American Civil Liberties Union (www.aclu.org)
Amnesty International
(http://web.amnesty.org/jobs)
Human Rights Watch (www.hrw.org/jobs/)
Human Rights First (www.humanrightsfirst.org)
International Center for Transitional Justice
(www.ictj.org)

Public Policy

Policy Jobs (www.policyjobs.net)
National Conference of State Legislatures
(www.ncsl.org)
Capitol Hill Jobs (www.rcjobs.com)
Capitol Hill Jobs (http://thehill.com/employment/)
Government Affairs Jobs
(www.brubach.com/ga.htm)
"Off-the-Hill" Jobs (http://hillzoo.com)
United States Institute of Peace (www.usip.org)

Real Estate

Land Trust Jobs (www.landtrustalliance.org)
Real Estate Investment Trust & Related Jobs
(www.nareit.org)
Pension Real Estate Association (www.prea.org)

Records Management

Association of Record Managers & Administrators
(www.arma.org)

Research Administration

National Council of University Research
Administrators (www.ncura.edu)

Risk Management
American Society for Healthcare Risk
Management (www.ashrm.org)
Risk & Insurance Management Society
(www.rims.org)
Public Risk Management Association
(www.primacentral.org)
Professional Risk Managers International
Association (www.prmia.org)

Securities
Broker Hunter (www.brokerhunter.com)
Financial Industry Regulatory Authority
(www.finra.org)

Sports & Entertainment
Entertainment Careers
(www.entertainmentcareers.net)
Show Business Jobs (www.showbizjobs.com)
Sports Job Opportunities
(www.collegesportscareers.com)
National Association of Collegiate Directors of
Athletics (http://nacda.cstv.com)
National Collegiate Athletic Association
(http://ncaa.thetask.com/market/jobs)
Jobs in Sports (www.jobsinsports.com)
TeamworkOnline (www.teamworkonline.com)
U.S. Olympic Committee & Olympic Sports
Governing Body Jobs (www.usoc.org)
Executive Sports Placement
(www.prosportsjobs.com)

Taxation
Tax Talent (www.taxtalent.com)

Trade & Professional Associations
Association Jobs
(http://asaenet.jobcontrolcenter.com)
Association Jobs
(http://jobs.associationtrends.com)

Trusts & Estates/Planned Giving
Chronicle of Philanthropy
(www.philanthropy.com)
Land Trust Jobs (www.landtrustalliance.org)
National Committee on Planned Giving
(www.ncpg.org)
Philanthropy News Digest
(http://foundationcenter.org)

EMPLOYER DIRECTORIES & DATABASES

Alternative Dispute Resolution
Dispute Resolution Web Directory
(http://consensus.fsu.edu/links.html)
Federal Alternative Dispute Resolution Resource
Guide (www.opm.gov/er/adrguide_2002/toc.asp)
University Ombudsmen
(http://www2.ku.edu/~ombuds/other.html)
International Ombudsman Association
(www.ombudsassociation.org)
United States Ombudsman Association:
www.usombudsman.org

Bar Associations
The Bar Guide (www.AttorneyJobs.com).
Children's Law
National Association of Counsel for Children
(www.naccchildlaw.org). Colleges &
universities
Index of American Universities
(www.clas.ufl.edu/au/)
Universities Outside the U.S.
(www.braintrack.com)
Academic 360 (www.academic360.com)

Compliance
Health Care Compliance Association
(http://hcca-info.org)
Society of Corporate Compliance & Ethics
(www.corporatecompliance.org)

Consulting Firms
Association of Management Consulting Firms
(www.amcf.org)
Accounting Firms (www.cpafirms.com)

Corporate Recovery and Turnaround
Turnaround Management Association
(www.turnaround.org)
Association of Certified Turnaround Professionals
(www.actp.org)
Association of Insolvency and Restructuring
Advisors (www.airacira.org)
Spinoff and Reorganization Profiles
(www.spinoffprofiles.com)

Corporations
In-House Counsel Directory of Top 500
Companies (www.law.com)
Directory of In-House Law Departments at the
Top 500 Companies (http://solis.365media.com/
alm/corpcounsel/search.asp)

Dun & Bradstreet Directories (www.dnb.com)

Society of Corporate Secretaries & Governance Professionals (www.governanceprofessionals.org)

Corporate Yellow Book (www.leadershipdirectories.com)

Federation of Defense and Corporate Counsel (www.thefederation.org)

Financial Yellow Book (www.leadershipdirectories.com)

Business Dateline (www.oclc.org)

Directory of Corporate Counsel (www.aspenpublishers.com)

Society of Corporate Compliance & Ethics (www.corporatecompliance.org)

Inc. 500 List of Fastest-Growing Private Companies (www.inc.com)

Fortune 500 (www.nyjobsource.com)

Global 2000 (www.forbes.com)

200 Best Small Companies (www.forbes.com)

The Nation's 100 Leading Media Companies (http://adage.com)

Business Book of Lists (for 66 major U.S. metropolitan areas) (www.bizjournals.com)

Edgar Database (www.sec.gov)

NASDAQ Company Finder (www.nasdaq.com)

Top 50 Bank Holding Companies (www.ffiec.gov/ nicpubweb/nicweb/Top50Form.aspx)

Largest Commercial Banks (www.americanbanker.com)

Vault.com (www.vault.com)

Wetfeet.com (www.wetfeet.com)

Eastern Technology Council Membership Directory (www.techcouncil.org)

Northern Virginia Technology Council Membership Directory (www.nvtc.org)

Austin Technology Council Member Directory (www.austintechnologycouncil.org)

Arizona Technology Council Member Directory (www.aztechcouncil.org)

Florida High Tech Corridor Member Directory (www.floridahightech.com)

Greater Baltimore Technology Council (www.gbtechcouncil.org)

Baton Rouge Technology Council (www.brtc.org)

Rochester (NY) High Tech Business Council Registry (www.htbc.org)

Massachusetts High Technology Council Member Database (www.mhtc.org)

Metroplex (Dallas-Fort Worth) Technology Business Council Directory (www.metroplextbc.org)

New York Software Industry Association Member Directory (www.nysia.com)

Northeast Tennessee Technology Council (www.netntech.org)

Pittsburgh Technology Council (www.pghtech.org)

San Diego Software Industry Council (www.sdsic.org)

Technology Council of Maryland (http://techcouncilmd.com)

Ben Franklin (Central & Northern Pennsylvania) Technology Partners (www.cnp.benfranklin.org)

Technology Gateway (St. Louis) (www.gotostlouis.org)

Technology Council of Southern California (www.tcosc.org)

Courts

Federal Court Web sites (www.uscourts.gov/courtlinks/)

State Court Web sites (www.ncsconline.org)

Education

Council of School Attorneys Directory (www.nsba.org)

Education Law Association (http://educationlaw.org)

National Association of College and University Attorneys (www.nacua.org)

National School Boards Association (www.nsba.org)

Environment

Environmental Law Institute (http://www2.eli.org)

Foundations

Foundation Directory Online (http://fconline.fdncenter.org)

Government

U.S. Government Agencies (www.usa.gov/ Agencies/Federal/All_Agencies/)

United States Government Manual (www.access.gpo.gov)

Federal Yellow Book (www.leadershipdirectories.com)

Federal Regulatory Directory (www.cqpress.com)

U.S. Government Selective Placement Program Coordinator (SPPC) Directory (http://apps. opm.gov/sppc_directory/searchlist.cfm)

U.S. News & World Report: Best Places to Work in the U.S. Government 2007 (http://bestplacestowork.org/BPTW/rankings/ list.php)

Federal Regional Yellow Book
(www.leadershipdirectories.com)
U.S. Government Ethics Offices (www.usoge.gov)
Federal Laboratory Consortium for Technology
Transfer (www.federallabs.org)
Congressional Yellow Book
(www.leadershipdirectories.com)
Members of Congress (http://clerk.house.gov/)
(www.gpoaccess.gov/cdirectory)
Judicial Yellow Book
(www.leadershipdirectories.com)
State Yellow Book
(www.leadershipdirectories.com)
State and Local Government Offices
(www.statelocalgov.net)
State Attorney General Offices (www.naag.org)
State Bank Regulatory Agencies
(http://consumeraction.gov/banking.shtml)
State Disability Organizations
(www.disabilityresources.org)
State Emergency Management Agencies
(www.fema.gov)
State Environmental Agencies
(www.epa.gov/epahome/state.htm)
State Health Agencies
(www.fda.gov/oca/sthealth.htm)
State/Local Housing Authorities
(www.nahro.org/reference/internethousing.cfm)
State Insurance Regulatory Agencies
(http://consumeraction.gov/insurance.shtml)
State Long-Term Care Ombudsmen
(www.ltcombudsman.org/static_pages/
ombudsmen_list.cfm)
State Public Service & Utilities Commissions
(www.statelocalgov.net/50states-regulatory.cfm)
State Tax Departments (www.irs.gov/taxpros/
article/0,,id=100236,00.html)
State Transportation Departments
(www.fhwa.dot.gov)
State Veterans Affairs Offices
(www.va.gov/statedva.htm)
State Vocational Rehabilitation Agencies
(http://wdcrobcolp01.ed.gov/Programs/EROD/
org_list.cfm?category_ID=SVR)
State Occupational Licensing Organizations
(www.brbpub.com/pubrecsitesOccStates.asp)
Municipal Yellow Book
(www.leadershipdirectories.com)
U.S. City Web sites (www.nlc.org)

Government Affairs
Government Affairs Yellow Book
(www.leadershipdirectories.com)

Lobbyist Databases
(www.opensecrets.org/lobbyists/)
(http://sopr.senate.gov/)
Top Lobbying Firms (www.publicintegrity.org)
State Lobbying (www.publicintegrity.org/
hiredguns/information.aspx)
Registered Foreign Agents
(www.usdoj.gov/criminal/fara/)
Foreign Representatives Yellow Book
(www.leadershipdirectories.com)

Graduate Law Degree & Certificate Programs
Graduate Law Degree Program Directory
(www.AttorneyJobs.com). Hospitals & Health
American Hospital Directory (www.ahd.com)
Hospital Web (http://adams.mgh.harvard.edu/
hospitalwebusa.html)
Healthcare Industry Organizations
(www.hospitalmanagement.net/industry/
united_states.html)
Duke Health Policy Gateway
(www.hpolicy.duke.edu/cyberexchange/)

Intellectual Property
International Anti-Counterfeiting Coalition
(www.iacc.org)
Licensing Executives Society
(www.usa-canada.les.org)
Coalition Against Counterfeiting and Piracy
(www.thecacp.com)

International Organizations
Northwestern University Library
(www.library.northwestern.edu/govinfo/
resource/internat/igo.html)
Universities Outside the U.S.
(www.braintrack.com)

Labor Unions
Labor Unions
(http://www.dol.gov/esa/regs/compliance/)

Law Firms
West Legal Directory (www.westlaw.com)
Martindale-Hubbell Law Directory
(www.martindale.com)
National Association of Law Placement (NALP)
Directory of Legal Employers (www.nalp.org)
The Top 250 Law Firms (www.law.com)
Chambers USA Guide to Law Firms
(www.chambersandpartners.co.uk/usa/firms.
aspx)
Vault.com (www.vault.com)
Wetfeet.com (www.wetfeet.com)

International Network of Boutique Law Firms
(http://www.inblf.com/index/page/60.html)

Municipal Law
International Municipal Lawyers Association
(www.imla.org). Non-Governmental
Organizations
Duke University Library (http://docs.lib.duke.edu/
igo/guides/ngo/db/a-e.asp)
NGO Global Network (www.ngo.org/index2.htm)

Nonprofits
Nonprofit Sector Yellow Book
(www.leadershipdirectories.com)

Pension Funds
Largest Pension Funds (www.pionline.com)

Public Policy
"Think Tanks" & Public Interest Organizations
(http://usinfo.state.gov/usa/infousa/politics/
thnktank.htm)
"Think Tanks" & Research Institutes
(http://people.virginia.edu/~rjb3v/T-tanks.html)

Research Administration
National Council of University Research
Administrators (www.ncura.edu)

Securities & Commodities
Stock Exchanges (www.tdd.lt)
Commodities Exchanges (www.cftc.gov)
Self-Regulatory Organizations (www.sec.gov)
International Swaps and Derivatives Association
(www.isda.org). Structured Settlements
National Structured Settlements Trade Association
(www.nssta.org). Trade & Professional
Associations
Encyclopedia of Associations (www.gale.com)
Associations Yellow Book
(www.leadershipdirectories.com)
Gateway to Associations (www.asaenet.org)

**Reports and Studies that Could Impact Legal
Employment**
Congressional Committee Reports
(www.gpoaccess.gov/serialset/creports/index.
html)
Government Accountability Office (www.gao.gov)
Congressional Research Service
(www.opencrs.com)
(http://fpc.state.gov/c4763.htm)
(www.ncseonline.org/NLE/CRS)
(http://digital.library.unt.edu/govdocs/crs)

Federal Judicial Center Reports
(www.fjc.gov/library/fjc_catalog.nsf)
White House Office of Science and Technology
Policy (www.ostp.gov)
National Technology Transfer Center
(www.nttc.edu)
Federal Laboratory Consortium for Technology
Transfer (www.federallabs.org)
U.S. Commission on Civil Rights
(www.usccr.gov/pubs/pubsndx.htm)
Office of Technology Assessment
(www.wws.princeton.edu/ota). Note: The
Office of Technology Assessment went out of
business in 1995. However, its reports are often
still timely and very insightful.

U.S. Government Contracts
Federal Business Opportunities
(www.fedbizopps.gov)
Federal, State and Local Government Contracts
(www.attorneyjobs.com)
U.S. Agency for International Development Yellow
Book (http://gemini.info.usaid.gov/yellowbook)

Law-Related Job Titles
JD Preferred! at AttorneyJobs.com
(www.attorneyjobs.com)

Commercial Legal Newspapers
American Lawyer (www.americanlawyer.com)
Legal Times (www.law.com/dc)
Lawyers Weekly Group
(www.lawyersweekly.com)

Self-Assessment Resources
Myers-Briggs Type Indicator®
(www.myersbriggs.org/)
Keirsey Temperament Sorter (free online)
(www.keirsey.com). Job-Seeker Support
Organizations
Forty-Plus (www.fortyplus.org)
Minority Corporate Counsel Association
(www.mcca.com)
American Health Lawyers Association
(www.healthlawyers.org)
National Organization of Social Security
Claimants' Representatives (www.nosscr.org)
National Academy of Elder Law Attorneys
(www.naela.org)

Solo Practice Resources
American Bar Association General Practice, Solo
& Small Firm Division.
http://www.abanet.org/genpractice/solo/)

Nader Anise Blog (www.NaderAnise.com)
Carolyn Elefant Blog (www.myshingle.com)
Law Practice Management and Technology CLE
Programs Online at West LegalEdCenter
(http://westlegaledcenter.com)
The Lawyer's Toolkit. James A. Calloway, Thomas
E. Kane, Natalie Kelly, Edward Poll, Catherine
Sanders Reach, and Jennifer J. Rose. 2006. ABA.
$221.00.
How to Build a Law Firm Brand (Downloadable
PDF). Corinne Cooper. 2005. ABA. $19.99.
How to Capture and Keep Clients: Marketing
Strategies for Lawyers (Also CD). Jennifer J.
Rose, Ed. 2005. ABA. $79.95.
Legal Marketing Association
(www.legalmarketing.org)
Legal Marketing Portal (www.lawmarketing.com)
Legal Marketing Blog
(www.legalmarketingblog.com)
ABA Legal Technology Resource Center
(www.abanet.org/tech/ltrc/lofftech.html)
Law Technology News
(www.lawtechnews.com/r5/home.asp)
American Prepaid Legal Services Institute
(www.aplsi.org)
A Concise Guide to Legal Plans. Alec M.
Schwartz, Ed. $24.50. Available from APLSI.

**Selected Resources for Analyzing Legal
Employment Trends**
The Economist (www.economist.com)
Oil & Gas Journal (www.ogj.com)
Aviation Week and Space Technology
(www.aviationnow.com)
Spinoff & Reorganization Profiles
(www.spinoffprofiles.com)
Venture Capital Firms (www.vfinance.com)
(www.nvca.org)
Chambers of Commerce
(www.uschamber.com)

Government Executive (www.govexec.com)
IRS Tax Statistics
(www.irs.gov/taxstats/index.html)
Federal Legislation (http://thomas.loc.gov)
Federal Regulations
(www.gpoaccess.gov/cfr/index.html)
Federal Budget Documents
(www.whitehouse.gov/omb)
House Ways & Means Committee Green Book
(excellent histories of Federal programs)
(www.gpoaccess.gov/wmprints/green/browse.
html)

Compensation Information
U.S. Government Salary Charts
(www.attorneyjobs.com)
Congressional Staff Salaries
(www.legistorm.com/)
Glass Door (www.glassdoor.com)
Law.com (www.law.com)
Altman Weil Pensa (www.altmanweil.com)
Findlaw (www.infirmation.com)
Society of American Law Teachers
(www.saltlaw.org)
College & University Faculty Salaries
(http://chronicle.com/stats/aaup/)
Bureau of Labor Statistics (http://stats.bls.gov/)
Executive PayWatch Database
(www.aflcio.org/corporatewatch/). Legal
Specialty Certification
The Bar Guide: The Attorney's Guide to State Bar
Admission Requirements
(www.attorneyjobs.com). State Bar Rules
Regarding In-House Counsel Practice
The Bar Guide: The Attorney's Guide to State Bar
Admission Requirements
(www.attorneyjobs.com)
Multijurisdictional Practice of Law Rules,
State-by-State
(www.abanet.org/cpr/jclr/in-house_rules.pdf)